LIFE

OF

TECUMSEH,

AND OF HIS BROTHER

THE PROPHET;

WITH A

HISTORICAL SKETCH

OF THE

SHAWANOE INDIANS.

BY BENJAMIN DRAKE,

AUTHOR OF "THE LIFE OF BLACK HAWK," "TALES FROM THE QUEEN CITY," &c. &c.

CINCINNATI:

ANDERSON, GATES & WRIGHT

112 MAIN STREET,

1858.

General Harrison's Victory over Proctor, at the Battle of the Thames.

Stereotyped by J. A. James
Cincinnati.

PREFACE.

MANY years have elapsed since the author of this volume determined to write the life of TECUMSEH and of his brother the PROPHET, and actually commenced the collection of the materials for its accomplishment. From various causes, the completion of the task has been postponed until the present time. This delay, however, has probably proved beneficial to the work, as many interesting incidents in the lives of these individuals are now embraced in its pages, which could not have been included had it been put to press at an earlier period.

In the preparation of this volume, the author's attention was drawn, to some extent, to the history of the Shawanoe tribe of Indians: and he has accordingly prefixed to the main work, a brief historical narrative of this wandering and warlike nation, with biographical sketches of several of its most distinguished chiefs.

The author is under lasting obligations to a number of gentlemen residing in different sections of the country, for the substantial assistance which they have kindly afforded him in the collection of the matter embraced in this volume. Other sources of information have not, however, been neglected. All the histories, magazines and journals within the reach of the author, containing notices of the subjects of this memoir, have been carefully consulted. By application at the proper department at Washington, copies of the numerous letters written by general Harrison to the Secretary of War in the years 1808, '9, '10, '11, '12 and '13, were ob-

iii

tained, and have been found of much value in the preparation
of this work. As governor of Indiana territory, superintend-
ant of Indian affairs, and afterwards commander-in-chief of
the north-western army, the writer of those letters possessed
opportunities of knowing Tecumseh and the Prophet enjoy
ed by no other individuals.

In addition to these several sources of information, the
author has personally, at different times, visited the frontiers
of Ohio and Indiana, for the purpose of conversing with the
Indians and the pioneers of that region, who happened to be
acquainted with Tecumseh and his brother; and by these
visits, has been enabled to enrich his narrative with some
amusing and valuable anecdotes.

In the general accuracy of his work the author feels considerable confidence : in its merit, as a literary production,
very little. Every line of it having been written while suffering under the depressing influence of ill health, he has
only aimed at a simple narrative style, without any reference
to the graces of a polished composition.   B. D.

Cincinnati, 1841.

CONTENTS.

THE LIFE OF TECUMSEH.

CHAPTER I.

Parentage of Tecumseh—his sister Tecumapease—his brother Cheesee-kau, Sauweeseekau, Nehasseemo, Tenskwautawa or the Prophet, and Kumskauka... 61

CHAPTER II.

Birth place of Tecumseh—destruction of the Piqua village—early habits of Tecumseh—his first battle—effort to abolish the burning of prisoners—visits the Cherokees in the south—engages in several battles—returns to Ohio in the autumn of 1790 66

CHAPTER III.

Tecumseh attacked near Big Rock by some whites under Robert M'Clelland—severe battle with some Kentuckians on the East Fork of the Little Miami—attack upon Tecumseh in 1793, on the waters of Paint creek—Tecumseh present at the attack on fort Recovery in 1794—participates in the battle of the Rapids of the Maumee, in 1794 71

CHAPTER IV.

Tecumseh's skill as a hunter—declines attending the treaty of Greenville in 1795—in 1796 removed to Great Miami—in 1798 joined a party of Delawares on White river, Indiana—in 1799 attended a council be-

A 2   v

CHAPTER V.

CHAPTER VI.

CHAPTER VII.

CHAPTER VIII.

CHAPTER IX.

CHAPTER X.

CHAPTER XI.

CHAPTER XII.

CHAPTER XIII.

CHAPTER XIV.

CHAPTER XV.

CHAPTER XVI.

HISTORY

OF THE

SHAWANOE INDIANS.

THERE is a tradition among the Shawanoes, in regard to their origin, which is said to be peculiar to that tribe. While most of the aborigines of this country believe that their respective races came out of holes in the earth at different places on this continent, the Shawanoes alone claim, that their ancestors once inhabited a foreign land; but having determined to leave it, they assembled their people and marched to the sea shore. Here, under the guidance of a leader of the Turtle tribe, one of their twelve original subdivisions, they walked into the sea, the waters of which immediately parted, and they passed in safety along the bottom of the ocean, until they reached this island.*

The Shawanoes have been known by different names. The Iroquois, according to Colden's history of the "Five Nations," gave them the appellation of Satanas. The Delawares, says Gallatin, in his synopsis of the Indian tribes, call them Shawaneu, which means *southern*. The French writers mention them under the name of Chaouanons; and occasionally they are denominated Massawomees.

The orthography of the word by which they are generally designated, is not very well settled. It has been written Shawanos, Sawanos, Shawaneu, Shawnees and Shawanoes, which last method of spelling the word, will be followed in the pages of this work.

---

* History of the Indian Tribes of North America, by James Hall and J. L. McKinney, a valuable work, containing one hundred and twenty richly colored portraits of Indian chiefs.

The original seats of the Shawanoes have been placed in different sections of the country. This has doubtless been owing to their very erratic disposition. Of their history, prior to the year 1680, but little is known. The earliest mention of them by any writer whose work has fallen under our observation, was in the beginning of the seventeenth century. Mr. Jefferson, in his "Notes on Virginia," says that when captain John Smith first arrived in America, a fierce war was raging against the allied Mohicans, residing on Long Island, and the Shawanoes on the Susquehanna, and to the westward of that river, by the Iroquois. Captain Smith first landed on this continent in April, 1607. In the following year, 1608, he penetrated down the Susquehanna to the mouth of it, where he met six or seven of their canoes, filled with warriors, about to attack their enemy in the rear. De Laet, in 1632, in his enumeration of the different tribes, on either side of the Delaware river, mentions the Shawanoes.— Charlevoix speaks of them under the name of Chaouanons, as neighbors and allies in 1672, of the Andastes, an Iroquois tribe, living south of the Senecas. Whether any of the Shawanoes were present at the treaty* made in 1682, under the celebrated Kensington elm, between William Penn and the Indians, does not positively appear from any authorities before us; that such, however, was the fact, may be fairly inferred, from the circumstance that at a conference between the Indians and governor Keith, in 1722, the Shawanoes exhibited a copy of this treaty written on parchment.

To the succeeding one made at Philadelphia, in February, 1701, the Shawanoes were parties, being represented on that occasion, by their chiefs, Wopatha, Lemoytungh and Pemoyajagh.† More than fifty years afterward, a manuscript copy of this treaty of commerce and friendship, was in the possession of the Shawanoes of Ohio, and was exhibited by them. In

* "This treaty," says Voltaire, "was the first made between those people (the Indians) and the Christians, that was not ratified with an oath, and that was never broken."
† Proud's History of Pennsylvania.

1684, the Iroquois, when complained of by the French
for having attacked the Miamis, justified their conduct
on the ground, that they had invited the Santanas
(Shawanoes) into the country, for the purpose of making war upon them.*   The Sauks and Foxes, whose
residence was originally on the St. Lawrence, claim the
Shawanoes as belonging to the same stock with themselves, and retain traditional accounts of their emigration to the south.†   In the "History of the Indian Tribes
of North America," when speaking of the Shawanoes,
the authors say, "their manners, customs and language
indicate a northern origin; and, upwards of two centu-
ries ago, they held the country south of Lake Erie.
They were the first tribe which felt the force and yielded to the superiority of the Iroquois. Conquered by
these, they migrated to the south, and from fear or
favor, were allowed to take possession of a region upon
the Savannah river; but what part of that stream,
whether in Georgia or Florida, is not known; it is pre-
sumed the former."   Mr. Gallatin speaks of the final
defeat of the Shawanoes and their allies, in a war with
the Five Nations, as having taken place in the year
1672. This same writer, who has carefully studied the
language of the aborigines, considers the Shawanoes as
belonging to the Lenape tribes of the north. From
these various authorities, it is apparent that the Shawanoes belonged originally to the Algonkin-Lenape nation; and that during the three first quarters of the
seventeenth century, they were found in eastern Pennsylvania, on the St. Lawrence, and the southern shore
of Lake Erie; and generally at war with some of the
neighboring tribes. Whether their dispersion, which is
supposed to have taken place about the year 1672,
drove them all to the south side of the Ohio, does not
very satisfactorily appear.

Subsequently to this period, the Shawanoes were
found on the Ohio river below the Wabash, in Kentucky, Georgia and the Carolinas. Lawson, in his history of Carolina in 1708, speaks of the Savanoes,

* Colden.   † Morse's Report.

removing from the Mississippi to one of the rivers of South Carolina. Gallatin quotes an authority which sustains Lawson, and which establishes the fact that at a very early period in the history of the south, there was a Shawanoe settlement on the head waters of the Catawba or Santee, and probably of the Yadkin. From another authority it appears, that for a time the Shawanoes had a station on the Savannah river, above Augusta; and Adair, who refers to the war between the Shawanoes and Cherokees, saw a body of the former in the wilderness, who, after having wandered for some time in the woods, were then returning to the Creek country. According to John Johnston,* a large party of the Shawanoes, who originally lived north of the Ohio, had for some cause emigrated as far south as the Suwanoe river, which empties into the Gulf of Mexico. From thence they returned, under the direction of a chief named Black Hoof, about the middle of the last century, to Ohio. It is supposed that this tribe gave name to the Suwanoe river, in 1750, by which name the Cumberland was also known, when Doctor Walker, (of Virginia) visited Kentucky.

Of the causes which led the Shawanoes to abandon the south, but little is known beyond what may be gleaned from their traditions. Heckewelder, in his contributions to the American Philosophical Society, says, "they were a restless people, delighting in wars, in which they were constantly engaged with some of the surrounding nations. At last their neighbors, tired of being continually harassed by them, formed a league for their destruction. The Shawanoes finding themselves thus dangerously situated, asked to be permitted to leave the country, which was granted to them; and they immediately removed to the Ohio. Here their main body settled, and then sent messengers to their elder brother,† the Mohicans, requesting them to intercede for them with their grandfather, the Lenni Lenape, to take them under his protection. This the Mohi-

---

* 1 Vol. Trans. Amer. Antiquarian Society.
† The Shawanoes call the Mohicans their *elder brother*, and the Delawares their *grandfather*.

cans willingly did, and even sent a body of their own people to conduct their younger brother into the country of the Delawares. The Shawanoes finding themselves safe under the protection of their grandfather, did not choose to proceed to the eastward, but many of them remained on the Ohio, some of whom settled as far up that river as the long island, above which the French afterwards built fort Duquesne, on the spot where Pittsburg now stands. Those who proceeded farther, were accompanied by their chief, named Gachgawatschiqua, and settled principally at and about the forks of the Delaware, between that and the confluence of the Delaware and Schuylkill; and some, even on the spot where Philadelphia now stands; others were conducted by the Mohicans into their own country, where they intermarried with them and became one people. When those settled near the Delaware had multiplied, they returned to Wyoming on the Susquehannah, where they resided for a great number of years."

Chapman, in his history of Wyoming, states, that after the Shawanoes were driven from Georgia and Florida, they built a town at the mouth of the Wabash, and established themselves in it. They then applied to the Delawares for some territory on which to reside. When granted, a council was held to consider the propriety of accepting the offer of the Delawares. On this question the Shawanoes divided—part of them remained on the Wabash,—the others, composing chiefly the Piqua tribe, formed a settlement in the forks of the Delaware. After a time, a disagreement arose between them and the Delawares, which induced the former to remove to the valley of the Wyoming, on the Susquehannah, on the west bank of which they built a town, and lived in repose many years. Subsequently to the treaty held at Philadelphia, in 1742, between the governor and the Six Nations, the Delawares were driven from that part of Pennsylvania; and a portion of them also removed to the Wyoming valley, then in possession of the Shawanoes, and secured the quiet occupancy of a part of it; built a town on the east bank of the river, which they called Waughwauwame, where they

B

lived for some time, on terms of amity with their new neighbors.

During the summer of 1742, count Zinzendorf of Saxony, came to America on a religious mission, con‧ nected with the ancient church of the United Brethren. Having heard of the Shawanoes at Wyoming, he determined to make an effort to introduce Christianity among them. He accordingly made them a visit, but did not meet with a cordial reception. The Shawanoes supposed that the missionary was in pursuit of their lands; and a party of them determined to assassinate him privately, for fear of exciting other Indians to hostility. The attempt upon his life was made, but strangely defeated. Chapman relates the manner of it, which he obtained from a companion of the count, who did not publish it in his memoirs, lest the United Brethren might suppose that the subsequent conversion of the Shawanoes was the result of their superstition. It is as follows:

"Zinzendorf was alone in his tent, seated upon a bundle of dry weeds, which composed his bed, and engaged in writing, when the assassins approached to execute their bloody commission. It was night, and the cool air of September had rendered a small fire necessary for his comfort and convenience. A curtain, formed of a blanket, and hung upon pins, was the only guard to his tent. The heat of his small fire had aroused a large rattlesnake, which lay in the weeds not far from it; and the reptile, to enjoy it the more effectually, had crawled slowly into the tent, and passed over one of his legs, undiscovered. Without, all was still and quiet, except the gentle murmur of the river, at the rapids about a mile below. At this moment, the Indians softly approached the door of his tent, and slightly removing the curtain, contemplated the venerable man, too deeply engaged in the subject of his thoughts, to notice either their approach, or the snake which lay before him. At a sight like this, even the heart of the savages shrunk from the idea of committing so horrid an act; and, quitting the spot, they hastily returned to the town, and informed their companions, that the Great Spirit protected the white man, for they had found him with no door but a blanket, and had seen a large rattlesnake crawl over his legs without attempting to injure him. This circumstance, together with the arrival soon afterwards of Conrad Weizer, the interpreter, procured the count the friendship of the Indians, and probably induced some of them to embrace Christianity."

When the war between the French and the English occurred in 1754, the Shawanoes on the Ohio took sides with the former; but the appeal to those residing at Wyoming to do the same, was ineffectual. The influence of the count's missionary efforts had made them averse to war. But an event which happened soon afterward, disturbed the peace of their settlement, and finally led to their removal from the valley. Occasional difficulties of a transient nature, had arisen between the Delawares and the Shawanoes at Wyoming. An unkind feeling, produced by trifling local causes, had grown up between the two tribes. At length a childish dispute about the possession of a harmless grasshopper, brought on a bloody battle; and a final separation of the two parties soon followed. One day, while most of the Delaware men were absent on a hunting excursion, the women of that tribe went out to gather wild fruits on the margin of the river, below their village. Here they met a number of Shawanoe women and their children, who had crossed the stream in their canoes, and were similarly engaged. One of the Shawanoe children having caught a large grasshopper, a dispute arose with some of the Delaware children, in regard to the possession of it. In this quarrel, as was natural, the mothers soon became involved. The Delaware women contended for the possession of the grasshopper on the ground that the Shawanoes possessed no privileges on that side of the river. A resort to violence ensued, and the Shawanoe women being in the minority, were speedily driven to their canoes, and compelled to seek safety by flight to their own bank of the stream. Here the matter rested until the return of the hunters, when the Shawanoes, in order to avenge the indignity offered to their women, armed themselves for battle. When they attempted to cross the river,

they found the Delawares duly prepared to receive
them and oppose their landing. The battle commenced while the Shawanoes were still in their canoes, but
they at length effected a landing, which was followed
by a general and destructive engagement. The Shawanoes having lost a number of their warriors before
reaching the shore, were too much weakened to sustain the battle for any length of time. After the loss
of nearly one half their party, they were compelled to
fly to their own side of the river. Many of the Delawares were killed. Shortly after this disastrous contest, the Shawanoes quietly abandoned their village,
and removed westward to the banks of the Ohio.*

After the Shawanoes of Pennsylvania had fallen back
upon the waters of the Ohio, they spread themselves
from the Alleghenies as far westward as the Big Miami.
One of their villages was seventeen miles below Pittsburg: it was called Log's Town, and was visited by
Croghan, in 1765. Another, named Lowertown, also
visited by the same traveler, stood just below the
mouth of the Scioto. It was subsequently carried away
by a great flood in that river, which overflowed the
site of the town, and compelled the Indians to escape
in their canoes. They afterwards built a new town on
the opposite side of the river, but soon abandoned it,
and removed to the plains of the Scioto and Paint creek,
where they established themselves, on the north fork
of the latter stream. They had also several other villages of considerable size in the Miami valley. One
was "Chillicothe," standing near the mouth of Massie's
creek, three miles north of Xenia. Another, called
Piqua, and memorable as the birth place of TECUMSEH,
the subject of our present narrative, stands upon the
north-west side of Mad river, about seven miles below
Springfield, in Clark county. Both of these villages
were destroyed in 1780, by an expedition from Kentucky, under the command of general George Rogers
Clark.

After the peace of 1763, the Miamis having removed from the Big Miami river, a body of Shawanoes

---

* Chapman.

established themselves at Lower and Upper Piqua, in Miami county, which places, being near together, became their great head-quarters in Ohio. Here they remained until driven off by the Kentuckians; when they crossed over to the St. Mary's and to Wapaka- notta. The Upper Piqua is said to have contained, at one period, near four thousand Shawanoes.*

From the geographical location of the Shawanoes, it will be perceived that they were placed under circumstances which enabled them, with great facility, to annoy the early settlements in Kentucky; and to attack the emigrants descending the Ohio. In this fierce border war, which was waged upon the whites for a number of years, and oftentimes with extreme cruelty, the Delawares, Wyandots, Mingoes and Miamis, united: the Shawanoes, however, were by far the most warlike and troublesome.

The Shawanoes were originally divided into twelve tribes or bands, each of which was sub-divided into families, known as the Eagle, the Turtle, the Panther, &c., these animals constituting their *totems*. Of these twelve, the names of but four tribes are preserved, the rest having become extinct, or incorporated with them. They are, 1st. the Mequachake,—2d. the Chillicothe,— 3d. the Kiskapocoke,—4th. the Piqua. When in council, one of these tribes is assigned to each of the four sides of the council-house, and during the continuance of the deliberations, the tribes retain their respective places. They claim to have the power of distinguishing, at sight, to which tribe an individual belongs; but to the casual observer, there are no visible shades of difference. In each of the four tribes, except the Mequachake, the chiefs owe their authority to merit, but in the last named, the office is hereditary. Of the origin of the Piqua tribe, the following tradition has been recited:† "In ancient times, the Shawanoes had occasion to build a large fire, and after it was burned down, a great puffing and blowing was heard, when up rose a

---

* John Johnston.
† Stephen Ruddell's manuscript account of the Shawanoes, in possession of the author.

B 2

man from the ashes!—hence the name **Piqua, which** means a man coming out of the ashes." Mequachake, signifies a perfect man. To this tribe the priesthood is confided. The members, or rather certain individuals of it, are alone permitted to perform the sacrifices and other religious ceremonies of the tribe.* The division of the tribe into bands or totems, is not peculiar to the Shawanoes, but is common to several other nations. One of the leading causes of its institution, was the prohibition of marriage between those related in a remote degree of consanguinity. Individuals are not at liberty to change their totems, or disregard the restraint imposed by it on intermarriages. It is stated in Tanner's narrative, that the Indians hold it to be criminal for a man to marry a woman whose totem is the same as his own; and they relate instances where young men, for a violation of this rule, have been put to death by their nearest relatives. Loskiel, in his history of the Moravian missions, says, the Delawares and Iroquois never marry near relatives. According to their own account, the Indian nations were divided into tribes for the sole purpose, that no one might, either through temptation or mistake, marry a near relation, which is now scarcely possible, for whoever intends to marry must take a person of a different totem. Another reason for the institution of these totems, may be found in their influence on the social relations of the tribe, in softening private revenge, and preserving peace. Gallatin, on the information derived from a former Indian agent † among the Creeks, says, "according to the ancient custom, if an offence was committed by one or another member of the same clan, the compensation to be made, on account of the injury, was regulated in an amicable way, by the other members of the clan. Murder was rarely expiated in any other way than by the death of the murderer; the nearest male relative of the deceased was the executioner; but this being done, as under the authority of the clan, there was no further retaliation. If the injury was committed by some one of another clan, it was not the injured party, but the

---

* John Johnston.   † Mitchell.

clan to which he belonged, that asked for reparation. This was rarely refused by the clan of the offender; but in case of refusal, the injured clan had a right to do itself justice, either by killing the offender, in case of murder, or inflicting some other punishment for lesser offences. This species of private war, was, by the Creeks, called, "to take up the sticks;" because, the punishment generally consisted in beating the offender. At the time of the annual corn-feast, the sticks were laid down, and could not be again taken up for the same offence. But it seems that originally there had been a superiority among some of the clans. That of the Wind, had the right to take up the sticks four times, that of the Bear twice, for the same offence; whilst those of the Tiger, of the Wolf, of the Bird, of the Root, and of two more whose names I do not know, could raise them but once. It is obvious that the object of the unknown legislation, was to prevent or soften the effects of private revenge, by transferring the power and duty from the blood relatives to a more impartial body. The father and his brothers, by the same mother, never could belong to the same clan, as their son or nephew, whilst the perpetual changes, arising from intermarriages with women of a different clan, prevented their degenerating into distinct tribes; and checked the natural tendency towards a subdivision of the nation into independent communities. The institution may be considered as the foundation of the internal policy, and the basis of the social state of the Indians."

One mode of ascertaining the origin of the Indian tribes, and of determining their relation to each other, as well as to other races of mankind, is the study of their language. This has, at different times, engaged the attention of several able philologists, who have done much to analyze the Indian languages, and to arrange in systematic order, the numerous dialects of this erratic people. The results of the investigation of one [*] of the most learned and profound of these individuals, may be summed up in the three following propositions :

---

[*] Mr. Duponceau.

1. "That the American languages in general, are rich in words and in grammatical forms, and that in their complicated construction, the greatest order, method and regularity prevail.

2. "That these complicated forms, which I call *poly synthetic*, appear to exist in all those languages, from Greenland to Cape Horn.

3. "That these forms appear to differ essentially from those of the ancient and modern languages of the old hemisphere."

In a late learned dissertation * on this subject, it is stated that in nearly the whole territory contained in the United States, and in British and Russian America, there are only eight great families, each speaking a distinct language, subdivided in many instances, into a number of dialects belonging to the same stock. These are the Eskimaux, the Athapascas (or Cheppeyans,) the Black Feet, the Sioux, the Algonkin-Lenape, the Iroquois, the Cherokee, and the Mobilian or Chahta-Muskhog. The Shawanoes belong to the Algonkin-Lenape family, and speak a dialect of that language. It bears a strong affinity to the Mohican and the Chippeway, but more especially the Kickapoo. Valuable vocabularies of the Shawanoe language have been given by Johnston and by Gallatin in their contributions to the American Antiquarian Society, which may be consulted by those disposed to prosecute the study of this subject.

The Shawanoes have been known since the first discovery of this country, as a restless, wandering people, averse to the pursuits of agriculture, prone to war and the chase. They have, within that period, successively occupied the southern shore of lake Erie, the banks of the Ohio and Mississippi, portions of Georgia, Florida, Tennessee, Kentucky, and eastern Pennsylvania; then again the plains of Ohio, and now the small remnant of them that remains, are established west of Missouri and Arkansas. They have been involved in numerous bloody wars with other tribes; and for near half a century, resisted with a bold, ferocious spirit, and an in-

---

* Mr. Gallatin.

domitable hatred, the progress of the white settlements
in Pennsylvania, western Virginia, and especially Kentucky. The Shawanoes have declined more rapidly in
numbers* than any other tribe of Indians known to the
whites. This has been, and we suppose justly, attributed to their wandering habits and their continual wars.
Although one of their villages is said once to have contained four thousand souls, their present number does
not exceed eighteen hundred. They have ever been
considered a courageous, powerful and faithless race;
who have claimed for themselves a pre-eminence not
only over other tribes, but also over the whites.† Their
views in regard to this superiority were briefly set
forth by one of their chiefs at a convention held at fort
Wayne, in 1803.

"The Master of Life," said he, "who was himself
an Indian, made the Shawanoes before any other of
the human race; and they sprang from his brain: he
gave them all the knowledge he himself possessed, and
placed them upon the great island, and all the other
red people are descended from the Shawanoes. After
he had made the Shawanoes, he made the French and
English out of his breast, the Dutch out of his feet, and
the long-knives out of his hands. All these inferior
races of men he made white and placed them beyond
the stinking lake.‡

"The Shawanoes for many ages continued to be
masters of the continent, using the knowledge they had
received from the Great Spirit in such a manner as to
be pleasing to him, and to secure their own happiness.
In a great length of time, however, they became cor-
rupt, and the Master of Life told them that he would
take away from them the knowledge which they possessed, and give it to the white people, to be restored,
when by a return to good principles they would de-
serve it. Many ages after that, they saw something
white approaching their shores; at first they took it for
a great bird, but they soon found it to be a monstrous

* John Johnston.
† General Harrison considers the Shawanoes, Delawares and Miamis,
as much superior to the other tribes of the west.
‡ Atlantic Ocean.

canoe filled with the very people who had got the knowledge which belonged to the Shawanoes. After these white people landed, they were not content with having the knowledge which belonged to the Shawanoes, but they usurped their lands also; they pretended, indeed, to have purchased these lands; but the very goods they gave for them, were more the property of the Indians than the white people, because the knowledge which enabled them to manufacture these goods actually belonged to the Shawanoes: but these things will soon have an end. The Master of Life is about to restore to the Shawanoes both their knowledge and their rights, and he will trample the long knives under his feet."

It has been already stated that, for a series of years, the several tribes of Indians residing in the territory now forming the state of Ohio, made violent opposition to the settlement of the whites, west of the Alleghanies. Among the most formidable of these were the Shawanoes. The emigrants, whether male or female, old or young, were every where met by the torch, the tomahawk and the scalping-knife. The war-cry of the savage was echoed from shore to shore of the beautiful Ohio, whose waters were but too often reddened with the blood of women and children. Many of those who escaped the perils of the river, and had reared their log-cabins amid the cane-brakes of Kentucky, were doomed to encounter the same ruthless foe, and fell victims to the same unrelenting cruelty. While the feelings are shocked at these dreadful scenes of blood and carnage, and the Indian character rises in hideous deformity before the mind, it is not to be forgotten that there are many mitigating circumstances to be pleaded in behalf of the aborigines. They were an ignorant people, educated alone for war, without the lights of civilization, without the attributes of mercy shed abroad by the spirit of christianity. They were contending for their homes and their hunting grounds—the tombs of their forefathers—the graves of their children. They saw the gradual, but certain, encroachments of the whites upon their lands; and they had the sagacity to perceive, that unless this mighty wave of emigration was arrested, it would overwhelm them. They fought as savage nature will fight, with unflinching courage and unrelenting cruelty. But it was not alone this encroachment upon their lands, which roused their savage passions. The wanton aggressions of the whites oftentimes provoked the fearful retaliation of the red-man. The policy of the United States towards the Indians has generally been of a pacific and benevolent character; but, in carrying out that policy, there have been many signal and inexcusable failures. The laws enacted by congress for the protection of the rights of the Indians, and to promote their comfort and civilization, have, in a great variety of cases, remained a dead letter upon the statute book. The agents of the government have often proved unfaithful, and have looked much more to their own pecuniary interests, than to the honest execution of the public trusts confided to them. Nor is this all. There has ever been found upon the western frontiers, a band of unprincipled men who have set at defiance the laws of the United States, debauched the Indians with ardent spirits, cheated them of their property, and then committed upon them aggressions marked with all the cruelty and wanton bloodshed which have distinguished the career of the savage. The history of these aggressions would fill a volume. It is only necessary to recall to the mind of the reader, the horrible murder of the Conestoga Indians, in December 1763, by some Pennsylvanians; the dark tragedy enacted on the banks of he Muskingum, at a later period, when the Moravian Indians, at the three villages of Schoenbrun, Salem, and Gnadenhuetten, were first disarmed and then deliberately tomahawked by Williamson and his associates; the unprovoked murder of the family of Logan; the assassination of Bald Eagle, of the gallant and high-souled Cornstalk, and his son Elinipsico: we need but recall these, from the long catalogue of similar cases, to satisfy every candid mind, that rapine, cruelty and a thirst for human blood are not peculiarly the attributes of the American Indian.

But there are still other causes which have aroused and kept in activity, the warlike passions of the Indians. They have been successively subjected to English,

Dutch, French and Spanish influence. The agents of these different powers, as well as the emigrants from them, either from interest or a spirit of mischievous hostility, have repeatedly prompted the Indians to arm themselves against the United States. The great principle of the Indian wars, for the last seventy years, has been the preservation of their lands. On this, the French, English and Spanish have in turn excited them to active resistance against the expanding settlement of the whites. It was on the principle of recovering their lands, that the French were their allies between the commencement of hostilities with the colonies, in 1754, and the peace of 1762; and subsequently kept up an excitement among them until the beginning of the revolution. From this period, the English took the place of the French, and instigated them in a similar manner. Their views and feelings on this point, may be gathered from their own words:

"It was we," say the Delawares, Mohicans and their kindred tribes, "who so kindly received the Europeans on their first arrival into our own country. We took them by the hand and bid them welcome to sit down by our side, and live with us as brothers; but how did they requite our kindness? They at first asked only for a little land, on which to raise bread for their families, and pasture for their cattle, which we freely gave them. They saw the game in the woods, which the Great Spirit had given us for our subsistence, and they wanted it too. They penetrated into the woods in quest of game, they discovered spots of land they also wanted, and because we were loth to part with it, as we saw they had already more than they had need of, they took it from us by force, and drove us to a great distance from our homes."*

It is matter of history, that for a period of near seventy years after it was planted, the colony of William Penn lived in peace and harmony with the neighboring Indians, among whom were bands of the warlike Shawanoes. It was an observation of this venerable and worthy man, when speaking of the Indians, that

---

* Heckewelder's historical account of the Indians.

"if you do not abuse them, but let them have justice, you will win them, when there is such a knowledge of good and evil." His kind treatment to them was repaid by friendly offices, both to himself and his followers. The Indians became indeed the benefactors of the colonists. When the latter were scattered in 1682, and without shelter or food, they were kind and attentive, and treated them as brothers.*

Proud, in his History of Pennsylvania, when explaining the aversion of the Indians to christianity, attributes it to the character and conduct of the whites residing near or among them, "many of whom were of the lowest rank and least informed of mankind, who flowed in from Germany, Ireland and the jails of Great Britain, or who had fled from the better inhabited parts of the colony, to escape from justice." The proceedings of the assembly of Pennsylvania show that, as early as 1722, an Indian was barbarously killed by some whites, within the limits of the province. The assembly proposed some measures for the governor's consideration in regard to the affair; and mentioned the repeated requests of the Indians, that strong liquors should not be carried nor sold among them. In a treatise published in London, in 1759, on the cause of the then existing difficulties between the Indians and the colonists, we find this paragraph. "It would be too shocking to describe the conduct and behavior of the traders, when among the Indians; and endless to enumerate the abuses the Indians received and bore from them, for a series of years. Suffice it to say, that several of the tribes were, at last, weary of bearing; and, as these traders were the persons who were, in some part, the representatives of the English among the Indians, and by whom they were to judge of our manners and religion, they conceived such invincible prejudices against both, particularly our holy religion, that when Mr. Sargeant, a gentleman in New England, took a journey in 1741, to the Shawanoes and some other tribes living on the Susquehanna, and offered to instruct them in the christian religion, they rejected

* Clarkson's Life of Penn.
C

his offer with disdain. They reproached Christianity.
They told him the traders would lie and cheat." In
1744, governor Thomas, in a message to the assembly
of Pennsylvania, says, " I cannot but be apprehensive
that the Indian trade, as it is now carried on, will in-
volve us in some fatal quarrel with the Indians. Our
traders, in defiance of the laws, carry spirituous liquors
among them, and take advantage of their inordinate
appetite for it, to cheat them of their skins, and their
wampum, which is their money." In 1753 governor
Hamilton appointed Richard Peters, Isaac Norris and
Benjamin Franklin, to hold a treaty with the Indians
at Carlisle, Pennsylvania. In the report of these commissioners they say : " But in justice to these Indians,
and the promises we made them, we cannot close our
report, without taking notice, that the quantity of strong
liquors sold to these Indians, in the places of their residence, and during their hunting season, have increased
to an inconceivable degree, so as to keep these poor
creatures continually under the force of liquors, that
they are thereby become dissolute, enfeebled and indolent when sober; and untractable and mischievous in
their liquor, always quarreling, and often murdering
one another." Some of the chiefs at this treaty said,
"these wicked whisky-sellers, when they have once got
the Indians in liquor, make them sell their very clothes
from their backs. In short, if this practice is continued,
we must be inevitably ruined ; we most earnestly, therefore, beseech you to remedy it."*

This brief sketch of the early intercourse between
the colonists and the aborigines of this country, is not
over-drawn, nor is it at all inapplicable to the period
which has elapsed since the formation of the federal
government. With an insatiable cupidity and a wanton disregard of justice, have the lands and property of
the Indians been sought by citizens of the United States.
The great agent of success in this unholy business, has
been ardent spirits, by means of which their savage reason has been overthrown, and their bad passions called
into action. The class of reckless and desperate charac-

* Proud's History of Pennsylvania.

ters, described by Proud, have hung upon the western frontiers, for the purpose of preying upon the Indians. If government itself be not to blame, for want of good faith towards this miserable race, is it not highly culpable for not having, by the strong arm of physical power, enforced the salutary laws, which from time to time, have been enacted for their protection? Impartial posterity will, we apprehend, answer this question in the affirmative.

The Shawanoes engaged in the war between the French and English, which commenced in 1755, and was terminated by the peace of 10th February, 1763. In this contest they took sides with the former, and rendered them essential service. They committed many depredations on the frontier settlements of Pennsylvania and Virginia. The peace of 1763, between France and England, did not terminate the Indian war against the colonies. The Indians were displeased with the provisions of this treaty, especially that which ceded the provinces of Canada to Great Britain. This dissatisfaction was increased when the British government began to build forts on the Susquehanna, and to repair or erect those of Bedford, Ligonier, Pittsburg, Detroit, Presque Isle, St. Joseph and Michilimakinac. By this movement the Indians found themselves surrounded, on two sides, by a cordon of forts, and were threatened with an extension of them into the very heart of their country. They had now to choose whether they would remove to the north and west, negociate with the British government for the possession of their own land, or take up arms for its defence. They chose the last alternative; and, a war of extermination against the English residents in the western country, and even those on the Susquehanna, was agreed upon and speedily commenced. Many of the British traders living among the Indians were murdered; the forts of Presque Isle, St. Joseph and Mackinac, were taken, with a general slaughter of their garrisons; while the forts of Bedford, Ligonier, Niagara, Detroit and Pitt, were barely preserved from falling into their hands. The contest was continued with resolute and daring spirit, and with much destruction of life and property, until December,

1764, when the war was brought to a close by a treaty at the German Flats, made between Sir William Johnston and the hostile Indians. Soon after the conclusion of this peace the Shawanoes became involved in a war with the Cherokees, which continued until 1768, when, pressed hard by the united force of the former tribe and the Delawares, the southern Indians solicit ed and obtained a peace.* For the ensuing six years, the Shawanoes remained quiet, living on amicable terms with the whites on the frontiers : in April, 1774 however, hostilities between these parties were renewed.

It is not our purpose in the present sketch of this tribe, to present a detail of all their conflicts with the whites; but the "Dunmore war," (as it is generally called,) of 1774, having been mainly prosecuted by Shawanoes, one of their distinguished chiefs having commanded in the battle of Point Pleasant, and another, Puckecheno, (the father of Tecumseh,) having fallen in this engagement, would seem to render a full account of the border feuds of this year, not out of place in the present narrative.

In the latter part of April, 1774, a report that the Indians had stolen some horses, from the vicinity of Wheeling, alarmed the whites who were making settlements on the Ohio below that place. For greater safety they immediately assembled on Wheeling creek, and learning that two Indians were with some traders above the town, they went up the river, and without stopping to enquire as to their guilt, deliberately put them to death. On the afternoon of the same day, they found a party of Indians on the Ohio, below Wheeling creek, on whom they fired, and killed several. The Indians returned the fire and wounded one of the assailing party. It is admitted by all the authorities on this subject, that the two Indians killed above Wheeling, were shot by men under the command of colonel Michael Cresap. Mr. Jefferson, in his Notes on Virginia, states that the second attack, in which one of Logan's family is alleged to have been killed, was also headed by

---

* Thatcher's Indian Biography.

Cresap; and, in this he is sustained by Doddridge, Heckewelder and others; but it is denied by Jacob. "Pursuing these examples," says Mr. Jefferson, "Daniel Greathouse and one Tomlinson, who lived on the opposite side of the river from the Indians, and were in habits of friendship with them, collected at the house of Polk, on Cross creek, about sixteen miles from Baker's bottom, a party of thirty-two men. Their object was to attack a hunting party of Indians, consisting of men, women and children, at the mouth of Yellow creek, some distance above Wheeling. They proceeded, and when arrived near Baker's bottom they concealed themselves, and Greathouse crossed the river to the Indian camp. Being among them as a friend, he counted them and found them too strong for an open attack with his force. While here, he was cautioned by one of the women not to stay, for that the Indian men were drinking; and having heard of Cresap's murder of their relatives at Grave creek, were angry; and she pressed him in a friendly manner to go home; whereupon, after inviting them to come over and drink, he returned to Baker's, which was a tavern, and desired that when any of them should come to his house, he would give them as much rum as they could drink. When this plot was ripe, and a sufficient number of them had collected at Baker's and become intoxicated, he and his party fell on them and massacred the whole except a little girl, whom they preserved as a prisoner. Among them was the very woman who had saved his life by pressing him to retire from the drunken wrath of her friends, when he was playing the spy in their camp at Yellow creek. Either she herself or some other one of the murdered women was the sister of Logan; there were others of his relations who fell at the same time. The party on the opposite side of the river, upon hearing the report of the guns, became alarmed for their friends at Baker's house, immediately manned two canoes and sent them over. They were met by a five from Greathouse's party, as they approached the shore, which kill ed some, wounded others, and obliged the remainde. to return. Baker subsequently stated, that six or eigh were wounded and twelve killed.

c 2

The settlers along the frontier, satisfied that the Indians would retaliate upon them, for these unprovoked aggressions, either returned to the interior of the country, or gathered in forts, and made preparation for resistance. The assembly of the colony of Virginia being then in session, an express was sent to the seat of government, announcing the commencement of hostilities with the Indians, and asking assistance. In the month of May, the excitement among the Indians was still further increased by the murder of the Delaware sachem, "Bald Eagle," and the wounding of "Silver Heels," a popular chief of the Shawanoe tribe. Bald Eagle was an aged, harmless man, who was in the habit of visiting the whites on the most friendly terms. At the period of his death, he was returning alone, in his canoe, from a visit to the fort at the mouth of the Kanawha. The individual who committed the murder, having scalped him, placed the body in a sitting posture in the canoe and suffered it to float down the stream, in which condition it was found by the Indians. Silver Heels was returning from Albany to the Ohio, having been to that city as the voluntary escort of some white traders, who were fleeing from the frontiers. He was fired upon and dangerously wounded while crossing Big Beaver in a canoe. Such were some of the causes which called into action the vindictive feelings of the Indians.

The distinguished Mingo chief, Logan, was roused to action by the murder of his relatives at Yellow creek; and in the course of the summer, led some war parties against the whites, and destroyed several families. The Earl of Dunmore, then governor of the colony of Virginia, made arrangements for a campaign against the Indians, but it was not until September, that his forces were brought into the field. He ordered three regiments to be raised west of the Blue Ridge, the command of which was given to general Andrew Lewis. A similar army was assembled from the interior, the command of which the Earl assumed in person. The mouth of the Great Kanawha was the point at which these two divisions of the army were to meet; from whence, under the command of governor Dunmore, they were to march against the Indian towns on the north side of the Ohio. General Lewis' division amount ed to eleven hundred men, most of whom were accus tomed to danger, and with their officers, familiar with the modes of Indian warfare. On the eleventh of September, general Lewis moved from his camp, in the vicinity of Lewisburg, and after a march of nineteen days, traversing a wilderness through the distance of one hundred and sixty-five miles, he reached the mouth of the Kanawha, and made an encampment at that point. Here he waited several days for the arrival of governor Dunmore, who, with the division under his command, was to have met him at this place. Disappointed in not hearing from Dunmore, general Lewis despatched some scouts, over land to Pittsburg, to obtain intelligence of him. On the ninth of October, and before the return of these scouts, an express from Dunmore arrived in camp, with information that he had changed his plan of operations; and intended to march directly against the Indian towns on the Scioto; and directing general Lewis to cross the Ohio and join him. Preparations were making to obey this order, when, about sunrise, on the morning of the tenth, a large body of Indians was discovered within a mile of the camp. Two detachments were ordered out by general Lewis, to meet the enemy, one under the command of colonel Charles Lewis, the other under colonel Fleming. The former marched to the right, some distance from the Ohio, the latter to the left, on the bank of that stream. Colonel Lewis had not proceeded half a mile from the camp, when, soon after sunrise, his front line was vigorously attacked by the united tribes of the Shawanoes, Delawares, Mingoes, Ioways, and some others, in number between eight hundred and one thousand. At the commencement of the attack, colonel Lewis received a wound, which in the course of a few hours proved fatal: several of his men were killed at the same time, and his division was forced to fall back. In about a minute after the attack upon Lewis, the enemy engaged the front of the other division, on the bank of the Ohio, and in a short time, colonel Fleming, the leader of it, was severely wounded, and compelled to retire to the camp. Colonel Lewis' division having now been reinforced from the camp, pressed upon the Indians until they had fallen back in a line with Fleming's division. During this time, it being now twelve o'clock, the action continued with unabated severity. The close underwood, the ravines and fallen trees, favored the Indians; and while the bravest of their warriors fought from behind these coverts, others were throwing their dead into the Ohio, and carrying off their wounded. In their slow retreat, the Indians, about one o'clock, gained a very advantageous position, from which it appeared to our officers so difficult to dislodge them, that it was deemed advisable to maintain the line as then formed, which was about a mile and a quarter in length. In this position, the action was continued, with more or less severity, until sundown, when, night coming on, the Indians effected a safe retreat.*

McClung, in his valuable Sketches of Western Adventure, in describing this sanguinary battle, speaks of the Indians fighting from behind a breastwork; Stone, in his Life of Brant, says the Indians were forced to avail themselves of a rude breastwork of logs and brushwood, which they had taken the precaution to construct for the occasion. There must be some mistake in regard to this breastwork, as it is evident from the circumstances of the case, that the Indians could not, before the battle, have erected one so near the camp without discovery; and after the action commenced, it was too fiercely prosecuted for a rampart of this kind to have been thrown up.

In regard to the number killed on either side, there is no very certain information. Doddridge, in his Notes on the Indian wars, places the number of whites killed in this action at seventy-five, and the wounded at one hundred and forty. Campbell, in his History of Virginia, says the number of whites who were killed was upwards of fifty, and that ninety were wounded, which is probably near the truth. The Indian force engaged in this action has been estimated by different

---

* Official Report, xii. vol., Niles Register.

writers, at from eight hundred to fifteen hundred men. It is probable that the number did not exceed eight hundred. They were led on by some bold and warlike chiefs, among them Cornstalk, Logan, Elenipsico, Red Eagle, and Packishenoah, the last of whom was killed. Cornstalk, the chief in command, was conspicuous for his bravery, and animated his followers in tones which rose above the clash of arms; and when a retreat became necessary, conducted it so successfully and with so much delay, as to give his men an opportunity of bearing off all their wounded and many of the killed, whose bodies were thrown into the river. The loss of the Indians was never ascertained. One of the historians already quoted, speaks of it as "comparatively trifling." The character of our troops, many of whom were experienced woods-men, familiar with Indian fighting, the long continuance of the action—from the rising to the going down of the sun—the equality in numbers and position of the contending parties, the known usage of the Indians in hiding their dead and carrying off the wounded, the number of killed found on the battle ground the following day, and the severe loss of the Virginians, all forbid the idea that the loss of the enemy could have been trifling. The Ohio and Kanawha rivers afforded them opportunities for concealing their dead, while the plan of retreat,—alternately giving ground and renewing the attack,—was no doubt adopted for the purpose of gaining time to remove the wounded across the Ohio. It is fair to assume that the loss of the Indians was not far short of that sustained by the whites.

All circumstances considered, this battle may be ranked among the most memorable, and well contested, that has been fought on this continent. The leaders, on either side, were experienced and able, the soldiers skilful and brave. The victorious party, if either could be so called, had as little to boast of as the vanquished. It was alike creditable to the Anglo-Saxon and the aboriginal arms.

After the Indians had recrossed the Ohio, they marched to the valley of the Scioto, and encamped on the east side of that stream, about eight miles north of

where Chillicothe now stands.   Here a council was
held to decide upon their future movements.   Cornstalk, although true to the interests of the Shawanoes,
was the friend of peace, and had been opposed to making the attack on the troops of general Lewis.   Being
overruled, he entered into the action determined to do
his duty.   He now rose in the council and demanded,
" *What shall we do now ?   The Long Knives are
coming upon us by two routes.   Shall we turn out
and fight them ?* "   No reply being made to his questions, he continued, " shall we kill all our women and
children, and then fight until we are all killed ourselves?"   The chiefs were still silent.   Cornstalk turned round, and striking his tomahawk into the war-post
standing in the midst of the council, said with his characteristic energy of manner, " *Since you are not inclined to fight, I will go and make peace.*"

In the meantime the earl of Dunmore, having procured
boats at fort Pitt, descended the river to Wheeling, where
the army halted for a few days, and then proceeded
down the river in about one hundred canoes, a few
keel boats and perogues, to the mouth of Hockhocking,
and from thence over land, until the army had got
within a few miles of the Shawanoe camp.   Here the
army halted, and made a breastwork of fallen trees,
and entrenchments of such extent as to include about
twelve acres of ground, with an enclosure in the centre containing about one acre.   This was the citadel,
which contained the markees of the earl and his superior officers.*   Before the army of Dunmore had reached this point, he had been met by messengers from the
Indians suing for peace.   General Lewis, in the meantime, did not remain inactive.   The day after the battle he proceeded to bury his dead, and to throw up a
rude entrenchment around his camp, and appoint a
guard for the protection of the sick and wounded.   On
the succeeding day he crossed the Ohio with his army,
and commenced his march through a trackless desert,
for the Shawanoe towns on the Scioto.   Governor Dunmore, having determined to make peace with the In-

---

* Doddridge's Indian Wars.

dians, sent an express to general Lewis, ordering him to retreat across the Ohio. The order was disregarded, and the march continued until the governor in person, met the general and peremptorily repeated it. General Lewis and his troops, burning with a desire of aveng- ing the Indian massacres, and the loss of their brave companions in the late battle, reluctantly obeyed the command of Dunmore; and turned their faces home- wards. When the governor and his officers had re- turned to their camp, on the following day, the treaty with the Indians was opened. For fear of treachery, only eighteen Indians were permitted to attend their chiefs within the encampment, and they were required to leave their arms behind them. The conference was commenced by Cornstalk, in a long, bold and spirited speech, in which the white people were charged with being the authors of the war, by their aggressions upon the Indians at Captina and Yellow creek. Logan, the celebrated Mingo chief, refused to attend, although wil- ling to make peace. His influence with the Indians made it important to secure his concurrence in the propo- sed treaty. Dunmore sent a special messenger, (colonel John Gibson,) to him. They met alone in the woods, where Logan delivered to him his celebrated speech. Colonel Gibson wrote it down, returned to Dunmore's camp, read the speech in the council, and the terms of the peace were then agreed on. What those terms were, is not fully known. No copy of the treaty can now be found, although diligent enquiry has been made for it. Burk, in his History of Virginia, says, that the peace was on "condition that the lands on *this side of the Ohio* should be for ever ceded to the whites; that their prisoners should be delivered up, and that four hostages should be immediately given for the faithful performance of these conditions." Campbell, in his History of Virginia, says, the Indians "agreed to give up their lands on this side of the Ohio, and set at liber- ty their prisoners." Butler, in his History of Kentucky, remarks that, " such a treaty appears at this day, to be utterly beyond the advantages which could have been claimed from Dunmore's expedition." This is undoubt- edly a reasonable conclusion. The statement in Doddridge, that "on our part we obtained at the treaty a cessation of hostilities and a surrender of prisoners, and nothing more," is most probably the true version of the terms of this peace. If an important grant of land had been obtained by this treaty, copies of it would have been preserved in the public archives, and references in subsequent treaties, would have been made to it; but such seems not to have been the case. The conclusion must be, that it was only a treaty for the cessation of hostilities and the surrender of prisoners.

There have been various speculations as to the causes which induced governor Dunmore to order the retreat of the army under general Lewis, before the treaty was concluded. However desirous of a peace, the presence of an additional force would only have rendered that result more certain. It was believed by some of the officers of the army, and the opinion has been held by several writers since, that after governor Dunmore started on this expedition, he was advised of the strong probability of a war between Great Britain and her colonies; and that all his subsequent measures were shaped with a reference to making the Indians the allies of England in the expected contest. On this supposition, his conduct in not joining general Lewis at the mouth of the Kanawha, in risking his own detachment in the enemy's country, and in positively forbidding the other wing of the army from uniting with his, at camp Charlotte, has been explained. There are certainly plausible grounds for believing that governor Dunmore at this time, had more at heart the interests of Great Britain than of the colonies.

Soon after the conclusion of this war, the Shawanoes, with other tribes of the north-western Indians, took part with England in the war with the colonies; nor did the peace of 1783 put an end to these hostilities. The settlement of the valley of the Ohio by the whites, was boldly and perseveringly resisted; nor was the tomahawk buried by the Indians, until after the decisive battle at the rapids of the Miami of the lakes, on the 20th of August, 1794. The proximity of the Shawanoe towns to the Ohio river—the great highway of emigration to the west—and the facility with which the infant settlements in Kentucky could be reached, rendered this warlike tribe an annoying and dangerous neighbor. Led on by some daring chiefs; fighting for their favorite hunting-grounds, and stimulated to action by British agents, the Shawanoes, for a series of years, pressed sorely upon the new settlements; and are supposed to have caused the destruction of more property and a greater number of lives, than all the other tribes of the north-west united. They participated in most of the predatory excursions into Kentucky. They were present at the celebrated attack on Bryant's station; they fought with their characteristic bravery in the battle of the Blue Licks, and participated in colonel Byrd's hostile excursion up Licking river, and the destruction of Martin's and Riddle's stations. In turn, they were compelled to stand on the defensive, and to encounter the gallant Kentuckians on the north side of the Ohio. Bowman's expedition in 1779, to the waters of Mad river; Clark's in 1780 and 1782, and Logan's in 1786, to the same point; Edwards' in 1787, to the head waters of the Big Miami; and Todd's in 1788, into the Scioto valley—not to name several minor ones—were chiefly directed against the Shawanoes; and resulted in the destruction of two or three of their principal villages, but not without a fierce and bloody resistance. The Shawanoes were likewise found in hostility to the United States, in the campaigns of Harmar, St. Clair and Wayne. They united in the treaty of Greenville, in 1795; and with the exception of a few who fought at Tippecanoe, remained at peace with this government until the war with Great Britain, in 1812, in which a considerable body of them became the allies of the latter power. Some of the tribe, however, remained neutral in that contest, and others joined the United States, and continued faithful until the peace of 1815.

WEYAPIERSENWAH, OR BLUE JACKET.

In the campaign of general Harmar, in the year 1790, Blue Jacket—an influential Shawanoe chief—was associated with the Miami chief, Little Turtle, in the command of the Indians. In the battle of the 20th

D

of August 1794, when the combined army of the Indians was defeated by general Wayne, Blue Jacket had the chief control. The night previous to the battle, while the Indians were posted at Presque Isle, a council was held, composed of chiefs from the Miamis, Potawatimies, Delawares, Shawanoes, Chippewas, Ottawas and Senecas—the seven nations engaged in the action. They decided against the proposition to attack general Wayne that night in his encampment. The expediency of meeting him the next day then came up for consideration. Little Turtle was opposed to this measure, but being warmly supported by Blue Jacket, it was finally agreed upon. The former was strongly inclined to peace, and decidedly opposed to risking a battle under the circumstances in which the Indians were then placed. "We have beaten the enemy," said he, "twice, under separate commanders. We cannot expect the same good fortune always to attend us. The Americans are now led by a chief who never sleeps. The night and the day are alike to him; and, during all the time that he has been marching upon our villages, notwithstanding the watchfulness of our young men, we have never been able to surprise him. Think well of it. There is something whispers me, it would be prudent to listen to his offers of peace." The councils of Blue Jacket, however, prevailed over the better judgment of Little Turtle. The battle was fought and the Indians defeated.

In the month of October following this defeat, Blue Jacket concurred in the expediency of sueing for peace, and at the head of a deputation of chiefs, was about to bear a flag to general Wayne, then at Greenville, when the mission was arrested by foreign influence. Governor Simcoe, colonel McKee and the Mohawk chief, captain John Brant, having in charge one hundred and fifty Mohawks and Messasagoes, arrived at the rapids of the Maumee, and invited the chiefs of the combined army to meet them at the mouth of the Detroit river, on the 10th of October. To this Blue Jacket assented, for the purpose of hearing what the British officers had to propose. Governor Simcoe urged the Indians to retain their hostile attitude towards the United States. In referring to the encroachments of the people of this country on the Indian lands, he said, "Children: I am still of the opinion that the Ohio is your right and title. I have given orders to the commandant of fort Miami to fire on the Americans whenever they make their appearance again. I will go down to Quebec, and lay your grievances before the great man. From thence they will be forwarded to the king, your father. Next spring you will know the result of every thing what you and I will do." He urged the Indians to obtain a cessation of hostilities, until the following spring, when the English would be ready to attack the Americans, and by driving them back across the Ohio, restore their lands to the Indians.[*] These counsels delayed the conclusion of peace until the following summer.

Blue Jacket was present at the treaty of Greenville in 1795, and conducted himself with moderation and dignity. Upon his arrival at that place, in excuse for not having met general Wayne at an earlier period, he said, "Brother, when I came here last winter, I did not mean to deceive you. What I promised you I did intend to perform. My wish to conclude a firm peace with you being sincere, my uneasiness has been great that my people have not come forward so soon as you, could wish, or might expect. But you must not be discouraged by these unfavorable appearances. Some of our chiefs and warriors are here; more will arrive in a few days. You must not, however, expect to see a great number. Yet, notwithstanding, our nation will be well represented. Our hearts are open and void of deceit."

On the second day of the council, Blue Jacket made a remark, showing the relation subsisting between the Shawanoes and some other tribes, to which allusion has been made already.

"Brothers: I hope you will not take amiss my changing my seat in this council. You all know the Wyandots are our uncles, and the Delawares our grand-

---

[*] Amer. State Papers, vol. 5, p. 529. Stone's Life of Brant, vol. 2, p. 392.

fathers, and that the Shawanoes are the elder brothers
of the other nations present. It is, therefore, proper
that I should sit next my grandfathers and uncles. I
hope, younger brothers, you are all satisfied with what
your uncles said yesterday, and that I have done every
thing in my power to advise and support you."

At the conclusion of the treaty Blue Jacket rose and
said :

"Elder Brother, and you, my brothers, present: you
see me now present myself as a war-chief to lay down
that commission, and place myself in the rear of my
village chiefs, who for the future will command me.
Remember, brothers, you have all buried your war
hatchet. Your brothers, the Shawanoes, now do the
same good act. We must think of war no more.

"Elder Brother: you see now all the chiefs and
warriors around you, have joined in the good work of
peace, which is now accomplished. We now request
you to inform our elder brother, general Washington,
of it; and of the cheerful unanimity which has marked
their determination. We wish you to enquire of him
if it would be agreeable that two chiefs from each nation should pay him a visit, and take him by the hand;
for your younger brothers have a strong desire to see
that great man and to enjoy the pleasure of conversing
with him."

We are indebted to major Galloway of Xenia, for
the following anecdote of this chief:

"In the spring of 1800, Blue Jacket and another
chief, whose name I have forgotten, boarded for several weeks at my father's, in Green county, at the
expense of a company of Kentuckians, who engaged
Blue Jacket, for a valuable consideration, to show them
a great silver mine, which tradition said was known to
the Indians, as existing on Red river, one of the head
branches of the Kentucky. A Mr. Jonathan Flack,
agent of this company, had previously spent several
months among the Shawanoes, at their towns and
hunting camps, in order to induce this chief to show
this great treasure. At the time agreed on, ten or
twelve of the company came from Kentucky to meet
Blue Jacket at my father's, where a day or two was

spent in settling the terms upon which he would accompany them; the crafty chief taking his own time
to deliberate on the offers made him, and rising in his
demands in proportion to their growing eagerness to
possess the knowledge which was to bring untold
wealth to all the company. At length the bargain
was made; horses, goods and money were given as
presents, and the two chiefs with their squaws, were
escorted in triumph to Kentucky, where they were
feasted and caressed in the most flattering manner, and
all their wants anticipated and liberally supplied. In
due time and with all possible secrecy, they visited the
region where this great mine was said to be embowel-
ed in the earth. Here the wily Shawanoe spent some
time in seclusion, in order to humble himself by fast-
ings, purifications and *pow-wowings*, with a view to
propitiate the Great Spirit; and to get His permission
to disclose the grand secret of the mine. An equivocal
answer was all the response that was given to him in
his dreams; and, after many days of fruitless toil and
careful research, the mine, the great object so devoutly
sought and wished for, could not be found. The cunning Blue Jacket, however, extricated himself with
much address from the anticipated vengeance of the
disappointed worshippers of Plutus, by charging his
want of success to his eyes, which were dimmed by
reason of his old age; and by promising to send his
son on his return home, whose eyes were young and
good, and who knew the desired spot and would show
it. The son, however, never visited the scene of his
father's failure; and thus ended the adventures of the
celebrated mining company of Kentucky."

CATAHECASSA, OR BLACK-HOOF.

AMONG the celebrated chiefs of the Shawanoes,
Black Hoof is entitled to a high rank. He was born
in Florida, and at the period of the removal of a portion of that tribe to Ohio and Pennsylvania, was old
enough to recollect having bathed in the salt water.
He was present with others of his tribe, at the defeat
of Braddock, near Pittsburg, in 1755, and was engaged

in all the wars in Ohio from that time until the treaty of Greenville, in 1795. Such was the sagacity of Black Hoof in planning his military expeditions, and such the energy with which he executed them, that he won the confidence of his whole nation, and was never at a loss for *braves* to fight under his banner. "He was known far and wide, as the great Shawanoe warrior, whose cunning, sagacity and experience were only equalled by the fierce and desperate bravery with which he carried into operation his military plans. Like the other Shawanoe chiefs, he was the inveterate foe of the white man, and held that no peace should be made, nor any negociation attempted, except on the condition that the whites should repass the mountains, and leave the great plains of the west to the sole occupancy of the native tribes.

"He was the orator of his tribe during the greater part of his long life, and was an excellent speaker. The venerable colonel Johnston of Piqua, to whom we are indebted for much valuable information, describes him as the most graceful Indian he had ever seen, and as possessing the most natural and happy faculty of expressing his ideas. He was well versed in the traditions of his people; no one understood better their peculiar relations to the whites, whose settlements were gradually encroaching on them, or could detail with more minuteness the wrongs with which his nation was afflicted. But although a stern and uncompromising opposition to the whites had marked his policy through a series of forty years, and nerved his arm in a hundred battles, he became at length convinced of the madness of an ineffectual struggle against a vastly superior and hourly increasing foe. No sooner had he satisfied himself of this truth, than he acted upon it with the decision which formed a prominent trait in his character. The temporary success of the Indians in several engagements previous to the campaign of general Wayne, had kept alive their expiring hopes; but their signal defeat by that gallant officer, convinced the more reflecting of their leaders of the desperate character of the conflict. Black Hoof was among those who decided upon making terms with the victorious American commander; and having signed the treaty of 1795, at Greenville, he continued faithful to his stipulations during the remainder of his life. From that day he ceased to be the enemy of the white man; and as he was not one who could act a negative part, he became the firm ally and friend of those against whom his tomahawk had been so long raised in vindictive animosity. He was their friend, not from sympathy or conviction, but in obedience to a necessity which left no middle course, and under a belief that submission alone could save his tribe from destruction; and having adopted this policy, his sagacity and sense of honor, alike forbade a recurrence either to open war or secret hostility.

"Black Hoof was the principal chief of the Shawanoe nation, and possessed all the influence and authority which are usually attached to that office, at the period when Tecumseh and his brother the Prophet commenced their hostile operations against the United States. Tecumseh had never been reconciled to the whites. As sagacious and as brave as Black Hoof, and resembling him in all the better traits of savage character, he differed widely from that respectable chief in his political opinions. They were both patriotic in the proper sense of the word, and earnestly desired to preserve the remnant of their tribe from the destruction that threatened the whole Indian race. Black Hoof, whose long and victorious career as a warrior placed his courage far above suspicion, submitted to what he believed inevitable, and endeavoured to evade the effects of the storm by bending beneath its fury; while Tecumseh, a younger man, an influential warrior, but not a chief, with motives equally public spirited, was, no doubt, unconsciously biassed by personal ambition, and suffered his hatred to the white man to master every other feeling and consideration. The one was a leader of ripened fame, who had reached the highest place in his nation, and could afford to retire from the active scenes of warfare; the other was a candidate for higher honors than he had yet achieved; and both might have been actuated by a common impulse of rivalry, which induced them to espouse different opinions in opposition to each other."*

When Tecumseh and the Prophet embarked in their scheme for the recovery of the lands as far south as the Ohio river, it became their interest as well as policy to enlist Black Hoof in the enterprise; and every effort which the genius of the one and the cunning of the other, could devise, was brought to bear upon him. But Black Hoof continued faithful to the treaty which he had signed at Greenville, in 1795, and by prudence and influence kept the greater part of his tribe from joining the standard of Tecumseh or engaging on the side of the British in the late war with England. In that contest he became the ally of the United States, and although he took no active part in it, he exerted a very salutary influence over his tribe. In January, 1813, he visited general Tupper's camp, at fort McArthur, and while there, about ten o'clock one night, when sitting by the fire in company with the general and several other officers, some one fired a pistol through a hole in the wall of the hut, and shot Black Hoof in the face : the ball entered the cheek, glanced against the bone, and finally lodged in his neck: he fell, and for some time was supposed to be dead, but revived, and afterwards recovered from this severe wound. The most prompt and diligent enquiry as to the author of this cruel and dastardly act, failed to lead to his detection. No doubt was entertained that this attempt at assassination was made by a white man, stimulated perhaps by no better excuse than the memory of some actual or ideal wrong, inflicted on some of his own race by an unknown hand of kindred colour with that of his intended victim.†

Black Hoof was opposed to polygamy, and to the practice of burning prisoners. He is reported to have lived forty years with one wife, and to have reared a numerous family of children, who both loved and esteemed him. His disposition was cheerful, and his conversation sprightly and agreeable. In stature he

* History of the Indian Tribes of N. America.   † James Galloway.

was smal., being not more than five feet eight inches in height. He was favored with good health, and unimpaired eye sight to the period of his death, which occurred at Wapakonatta, in the year 1831, at the age of one hundred and ten years.

CORNSTALK.

THE reader of these pages is already familiar with the name of Cornstalk, " the mighty Cornstalk, sachem of the Shawanoes, and king of the Northern Confederacy." His conduct in the memorable battle of Point Pleasant establishes his fame as an able and gallant warrior. He carried into that action the skill of an accomplished general, and the heroism of a dauntless brave. Neither a thirst for blood, nor the love of renown, ever prompted him to arms. He was the open advocate for honorable peace—the avowed and devoted friend of the whites. But he loved his own people and the hunting grounds in which they roamed ; and, when his country's wrongs demanded redress, he became the " thunderbolt of war," and avenged the aggressions upon his tribe with energy and power. He fought, however, that peace might reign ; and, after the battle in which he so highly distinguished himself, was the first among his associated chiefs to propose a cessation of hostilities. While he mourned over the inevitable doom of the Indians, he had the sagacity to perceive that all efforts to avert it, were not only useless, but, in the end, reacted upon them with withering influence.

He has been justly called a great and a good man. He was the zealous friend of the Moravian missions; and warmly encouraged every effort to ameliorate the moral and physical condition of his people. " His noble bearing," says Mr. Withers, " his generous and disinterested attachment to the colonies, when the thunder of British cannon was reverberating through the land, his anxiety to preserve the frontier of Virginia from desolation and death, (the object of his visit to Point Pleasant,) all conspired to win for him the esteem and respect of others; while the untimely and perfidious manner of his death, caused a deep and lasting regret to pervade the bosoms even of those who were enemies to his nation; and excited the just indignation of all towards his inhuman and barbarous murderers." The strong native powers of his mind had been more enriched by observation, travel and intercourse with the whites, than is usual among the Indian chiefs. He was familiarly acquainted with the topography and geography of the north-west, even beyond the Mississippi river, and possessed an accurate knowledge of the various treaties between the whites and the Indian tribes of this region, and the relative rights of each party.

At the treaty with Dunmore, he made a speech alike creditable to his love of country and his sense of justice. He pourtrayed, in living colors, the wrongs inflicted upon the Indians by the colonists, and placed in strong contrast the former and present condition of his nation, the one being happy and prosperous, the other degraded and oppressed. He spoke in a strain of manly boldness of the repeated perfidy of the white people; and especially, of the unblushing dishonesty of the traders; and, finally concluded by proposing as one of the fundamental provisions of the treaty, that no commerce with the Indians should be carried on for individual profit, but that honest men should be sent among them by their white brother, with such things as they needed, to be exchanged, at a fair price, for their skins and furs: and still further, that no "fire-water," of any kind, should be introduced among them, inasmuch as it depraved his people and stimulated them to aggressions upon their white brethren.

As an orator, the fame of Cornstalk stands high. Colonel Benjamin Wilson, an officer in Dunmore's campaign, in 1774, who was present at the interview (at camp Charlotte) between the chiefs and the governor, in speaking of Cornstalk, says, "when he arose, he was in no wise confused or daunted, but spoke in a distinct and audible voice, without stammering or repetition, and with peculiar emphasis. His looks, while addressing Dunmore, were truly grand and majestic, yet graceful and attractive. I have heard the first orators in Virginia,—Patrick Henry and Richard Henry Lee,—

SHAWANOE INDIANS.   47

but never have I heard one whose powers of delivery surpassed those of Cornstalk."

The treaty at camp Charlotte did not bring much repose to the frontier. In the course of the two years succeeding it, new difficulties arose between the Indians and the inhabitants of western Virginia. Early in the spring of 1777, several tribes joined in an offensive alliance against the latter. Cornstalk exerted all his influence to arrest it, but in vain. Sincerely desirous of averting war, he resolved to communicate this condition of affairs to the Virginians, in the hope that they might dissipate the impending war-cloud. This information he determined to give in person. Taking with him Red Hawk, and one other Indian, he went secretly to the fort at Point Pleasant, with a flag of peace, and presented himself to the commander of that post. After stating to him the object of the mission, and fully explaining the situation of the confederate tribes and their contemplated attack upon the whites, he remarked, in regard to his own, "the current sets (with the Indians,) so strong against the Americans, in consequence of the agency of the British, that they (the Shawanoes) will float with it, I fear, in spite of all my exertions." No sooner had this information been given to the commander, captain Matthew Arbuckle, than he decided, in violation of all good faith, to detain the two chiefs as hostages, to prevent the meditated attack on the settlements. This he did; and immediately gave information to the executive of Virginia, who ordered additional troops to the frontier. In the mean time, the officers in the fort held frequent conversations with Cornstalk, whose intelligence equally surprised and pleased them. He took pleasure in giving them minute descriptions of his country, its rivers, prairies and lakes, its game and other productions. One day, as he was drawing a rude map on the floor, for the gratification of those present, a call was heard from the opposite shore of the Ohio, which he at once recognized as the voice of his favorite son, Elenipsico, a noble minded youth, who had fought by his father's side in the battle of Point Pleasant. At the request of Cornstalk, Elenipsico crossed over the river, and joined him in the fort,

where they had an affectionate and touching meeting.
The son had become uneasy at his father's long absence; and regardless of danger, had visited this place
in search of him. It happened on the following day
that two white men, belonging to the fort, crossed over
the Kanawha, upon a hunting excursion; as they were
returning to their boat, they were fired upon by some
Indians in ambush, and one of the hunters, named Gilmore, was killed, the other making his escape. The
news of this murder having reached the fort, a party
of captain Hall's men crossed the river and brought in
the body of Gilmore; whereupon the cry was raised,
"let us go and kill the Indians in the fort." An in-
furiated gang, with captain Hall at their head, instantly
started, and in despite of all remonstrance, and the most
solemn assurances that the murderers of Gilmore had
no connection whatever with the imprisoned chiefs,
they persisted in their cruel and bloody purpose, swear-
ing, with guns in their hands, that they would shoot
any one who attempted to oppose them. In the mean
time, the interpreter's wife, who had been a captive
among the Indians, and had a feeling of regard for
Cornstalk and his companions, perceiving their danger,
ran to the cabin to tell them of it; and to let them know
that Hall and his party charged Elenipsico with having
brought with him the Indians who had killed Gilmore.
This, however, the youthful chief denied most positively, asserting that he came unattended by any one,
and for the single purpose of learning the fate of his
father. At this time captain Hall and his followers, in
despite of the remonstance and command of captain
Arbuckle, were approaching the cabin of the prisoners.
For a moment, Elenipsico manifested some agitation.
His father spoke and encouraged him to be calm, saying,
"my son, the Great Spirit has seen fit that we should
die together, and has sent you here to that end. It is
his will, and let us submit; it is all for the best;" and
turning round to meet the assassins at the door, was
shot with seven bullets, and expired without a groan.
The momentary agitation of Elenipsico passed off, and
keeping his seat, he met his death with stern and heroic apathy. Red Hawk manifested less resolution, and

made a fruitless effort to conceal himself in the chimney of the cabin. He was discovered and instantly shot. The fourth Indian was then slowly and cruelly put to death. Thus terminated this dark and fearful tragedy—leaving a foul blot on the page of history, which all the waters of the beautiful Ohio, on whose banks it was perpetrated, can never wash out, and the remembrance of which will long outlive the heroic and hapless nation which gave birth to the noble Cornstalk

SPEMICA-LAWBA—THE HIGH HORN,

generally known as

CAPTAIN LOGAN

In September, 1786, captain Benjamin Logan, of Kentucky, led an expedition of mounted men from that state against the Shawanoes, on the north side of the Ohio, and destroyed the Machachac towns on the waters of Mad river. Most of the warriors happened to be absent from the villages when the invading army reached them. About thirty persons were captured, chiefly women and children. After the slight resistance which was made by the Indians had ceased, captain Logan's men were both annoyed and endangered by some arrows, shot among them by an invisible but not unpractised hand. After considerable search, in the tall grass around the camp, an Indian youth was discovered, who with his bow and a quiver of arrows, had concealed himself in a position from which he could successfully throw his darts against the enemy: that intrepid boy was Logan, the subject of the present biographical sketch. He likewise was made prisoner, and with the others carried to Kentucky. The commander of the expedition was so much pleased with the bold conduct of this boy, that upon returning home, he made him a member of his own family, in which he resided some years, until at length, at a council for the exchange of prisoners, held on the bank of the Ohio, opposite to Maysville, between some Shawanoe chiefs and a deputation of citizens from Kentucky, our young hero was permitted to return to his

E

native land. He was ever afterwards known by the name of Logan.

Of the family of this distinguished individual, we have been enabled to glean but few particulars. In M'Afee's History of the Late War, and in Butler's History of Kentucky, he is represented to have been the son of Tecumseh's sister: this is manifestly an error; there was no relationship between them, either by blood or marriage.

Logan was a member of the Machachac tribe of the Shawanoes, and was elevated to the rank of a civil chief on account of his many estimable qualities, both intellectual and moral. He was a married man, and left behind him a wife and several children—requesting on his death bed that they might be sent into Kentucky, and placed under the patronage of his friend, colonel Hardin, who had married the daughter of his early patron, captain Logan. This, however, was not done, owing to objections interposed by the wife. The personal appearance of Logan was remarkably good, being six feet in height, finely formed and weighing near two hundred pounds.

From the period of his residence in Kentucky, to that of his death, Logan was the unwavering friend of the United States. He was extensively and favorably known on the frontier of Ohio, and the Indiana territory; and, immediately after the declaration of war against England in 1812, he joined the American service. He acted as one of the guides of general Hull's army to Detroit; and, prior to the actual investment of fort Wayne,—an account of which will be presently given—he was employed by the Indian agent at Piqua, on an important and delicate mission. The Indians around fort Wayne were giving indications of a disposition to abandon their neutrality. This rendered it expedient that the women and children then at that point, should be removed within the inhabited portions of Ohio. John Johnston, the Indian agent at Piqua, knowing Logan intimately, and having great confidence in his judgment as well as his fidelity, selected him to perform this duty. He was accordingly furnished with a letter to the commandant of that fort, in which assurances were given, that the persons about to be removed might confidently rely upon the discretion and enterprise of Logan. He proceeded on his mission, and executed it successfully: bringing into Piqua—near one hundred miles distant from fort Wayne—twenty-five women and children; the former, without an exception, bearing testimony to the uniform delicacy and kindness with which he treated them. Deeply impressed with the dangerous responsibility of the office he had assumed, he is said not to have slept from the time the party left fort Wayne, until it reached Piqua.

We next hear of Logan, in connection with the memorable siege of fort Wayne. This post, which was erected in 1794, stood at the junction of the St. Joseph's and St. Mary's rivers, and, although not within the limits of Ohio, its preservation was all-important to the peace and safety of our north-western frontier. Having been built of wood, it was, in 1812, a pile of combustible matter. Immediately after the surrender of general Hull, in August, 1812, the Indians, to the number of four or five hundred, closely invested this place. The garrison at that time, including every description of persons, amounted to less than one hundred persons, of whom not more than sixty or seventy were capable of performing military duty. These were commanded by captain Rhea, an officer who, from several causes, was but ill qualified for the station. His lieutenants were Philip Ostrander and Daniel Curtis, both of whom, throughout the siege, discharged their duty in a gallant manner.

At the time of the investment of this place, there was a considerable body of Ohio troops in the neighborhood of Piqua. These had been ordered out by governor Meigs, for the relief of Detroit; but, upon hearing of the surrender of that place, their course was directed towards fort Wayne. They were, however, almost in a state of disorganization, and manifested but little ardor in entering upon this new duty. Perceiving this state of things, and aware that the fort was in imminent danger, a young man, now major William Oliver, of Cincinnati, determined upon making

an effort to reach the garrison. Young Oliver was a
resident of fort Wayne, and was on his return from a
visit to Cincinnati when, at Piqua, he learned that the
place was besieged. He immediately joined a rifle
company of the Ohio militia; but seeing the tardy
movements of the troops, in advancing to the relief of
the fort, he resolved in the first place to return with all
possible expedition, to Cincinnati, for the purpose of
inducing colonel Wells, of the 17th U. S. infantry, to
march his regiment to the relief of the fort; and, in the
second place, to make an effort to reach it in person,
that the garrison might be encouraged to hold out until
reinforcements should arrive. When Oliver arrived
in Cincinnati, he found that general Harrison had just
crossed the Ohio, from Kentucky, and assumed the
command of the troops composing the north-western
army. He called upon the general, stated the condition
of things on the frontier, and avowed his intention of
passing into the fort in advance of the reinforcements.
The general informed him that the troops then at Cincinnati would be put in motion that day, and marched
with all practicable expedition to the invested point.
This was on the 27th of August; on the 31st Oliver
overtook the Ohio militia at the St. Mary's river.
Here he learned that Adrian and Shane, two experienced scouts, had been sent in the direction of fort
Wayne, and had returned with information that the
hostile Indians were in great force on the route to that
place. On the next day, general Thomas Worthington,
of Chillicothe, who was then on the frontier as Indian
commissioner, seeing the great importance of communicating with the garrison, determined to unite with
Oliver in the attempt to reach it. These two enterpri
sing individuals induced sixty-eight of the Ohio troops
and sixteen Shawanoe Indians, among whom was Logan, to accompany them. They marched eighteen
miles that day, and camped for the night at Shane's
crossing.

Next morning they again moved forward, but in the
course of the day, some thirty-six of their party abandoned the hazardous enterprise, and returned to the
main army. The remainder pursued their route, and

encamped that evening within twenty-four miles of fort Wayne. As the party was not strong enough in its present condition to encounter the besieging enemy, general Worthington was very reluctantly induced to remain at this point, while Oliver, with Logan, captain Johnny and Brighthorn, should make an effort to reach the fort. Being well armed and mounted, they started at daybreak next morning upon this daring adventure. Proceeding with great caution, they came within five miles of the fort, before they observed any fresh Indian signs. At this point the keen eye of Logan discovered the cunning strategy of the enemy: for the purpose of concealing their bodies, they had dug holes on either side of the road, alternately, at such distances as to secure them from their own fire: these were intended for night watching, in order to cut off all communication with the fort. Here the party deemed it advisable to leave the main road, and strike across the country to the Maumee river, which was reached in safety at a point one and a half miles below the fort. Having tied their horses in a thicket, the party proceeded cautiously on foot, to ascertain whether our troops or the Indians were in possession of the fort. Having satisfied themselves on this point, they returned, remounted their horses, and taking the main road, moved rapidly to the fort. Upon reaching the gate of the esplanade, they found it locked, and were thus compelled to pass down the river bank, and then ascend it at the northern gate. They were favored in doing so by the withdrawal of the hostile Indians from this point, in carrying out a plan, then on the point of consummation, for taking the fort by an ingenious stratagem. For several days previous to this time, the hostile chiefs under a flag of truce, had been holding intercourse with the garrison; and had, it is supposed, discovered the unsoldier-like condition of the commander. They had accordingly arranged their warriors in a semicircle, on the west and south sides of the fort, and at no great distance from it. Five of the chiefs, under pretence of treating with the officers of the garrison, were to pass into the fort, and when in council were to assassinate the subaltern officers with pistols and knives, concealed under

E 2

their blankets; and then to seize captain Rhea, who, in his trepidation, and under a promise of personal safety, would, they anticipated, order the gates of the fort to be thrown open for the admission of the besiegers. The plan, thus arranged, was in the act of being carried into execution at the moment when Oliver and his companions reached the gate. In speaking of the opportune approach of this party, lieutenant Curtis says, "the safe arrival of Mr. Oliver at that particular juncture, may justly be considered most miraculous. One hour sooner or one later, would no doubt have been inevitable destruction both to himself and escort: the parties of Indians who had been detached to guard the roads and passes in different directions, having all at that moment been called in, to aid in carrying the fort. It is generally believed by those acquainted with the circumstances, that not one hour, for eight days and nights preceding or following the hour in which Mr. Oliver arrived, would have afforded an opportunity of any probable safety." Winnemac, Five Medals, and three other hostile chiefs, bearing the flag under which they were to gain admittance to the fort to carry out their treacherous intentions, were surprised by suddenly meeting at the gate, Oliver and his companions. Coming from different directions and screened by the angles of the fort, the parties were not visible to each other until both were near the gate. On meeting, they shook hands, but it was apparent that Winnemac was greatly disconcerted; he immediately wheeled and returned to his camp, satisfied that this accession of strength to the garrison—the forerunner, in all probability, of a much larger force—had defeated his scheme. The others of his party entered the fort, and remained some little time, during which they were given to understand that Logan and his two Indian companions were to remain with the garrison. Oliver, in the mean time, having written a hasty letter, describing the condition of the fort, to general Worthington; and the Indians being equipped with new rifles from the public stores, they prepared to leave the fort without delay. Fortunately their movements were not observed by the enemy, until they had actually started from the garrison gate. They now put spurs to their horses and dashed off at full speed. The hostile Indians were instantly in motion to intercept them; the race was a severe and perilous one, but Logan and his companions cleared the enemy's line in safety, and this accomplished, his loud shout of triumph rose high in the air, and fell like music upon the ears of the beleaguered garrison. The party reached general Worthington's camp early the next morning, and delivered Oliver's letter to him. Notwithstanding the perilous condition of the garrison, however, the Ohio troops delayed moving for its relief, until they were overtaken by general Harrison, who, with his reinforcements, was unable to reach the fort until the twelfth. In the mean time the Indians kept up an incessant firing, day and night, upon the fort, killing on one occasion, two of the garrison who passed out of the gate on police duty. Several times the buildings of the fort were set on fire by the burning arrows which were shot upon them, but by the vigilance of the garrison in extinguishing the flames, a general conflagration was prevented. Some days after the arrival of Oliver, the Indians appeared to be making preparations for some uncommon movement, and one afternoon, just before night-fall, succeeded in getting possession of one of the trading houses standing near the fort. From this point they demanded a surrender of the garrison, under a promise of protection; and with a threat of extermination if they were compelled to carry the fort by storm : they alleged, further, that they had just been reinforced by a large number of warriors, some pieces of British cannon, and artillerists to man them. Their demand being promptly refused, they immediately closed in upon the fort, yelling hideously, firing their guns and also a couple of cannon. Every man in the fort capable of doing duty, now stood at his post, having several stands of loaded arms by his side. They were directed by the acting lieutenant, Curtis,* not to fire until the Indians had approached within twenty-five paces of the fort: the

---

* Captain Rhea, by common consent, was suspended for incapacity, and lieutenant Ostrander was on the sick list.

fire was at length opened upon the entire Indian lines, and in a manner so destructive, that in twenty minutes the enemy retreated with the loss of eighteen of their warriors, killed. It was discovered, subsequently, that the cannon used on this occasion by the Indians, had been made of wood by some British traders who were with them; one of the pieces burst upon the first, and the other on the second, fire.

The day before general Harrison reached this place, the Indians concentrated at a swamp, five miles south of the fort, for the purpose of giving him battle; but after reconnoitering his force, and finding it too strong for them, they fell back, passing by the fort in great disorder, in the hope, it is supposed, of drawing out the garrison, under a belief that they, (the Indians,) had been defeated by general Harrison's army. To promote this idea, they had, while lying at the swamp, kindled extensive fires, that the rising volume of smoke might be mistaken for that which usually overhangs the field of battle. This device proving unavailing, the Indians, after a vigorous investment, running through more than twenty days, withdrew forever from the siege of fort Wayne.

The enterprise of young Oliver, just related, reflected the highest credit on his bravery and patriotism: being wholly voluntary on his part, the moral heroism of the act was only surpassed by its fortunate results; as it prevented, in all probability, the fall of an important frontier post, and saved its garrison from the tomahawk and scalping knife. So hazardous was the effort deemed, indeed, that experienced frontier's-men endeavored to dissuade him from the undertaking; and even Logan considered it one of great peril; but when once resolved upon, he gallantly incurred the hazard of the deed, and showed himself worthy of the trust reposed in him.

In November of this year, general Harrison directed Logan to take a small party of his tribe, and reconnoitre the country in the direction of the Rapids of the Maumee. When near this point, they were met by a body of the enemy, superior to their own in number, and compelled to retreat. Logan, captain Johnny and

Bright-horn, who composed the party, effected their escape, to the left wing of the army, then under the command of general Winchester, who was duly informed of the circumstances of their adventure. An officer of the Kentucky troops, general P., the second in command, without the slightest ground for such a charge, accused Logan of infidelity to our cause, and of giving intelligence to the enemy. Indignant at this foul accusation, the noble chief at once resolved to meet it in a manner that would leave no doubt as to his faithfulness to the United States. He called on his friend Oliver, and having told him of the imputation that had been cast upon his reputation, said that he would start from the camp next morning, and either leave his body bleaching in the woods, or return with such trophies from the enemy, as would relieve his character from the suspicion that had been wantonly cast upon it by an American officer.

Accordingly, on the morning of the 22d he started down the Maumee, attended by his two faithful companions, captain Johnny and Bright-horn. About noon, having stopped for the purpose of taking rest, they were suddenly surprised by a party of seven of the enemy, amongst whom were young Elliott, a half-breed, holding a commission in the British service, and the celebrated Potawatamie chief, Winnemac. Logan made no resistance, but with great presence of mind, extending his hand to Winnemac, who was an old acquaintance, proceeded to inform him, that he and his two companions, tired of the American service, were just leaving general Winchester's army, for the purpose of joining the British. Winnemac, being familiar with Indian strategy, was not satisfied with this declaration, but proceeded to disarm Logan and his comrades, and placing his party around them, so as to prevent their escape, started for the British camp at the foot of the Rapids. In the course of the afternoon, Logan's address was such as to inspire confidence in his sincerity, and induce Winnemac to restore to him and his companions their arms. Logan now formed the plan of attacking his captors on the first favorable opportunity, and whilst marching along, succeeded in communicat-

ing the substance of it to captain Johnny and Bright-
horn. Their guns being already loaded, they had little
further preparation to make, than to put bullets into
their mouths, to facilitate the reloading of their arms.
In carrying on this process, captain Johnny, as he afterwards related, fearing that the man marching by his
side had observed the operation, adroitly did away the
impression by remarking, "me chaw heap tobac."

The evening being now at hand, the British Indians
determined to encamp on the bank of Turkeyfoot creek,
about twenty miles from fort Winchester. Confiding
in the idea that Logan had really deserted the American service, a part of his captors rambled around the
place of their encampment, in search of blackhaws.
They were no sooner out of sight, than Logan gave
the signal of attack upon those who remained behind;
they fired and two of the enemy fell dead—the third,
being only wounded, required a second shot to despatch him; and in the mean time, the remainder of the
party, who were near by, returned the fire, and all of
them "treed." There being four of the enemy, and
only three of Logan's party, the latter could not watch
all the movements of their antagonists. Thus circum-
stanced, and during an active fight, the fourth man of
the enemy passed round until Logan was uncovered
by his tree, and shot him through the body. By this
time Logan's party had wounded two of the surviving
four, which caused them to fall back. Taking advantage of this state of things, captain Johnny mounted
Logan—now suffering the pain of a mortal wound—
and Bright-horn—also wounded—on two of the enemy's horses, and started them for Winchester's camp,
which they reached about midnight. Captain Johnny,
having already secured the scalp of Winnemac, followed
immediately on foot, and gained the same point early
on the following morning. It was subsequently ascertained that the two Indians of the British party, who
were last wounded, died of their wounds, making in
all five out of the seven, who were slain by Logan
and his companions.

When the news of this gallant affair had spread
through the camp, and especially after it was known

that Logan was mortally wounded, it created a deep and mournful sensation. No one, it is believed, more deeply regretted the fatal catastrophe, than the author of the charge upon Logan's integrity, which had led to this unhappy result.

Logan's popularity was very great; indeed he was almost universally esteemed in the army, for his fidelity to our cause, his unquestioned bravery, and the nobleness of his nature. He lived two or three days after reaching the camp, but in extreme bodily agony; he was buried by the officers of the army, at fort Winchester, with the honors of war. Previous to his death, he related the particulars of this fatal enterprise to his friend Oliver, declaring to him that he prized his honor more than life; and, having now vindicated his reputation from the imputation cast upon it, he died satisfied. In the course of this interview, and while writhing with pain, he was observed to smile; upon being questioned as to the cause, he replied, that when he recalled to his mind the manner in which captain Johnny took off the scalp of Winnemac, while at the same time dexterously watching the movements of the enemy, he could not refrain from laughing—an incident in savage life, which shows the "ruling passion strong in death." It would perhaps be difficult in the history of savage warfare, to point out an enterprise the execution of which reflects higher credit upon the address and daring conduct of its authors, than this does upon Logan and his two companions. Indeed a spirit even less indomitable, a sense of honor less acute, and a patriotic devotion to a good cause less active, than were manifested by this gallant chieftain of the woods, might, under other circumstances, have well conferred immortality upon his name.

The Shawanoe nation has produced a number of distinguished individuals, besides those who have been noticed in this brief sketch of that people. The plan of our work does not permit a more extended enumeration of them. When a full and faithful history of this tribe shall be written, it will be found, we think, that no tribe of aborigines on this continent, has given birth to so many men, remarkable for their talents, energy of character, and military prowess, as the Shawanoe.

Under a treaty held at the rapids of the Miami of the lakes, in 1817, by Duncan McArthur and Lewis Cass, commissioners on the part of the United States, for extinguishing Indian titles to lands in Ohio, the Shawanoes ceded to the government the principal portion of their lands within the limits of this state. After this period they resided principally on the reserve made by them at and around Wapakanotta, on the Auglaize river. Here the greater part of them remained, until within a few years past, when, yielding to the pressing appeals of the government, they sold their reserved lands to the United States, and removed west of the Mississippi.

For a number of years prior to their final departure from Ohio, the society of Friends, with their characteristic philanthropy towards the Indians, maintained a mission at Wapakanotta, for the purpose of giving instruction to the Shawanoe children, and inducing the adults to turn their attention to agricultural pursuits. Notwithstanding the wandering and warlike character of this tribe, such was the success attending this effort of active benevolence, that the Friends composing the Yearly Meetings of Baltimore, Ohio and Indiana, still continue a similar agency among the Shawanoes, although they are now the occupants of the territory lying beyond the distant Arkansas.

Whether the new position west of the Mississippi, in which the Indian tribes have been placed, will tend to promote their civilization, arrest their deterioration in morals, or their decline in numbers, we think extremely problematical. Should such, however, be the happy result, it may be anticipated that the tribe which has produced a Logan, a Cornstalk and a Tecumseh, will be among the first to rise above the moral degradation in which it is shrouded, and foremost to exhibit the renovating influences of christian civilization.

THE LIFE OF TECUMSEH.

CHAPTER I.

Parentage of Tecumseh—his sister Tecumapease—his brothers Cheesee-kau, Sauweeseekau, Nehasseemo, Tenskwautawa or the Prophet, and Kumskaukau.

THERE are not wanting authorities for the assertion that both the Anglo-Saxon and Creek blood ran in the veins of TECUMSEH.* It has been stated that his paternal grandfather was a white man, and that his mother was a Creek. The better opinion, however, seems to be, that he was wholly a Shawanoe. On this point we have the concurrent authority of John Johnston, late Indian agent at Piqua; and of Stephen Ruddell, formerly of Kentucky, who for near twenty years was a prisoner among the Shawanoes. They both possessed ample opportunities for ascertaining the fact, and unite in asserting that Puckeshinwa, the father of Tecumseh, was a member of the Kiscopoke, and Methoataske, the mother, of the Turtle tribe of the Shawanoe nation.

The parents of Tecumseh removed from Florida to the north side of the Ohio, about the middle of the eighteenth century. The father rose to the rank of a chief, and fell in the celebrated battle of the Kanawha, in 1774, leaving six sons and one daughter. Of these, one or two were born at the south, the others within what now constitutes the state of Ohio. They will be briefly noticed in the order of their birth.

Cheeseekau, the eldest, is represented to have taken great pains with his brother Tecumseh, laboring not only to make him a distinguished warrior, but to instil into his mind a love of truth, and a contempt for every

* The Indian orthography of this name is Tecumthà, but the public have been so long under a different impression, that no attempt has been made in this work to restore the original reading.

thing mean and sordid. Cheeseekau fought by the side of his father in the battle of Kanawha; and, some years afterwards, led a small band of Shawanoes on a predatory expedition to the south, Tecumseh being one of the party. While there, they joined some Cherokees, in an attack upon a fort, garrisoned by white men. A day or two before the attack, Cheeseekau made a speech to his followers, and predicted that at such an hour, on a certain morning, they would reach the fort, and that he should be shot in the forehead and killed; but that the fort would be taken, if the party persevered in the assault, which he urged them to do. An effort was made by his followers to induce him to turn back, but he refused. The attack took place at the time predicted, and Cheeseekau fell. His last words expressed the joy he felt at dying in battle; he did not wish, he said, to be buried at home, like an old woman, but preferred that the fowls of the air should pick his bones. The fall of their leader created a panic among the assaulting party, and they suddenly retreated.*

Tecumapease, known also by the name of Menewaulakoosee, was a sister worthy of her distinguished brother Tecumseh, with whom, up to the period of his death, she was a great favorite. Sensible, kind hearted, and uniformly exemplary in her conduct, she obtained and exercised a remarkable degree of influence over the females of her tribe. She was united in marriage to a *brave,* called Wasegoboah, (stand firm,) who fell in the battle of the Thames, fighting courageously by the side of his brother-in-law, Tecumseh. In 1814, Tecumapease visited Quebec, in company with some other members of her tribe, from whence, after the close of the war between this country and England, she returned to the neighborhood of Detroit, where, not long afterwards, she died. Tecumseh is represented to have entertained for her a warm affection, and to have treated her, uniformly, with respect. He was in the habit of making her many valuable presents.

Sauwaseekau, is supposed to have been born while his parents were removing from the south to the Ohio.

---

* Stephen Ruddell's manuscript narrative.

Concerning him few particulars have been preserved. He stood well as a warrior, and was killed in battle during Wayne's campaign in 1794.

The fourth child, Tecumseh, or the Shooting Star, is the subject of this biography.

Of the fifth, Nehaseemo, no information has been obtained.

The two remaining children, Laulewasikaw, called after he became a prophet Tenskwautawa, and Kumskaukau, were twins. Such is understood to have been the statement of the former, in giving the family pedigree. Other authorities* say that Tecumseh, Laulewasikaw, and Kumskaukau were all three born at the same time. The last named lived to be an old man, and died without distinction.

Laulewasikaw, as will appear in the course of this work, lived to attain an extraordinary degree of notoriety. He became, under the influence of his brother Tecumseh, a powerful agent in arousing the superstitious feelings of the north-western Indians, in that memorable period of their history, between the year 1805, and the battle of Tippecanoe, in 1811, which dissolved, in a great measure, the charm by which he had successfully played upon their passions and excited them to action. The character and prophetical career of this individual will necessarily be fully displayed in the progress of this work. There is, however, one trait of his character which may be appropriately mentioned in this place—his disposition to boast, not only of his own standing and importance, but also of the rank and respectability of the family to which he belonged. As an instance of this peculiarity, and of his tact in telling a plausible tale, the following narration may be cited. It is an ingenious mixture of truth and fiction; and was written down by the gentleman to whom it was related by Laulewasikaw. The language is that of the individual to whom the narrative was made.

"His paternal grandfather, (according to his statement of the family pedigree) was a Creek, who, at a period which is not defined in the manuscript before

---

* John Johnston and Anthony Shane.

us, went to one of the southern cities, either Savannah or Charleston, to hold a council with the English governor, whose daughter was present at some of the interviews. This young lady had conceived a violent admiration for the Indian character; and, having determined to bestow herself upon some " warlike lord" of the forest, she took this occasion to communicate her partiality to her father. The next morning, in the council, the governor enquired of the Indians which of them was the most expert hunter; and the grandfather of Tecumseh, then a young and handsome man, who sat modestly in a retired part of the room, was pointed out to him. When the council broke up for the day, the governor asked his daughter if she was really so partial to the Indians, as to prefer selecting a husband from them, and finding that she persisted in this singular predilection, he directed her attention to the young Creek warrior, for whom, at first sight, she avowed a decided attachment. On the following morning the governor announced to the Creeks that his daughter was disposed to marry one of their number; and, having pointed out the individual, added, that his own consent would be given. The chiefs at first very naturally doubted whether the governor was in earnest; but upon assuring them that he was sincere, they advised the young man to embrace the lady and her offer. He was not so ungallant as to refuse; and having consented to the fortune that was thus buckled on him, was immediately taken to another apartment, where he was disrobed of his Indian costume by a train of black servants, washed, and clad in a new suit, and the marriage ceremony was immediately performed.

" At the close of the council the Creeks returned home, but the young hunter remained with his wife. He amused himself in hunting, in which he was very successful, and was accustomed to take a couple of black servants with him, who seldom failed to bring in large quantities of game. He lived among the whites until his wife had borne him two daughters and a son. Upon the birth of the latter, the governor went to see his grandson, and was so well pleased, that he called his friends together, and caused thirty guns to be fired.

When the boy was seven or eight years old his father
died, and the governor took charge of the child, who
was often visited by the Creeks. At the age of ten or
twelve, he was permitted to accompany the Indians to
their nation, where he spent some time; and two years
after, he again made a long visit to the Creeks, who
then, with a few Shawanoes, lived on a river called
Pauseekoalaakee, and began to adopt their dress and
customs. They gave him an Indian name, Puckeshinwau, which means *something that drops;* and after
learning their language, he became so much attached
to the Indian life, that when the governor sent for him
he refused to return."

Such is the pleasant and artful story, narrated with
solemn gravity by Laulewasikaw, to emblazon the family pedigree by connecting it with the governor of
one of the provinces: and here, for the present, we
take our leave of the "Open Door."

The band of Shawanoes with whom Puckeshinwau
and his family emigrated to the Ohio, established themselves, in the first place, in the valley of the Scioto,
from whence they subsequently removed to the waters
of Mad River, one of the tributaries of the Great Miami.
After the death of Puckeshinwau, his wife Methoataas-
kee, returned to the south, where she died at an advanced age, among the Cherokees. She belonged to the
Turtle tribe of the Shawanoes, and her name signifies,
a turtle laying eggs in the sand. That she was a respectable woman, is the testimony of those who knew
her personally: that she was naturally a superior one,
may be fairly inferred from the character of at least a
part of her children.

With this brief account of an aboriginal family,
highly reputable in itself, but on which the name of
Tecumseh has conferred no small degree of distinction,
we now proceed to the immediate subject of this memoir.

F 2

CHAPTER II.

Birth place of Tecumseh—destruction of the Piqua village—early habits
   of Tecumseh—his first battle—effort to abolish the burning of prisoners—visits the Cherokees in the south—engages in several battles—returns to Ohio in the autumn of 1790.

SOME diversity of opinion has prevailed as to the
birth place of Tecumseh. It is generally supposed,
and indeed is stated by several historians to have been
in the Scioto valley, near the place where Chillicothe
now stands. Such, however, is not the fact. He was
born in the valley of the Miamis, on the bank of Mad
River, a few miles below Springfield, and within the
limits of Clark county. Of this there is the most satisfactory evidence. In the year 1805, when the Indians
were assembling at Greenville, as it was feared with
some hostile intention against the frontiers, the governor of Ohio sent Duncan McArthur and Thomas Worthington to that place, to ascertain the object and disposition of these Indians. Tecumseh and three other
chiefs agreed to return with these messengers to Chillicothe, then the seat of government, for the purpose of
holding a "talk" with the governor. General McArthur, in a letter to the author of this work, under date
of 19th November, 1821, says, "When on the way
from Greenville to Chillicothe, Tecumseh pointed out
to us the place where he was born. It was in an old
Shawanoe town, on the north-west side of Mad River,
about six miles below Springfield." This fact is corrob-
orated by Stephen Ruddell, the early and intimate associate of Tecumseh, who states that he was "born in the
neighborhood of "old Chillicothe," in the year 1768."
The "old Chillicothe" here spoken of was a Shawanoe
village, situated on Massie's creek, three miles north
of where Xenia now stands, and about ten or twelve
miles south of the village pointed out by Tecumseh, to
general McArthur, as the spot of his nativity. This
village was the ancient Piqua of the Shawanoes, and
occupied the site on which a small town called West
Boston has since been built. The principal part of

Piqua stood upon a plain, rising fifteen or twenty feet above the river. On the south, between the village and Mad River, there was an extensive prairie—on the north-east some bold cliffs, terminating near the river—on the west and south-west, level timbered land; while on the opposite side of the stream, another prairie, of varying width, stretched back to the high grounds. The river sweeping by in a graceful bend—the precipitous rocky cliffs—the undulating hills with their towering trees—the prairies garnished with tall grass and brilliant flowers—combined to render the situation of Piqua both beautiful and picturesque.

At the period of its destruction, Piqua was quite populous. There was a rude log fort within its limits, surrounded by pickets. It was, however, sacked and burnt on the 8th of August, 1780, by an army of one thousand men from Kentucky, after a severe and well conducted battle with the Indians who inhabited it. All the improvements of the Indians, including more than two hundred acres of corn and other vegetables, then growing in their fields, were laid waste and destroyed. The town was never afterwards rebuilt by the Shawanoes. Its inhabitants removed to the Great Miami river, and erected another town which they called Piqua, after the one that had just been destroyed; and in defence of which they had fought with the skill and valor characteristic of their nation.*

The birth of Tecumseh has been placed by some writers in the year 1771. Ruddell states that it occurred in 1768, three years earlier, and this, we think, is probably the true period. His early boyhood gave promise of the renown of his maturer years. After the death of his father, which occurred when he was in his sixth year, he was placed under the charge of his oldest brother, Cheeseekau, who taught him to hunt, led him to battle, and labored zealously to imbue his mind with a love for truth, generosity, and the practice of those cardinal Indian virtues, courage in battle and fortitude in suffering. From his boyhood,

---

* For this sketch of Piqua, the author is chiefly indebted to his venerable friend, Major James Galloway, of Xenia, Ohio.

Tecumseh seems to have had a passion for war. His pastimes, like those of Napoleon, were generally in the sham-battle field. He was the leader of his companions in all their sports, and was accustomed to divide them into parties, one of which he always headed, for the purpose of fighting mimic battles, in which he usua.ly distinguished himself by his activity, strength and skill.* His dexterity in the use of the bow and arrow exceeded that of all the other Indian boys of his tribe, by whom he was loved and respected, and over whom he exercised unbounded influence. He was generally surrounded by a set of companions who were ready to stand or fall by his side.† It is stated that the first battle in which he was engaged, occurred on Mad River, near where Dayton stands, between a party of Kentuckians, commanded by colonel Benjamin Logan, and some Shawanoes. At this time Tecumseh was very young, and joined the expedition under the care of his brother, who was wounded at the first fire. It is related by some Indian chiefs that Tecumseh, at the commencement of the action, became frightened and ran.‡ This may be true, but it is the only instance in which he was ever known to shrink from danger, or to loose that presence of mind for which he was ever afterwards remarkably distinguished.

The next action in which Tecumseh participated, and in which he manifested signal prowess, was an attack made by the Indians upon some flat boats, descending the Ohio, above Limestone, now Maysville. The year in which it occurred is not stated, but Tecumseh was not probably more than sixteen or seventeen years of age. The boats were captured, and all the persons belonging to them killed, except one, who was taken prisoner, and afterwards burnt. Tecumseh was a silent spectator of the scene, having never witnessed the burning of a prisoner before. After it was over, he expressed in strong terms, his abhorrence of the act, and it was finally concluded by the party that they

---

* Stephen Ruddell's MS. account.   † Anthony Shane.
‡ A similar statement is made in regard to the first battle of the celebrated Red Jacket.

would never burn any more prisoners;* and to this resolution, he himself, and the party also, it is believed, ever afterwards scrupulously adhered. It is not less creditable to the humanity than to the genius of Tecumseh, that he should have taken this noble stand, and by the force and eloquence of his appeal, have brought his companions to the same resolution. He was then but a boy, yet he had the independence to attack a cherished custom of his tribe, and the power of argument to convince them, against all their preconceived notions of right and the rules of warfare, that the custom should be abolished. That his effort to put a stop to this cruel and revolting rite, was not prompted by any temporary expediency, but was the result of a humane disposition, and a right sense of justice, is abundantly shown by his conduct towards prisoners in after life.

The boats were owned by traders. The number of whites killed in the engagement has not been ascertained. In the attack upon them, Tecumseh not only behaved with great courage, but even left in the back ground some of the oldest and bravest warriors of the party. From this time his reputation as a brave, and his influence over other minds, rose rapidly among the tribe to which he belonged.

About the year 1787, Cheeseekau and Tecumseh, with a party of Kiscopokes, one of the tribes of the Shawanoe nation, moved westward on a hunting and predatory expedition. They made a stand for some months on the waters of the Mississinnaway, and then crossed over to the Mississippi, opposite the mouth of Apple creek, where they encamped and remained for eight or nine months. From thence they proceeded towards the Cherokee country. On their route, while opposite fort Massac, they engaged in a buffalo chase, during which Tecumseh was thrown from his horse, and had his thigh broken.† This accident detained them for some months at the place where it occurred. So soon as he had recovered, the party, headed by Cheeseekau, pro-

* Stephen Ruddell.
† Shane thinks both thighs were broken, Ruddell says but one.

ceeded on their way to the country of the Cherokees, who were then at hostilities with the whites. With that fondness for adventure and love of war, which have ever marked the Shawanoe character, they immediately offered assistance to their brethren of the south, which being accepted, they joined in the contest.

The engagement in which they participated was an attack upon a fort, the name and position of which were not known to our informant. The Indians, it is well known are always superstitious, and from the fact of Cheeseekau, having foretold his death, its occurrence disheartened them, and in despite of the influence of Tecumseh and the Cherokee leaders, who rose above the superstition of their comrades, the attack was given up, and a sudden retreat followed.

Tecumseh, who had left the banks of the Miami in quest of adventures, and for the purpose of winning renown as a warrior, told the party that he was determined not to return to his native land, until he had achieved some act worthy of being recounted. He accordingly selected eight or ten men and proceeded to the nearest settlement, attacked a house, killed all the men in it, and took the women and children prisoners. He did not immediately retreat, but engaged in some other similar adventures. During this expedition he was three times attacked in the night in his encampment; but owing to his good judgment in the choice of his camping ground, and his habitual watchfulness when in an enemy's country, no advantage was gained over him. On one occasion, while encamped in the edge of a cane-brake on the waters of the Tennessee, he was assaulted by a party of whites, about thirty in number. Tecumseh had not lain down, but was engaged at the moment of the attack, in dressing some meat. He instantly sprang to his feet, and ordering his small party to follow him, rushed upon his foes with perfect fearlessness; and, having killed two, put the whole party to flight, he losing none of his own men.

Tecumseh and his party remained at the south nearly two years, traversing that region of country, visiting the different tribes of Indians, and engaging in the border forays which at that period were constantly occurrmg between the whites and the native possessors of the soil. He now determined to return home, and accordingly set out with eight of his party. They passed through western Virginia, crossed the Ohio near the mouth of the Scioto, and visiting the Machichac towns on the head waters of Mad River, from thence proceeded to the Auglaize, which they reached in the fall of 1790, shortly after the defeat of general Harmar, having been absent from Ohio upwards of three years.

CHAPTER III.

Tecumseh attacked near Big Rock by some whites under Robert M'Clelland—severe battle with some Kentuckians on the East Fork of the Little Miami—attack upon Tecumseh in 1793, on the waters of Paint creek—Tecumseh present at the attack on fort Recovery in 1794—participates in the battle of the Rapids of the Maumee, in 1794.

FROM the period of his return, until August of the following year, 1791, Tecumseh spent his time in hunting. In the autumn of this year, when information reached the Indians, that general St. Clair and his army were preparing to march from fort Washington, into their country, this chief headed a small party of spies, who went out for the purpose of watching the movements of the invading force.* While lying on Nettle creek, a small stream which empties into the Great Miami, general St. Clair and his army passed out through Greenville to the head waters of the Wabash, where he was defeated. Tecumseh, of course, had no personal participation in this engagement, so creditable to the valor of the Indians, and so disastrous to the arms and renown of the United States.

In December, 1792, Tecumseh, with ten other warriors and a boy, were encamped near Big Rock, between Loramie's creek and Piqua, for the purpose of hunting. Early one morning, while the party were seated round the fire, engaged in smoking, they were fired upon by a company of whites near treble their

* Stephen Ruddell.

number. Tecumseh raised the war-whoop, upon which the Indians sprang to their arms, and promptly returned the fire. He then directed the boy to run, and in turning round a moment afterwards, perceived that one of his men, Black Turkey, was running also. He had already retreated to the distance of one hundred yards, yet such was his fear of Tecumseh, he instantly obeyed the order to return, indignantly given him, and joined in the battle. Two of the whites were killed—one of them by Tecumseh—before they retreated. While pursuing them Tecumseh broke the trigger of his rifle, which induced him to give up the chase, or probably more of the whites would have fallen. They were commanded by Robert M'Clelland. Tecumseh lost none of his men; two of them, however, were wounded, one of whom was Black Turkey.*

In the month of March, 1792, some horses were stolen by the Indians, from the settlements in Mason county, Kentucky. A party of whites to the number of thirty-six, was immediately raised for the purpose of pursuing them. It embraced Kenton, Whiteman, M'Intire, Downing, Washburn, Calvin and several other experienced woodsmen. The first named, Simon Kenton, a distinguished Indian fighter, was placed in command. The trail of the Indians being taken, it was found they had crossed the Ohio just below the mouth of Lee's creek, which was reached by the pursuing party towards evening. Having prepared rafts, they crossed the Ohio that night, and encamped. Early next morning the trail was again taken and pursued, on a north course, all day, the weather being bad and the ground wet. On the ensuing morning twelve of the men were unable to continue the pursuit, and were permitted to return. The remainder followed the trail until eleven o'clock, A. M., when a bell was heard, which they supposed indicated their approach to the Indian camp. A halt was called, and all useless baggage and clothing laid aside. Whiteman and two others were sent ahead as spies, in different directions, each being followed by a detachment of the party.

---

* Anthony Shane.

After moving forward some distance, it was found that the bell was approaching them. They halted and soon perceived a solitary Indian riding towards them. When within one hundred and fifty yards, he was fired at and killed. Kenton directed the spies to proceed, being now satisfied that the camp of the Indians was near at hand. They pushed on rapidly, and after going about four miles, found the Indians encamped, on the south-east side of the east fork of the Little Miami, a few miles above the place where the town of Williamsburg has since been built. The indications of a considerable body of Indians were so strong, that the expediency of an attack at that hour of the day was doubted by Kenton. A hurried council was held, in which it was determined to retire, if it could be done without discovery, and lie concealed until night, and then assault the camp. This plan was carried into execution. Two of the spies were left to watch the Indians, and ascertain whether the pursuing party had been discovered. The others retreated for some distance and took a commanding position on a ridge. The spies watched until night, and then reported to their commander, that they had not been discovered by the enemy. The men being wet and cold, they were now marched down into a hollow, where they kindled fires, dried their clothes, and put their rifles in order. The party was then divided into three detachments,— Kenton commanding the right, M'Intire the centre, and Downing the left. By agreement, the three divisions were to move towards the camp, simultaneously, and when they had approached as near as possible, without giving an alarm, were to be guided in the commencement of the attack, by the fire from Kenton's party. When Downing and his detachment had approached close to the camp, an Indian rose upon his feet, and began to stir up the fire, which was but dimly burning. Fearing a discovery, Downing's party instantly shot him down. This was followed by a general fire from the three detachments, upon the Indians who were sleeping under some marquees and bark tents, close upon the margin of the stream. But unfortunately, as it proved in the sequel, Kenton's party had taken

G

" Boone," as their watch-word. This name happening to be as familiar to the enemy as themselves, led to some confusion in the course of the engagement. When fired upon, the Indians instead of retreating across the stream as had been anticipated, boldly stood to their arms, returned the fire of the assailants and rushed upon them. They were reinforced moreover from a camp on the opposite side of the river,* which until then, had been unperceived by the whites. In a few minutes the Indians and the Kentuckians were blended with each other, and the cry of " Boone," and " Che Boone," arose simultaneously from each party.

It was after midnight when the attack was made, and there being no moon, it was very dark. Kenton perceiving that his men were likely to be overpowered, ordered a retreat after the attack had lasted for a few minutes; this was continued through the remainder of the night and part of the next day, the Indians pursuing them, but without killing more than one of the retreating party. The Kentuckians lost but two men, Alexander McIntire and John Barr.† The loss of the Indians was much greater, according to the statements of some prisoners, who, after the peace of 1795, were released and returned to Kentucky. They related that fourteen Indians were killed, and seventeen wounded. They stated further, that there were in the camp about one hundred warriors, among them several chiefs of note, including Tecumseh, Battise, Black Snake, Wolf and Chinskau; and that the party had been formed for the purpose of annoying the settlements in Kentucky, and attacking boats descending the Ohio river. Kenton and his party were three days in reaching Limestone, during two of which they were without food, and destitute of sufficient clothing to protect them from the cold winds and rains of March. The foregoing particulars of this expedition are taken from the manuscript narrative of general Benjamin Whiteman, one

---

* M'Donald, in his interesting " Biographical Sketches," of some of the western pioneers, says this " second line of tents" was on the lower bottom of the creek and not on the opposite side of it.

† The father of the late Major William Barr, for many years a citizen of Cincinnati.

of the early and gallant pioneers to Kentucky, now a resident of Green county, Ohio.

The statements of Anthony Shane and of Stephen Ruddell, touching this action, vary in some particulars from that which has been given above, and also from the narrative in McDonald's Sketches. The principal difference relates to the number of Indians in the engagement, and the loss sustained by them. They report but two killed, and that the Indian force was less than that of the whites. Ruddell states that at the commencement of the attack, Tecumseh was lying by the fire, outside of the tents. When the first gun was heard he sprang to his feet, and calling upon Sinnamatha* to follow his example and charge, he rushed forward, and killed one of the whites† with his warclub. The other Indians, raising the war-whoop, seized their arms, and rushing upon Kenton and his party, compelled them, after a severe contest of a few minutes, to retreat. One of the Indians, in the midst of the engagement, fell into the river, and in the effort to get out of the water, made so much noise, that it created a belief on the minds of the whites that a reinforcement was crossing the stream to aid Tecumseh. This is supposed to have hastened the order from Kenton, for his men to retreat. The afternoon prior to the battle, one of Kenton's men, by the name of McIntire, succeeded in catching an Indian horse, which he tied in the rear of the camp; and, when a retreat was ordered, he mounted and rode off. Early in the morning, Tecumseh and four of his men set off in pursuit of the retreating party. Having fallen upon the trail of McIntire, they pursued it for some distance, and at length overtook him. He had struck a fire and was cooking some meat. When McIntire discovered his pursuers, he instantly fled at full speed. Tecumseh and two others followed, and were fast gaining on him, when he turned and raised his gun. Two of the Indians, who happened to be in advance of Tecumseh, sprung behind trees, but he

---

* Or Big Fish, the name by which Stephen Ruddell, then fighting with Tecumseh, was called.

† John Barr, referred to in a preceding note.

rushed upon McIntire and made him prisoner. He was tied and taken back to the battle ground. Upon reaching it, Tecumseh deemed it prudent to draw off his men, lest the whites should rally and renew the attack. He requested some of the Indians to catch the horses, but they, hesitating, he undertook to do it himself, assisted by one of the party. When he returned to camp with the horses, he found that his men had killed McIntire. At this act of cruelty to a prisoner, he was exceedingly indignant; declaring that it was a cowardly act to kill a man when tied and a prisoner. The conduct of Tecumseh in this engagement, and in the events of the following morning, is creditable alike to his courage and humanity. Resolutely brave in battle, his arm was never uplifted against a prisoner, nor did he suffer violence to be inflicted upon a captive without promptly rebuking it.

McDonald, in speaking of this action, says:

"The celebrated Tecumseh commanded the Indians. His cautious and fearless intrepidity made him a host wherever he went. In military tactics, night attacks are not allowable, except in cases like this, when the assailing party are far inferior in numbers. Sometimes in night attacks, panics and confusion are created in the attacked party, which may render them a prey to inferior numbers. Kenton trusted to something like this on the present occasion, but was disappointed; for when Tecumseh was present, his influence over the minds of his followers infused that confidence in his tact and intrepidity, that they could only be defeated by force of numbers."

Some time in the spring of 1793, Tecumseh and a few of his followers, while hunting in the Scioto valley on the waters of Paint creek, were unexpectedly attacked by a party of white men from Mason county, Kentucky. The circumstances which led to this skirmish were the following. Early in the spring of this year, an express reached the settlement in Mason, that some stations had been attacked and captured on Slate creek, in Bath county, Kentucky, and that the Indians were returning with their prisoners to Ohio. A party of thirty-three men was immediately raised to cut off their retreat. These were divided into three companies, of ten men each;—Simon Kenton commanding one, —— Baker another, and James Ward the third. The whole party crossed the Ohio river at Limestone, and aimed to strike the Scioto above the mouth of Paint creek. After crossing this latter stream, near where the great road from Maysville to Chillicothe now crosses it, evening came on, and they halted for the night. In a short time they heard a noise, and a little examination disclosed to them that they were in the immediate vicinity of an Indian encampment. Their horses were promptly taken back some distance and tied, to prevent an alarm. A council was held,—captain Baker offered to go and reconnoitre, which being agreed to, he took one of his company and made the examination. He found the Indians encamped on the bank of the creek, their horses being between them and the camp of the whites. After Baker's report was made, the party determined to remain where they were until near daylight the next morning; and then to make an attack in the following manner. Captain Baker and his men were to march round and take a position on the bank of the stream, in front of the Indian camp: captain Ward was to occupy the ground in the rear; and captain Kenton one side, while the river presented a barrier on the fourth, thus guarding against a retreat of the Indians. It was further agreed that the attack was not to commence until there was light enough to shoot with accuracy. Before Kenton and Ward had reached the positions they were respectively to occupy, the bark of a dog in the Indian camp was heard, and then the report of a gun. Upon this alarm, Baker's men instantly fired, and captains Kenton and Ward, with their companies, raising the battle cry, rushed towards the camp. To their surprise, they found Baker and his men in the rear, instead of the front of the Indians, thus deranging the plan of attack, whether from design or accident is unknown. The Indians sent back the battle cry, retreated a few paces, and treed. It was still too dark to fire with precision, but random shots were made, and a terrible shouting kept up by the Indians. While the parties were thus at bay, Tecumseh had the address

G 2

to send a part of their men to the rear of the Kentuckians for the horses; and when they had been taken
to the front, which was accomplished without discovery, the Indians mounted and effected their escape, carrying with them John Ward, the only one of their party
who was shot. This individual, a white man, had
been captured when three years old, on Jackson, one
of the tributaries of James river, in Virginia. He had
been raised by the Indians, among whom he had married, and reared several children. He was the brother
of James Ward, one of the leaders of this expedition,
and died of his wound a few days after the engagement, as was subsequently ascertained. No Indian
was killed in this skirmish, and but one of the Kentuckians, Jacob Jones, a member of Baker's detachment.
No pursuit of the Indians was made from this point,
nor did they prove to be the same party who had been
engaged in the attack upon the Slate creek station.*

In McDonald's Sketches, it is stated that "three Indians were killed in this action; and that when fired
upon by their assailants, they dashed through the creek,
and scattered through the woods, like a flock of young
partridges."

On these points, the worthy author of the "Sketches"
has undoubtedly been misinformed. The Indians lost
but one man, John Ward; and after having treed, maintained their ground until they had adroitly obtained
possession of their horses, and then succeeded in making their escape, carrying off not only the wounded
man, but also the women and children who were with
them when attacked. This we learn from authorities
before us, on which reliance may be placed.† By one
of these, it appears that there were but six or seven
warriors in the party; and, that when the attack was
made, Tecumseh called out to them that the women
and children must be defended, and it was owing
to his firmness and influence that the assailants were
kept at bay until the horses of his party were secured,

---

* For the foregoing details of this little expedition, the author is indebted to captain James Ward, of Mason county, Kentucky, who commanded
one of the detachments on this occasion.

† Anthony Shane. Stephen Ruddell.

and the necessary arrangements made for a hasty retreat.

After this engagement, it is not known that Tecumseh was a party to any warlike movement, until the summer of the following year. He returned to the waters of the Miami, and spent his time in hunting, for which he had a great fondness, and in which he was generally more successful than any other member of his tribe.

After general Wayne assumed the command of the north-western army, he caused a fort to be built on the spot where the unfortunate defeat of his predecessor, general Arthur St. Clair, had occurred. This fort was named Recovery.

In the summer of 1794, an attack was made upon it by a numerous body of Indians, among whom was Tecumseh. They were accompanied by a British officer, and some artillerists, furnished with fixed ammunition, suited to the calibre of some field pieces which the Indians had taken from general St. Clair, at the time of his defeat.* In referring to this attack and the movements of general Wayne, Withers, in his " Chronicles of Border Warfare," says:

" Before the troops marched from fort Washington, it was deemed advisable to have an abundant supply of provisions in the different forts in advance of this, as well for the support of their respective garrisons, as for the subsistence of the general army, in the event of its being driven into them, by untoward circumstances. With this view, three hundred pack horses, laden with flour, were sent on to fort Recovery; and as it was known that considerable bodies of the enemy were constantly hovering about the forts, and awaiting opportunities of cutting off any detachments from the main army, major McMahon, with ninety riflemen under captain Hartshorn, and fifty dragoons under captain Taylor, was ordered on as an escort. This force was so large as to discourage the savages from making an attack, until they should unite their several war parties,

* For this fact see general Harrison's Address on the 50th Anniversary of the first settlement of Ohio.

and before this could be effected, major McMahon reached the place of his destination.

"On the 30th of July, as the escort was about leaving fort Recovery, it was attacked by a body of one thousand Indians, in the immediate vicinity of the fort. Captain Hartshorn had advanced only three or four hundred yards, at the head of the riflemen, when he was unexpectedly beset on every side. With the most consummate bravery and good conduct, he maintained the unequal conflict, until major McMahon, placing himself at the head of the cavalry, charged upon the enemy, and was repulsed with considerable loss. Major McMahon, captain Taylor and cornet Torrey fell, upon the first onset, and many of the privates were killed or wounded. The whole savage force being now brought to press on captain Hartshorn, that brave officer was forced to try and regain the fort; but the enemy interposed its strength to prevent this movement. Lieutenant Drake and ensign Dodd, with twenty volunteers, marched from the fort, and forcing a passage through a column of the enemy, at the point of the bayonet, joined the rifle corps at the instant that captain Hartshorn received a shot which broke his thigh. Lieutenant Craig being killed, and lieutenant Marks taken prisoner, lieutenant Drake conducted the retreat; and while endeavoring for an instant to hold the enemy in check, so as to enable the soldiers to bring off their wounded captain, himself received a shot in the groin, and the retreat was resumed, leaving captain Hartshorn on the field.

"When the remnant of the troops came within the walls of the fort, lieutenant Michael, who had been detached at an early period of the battle by captain Hartshorn to the flank of the enemy, was found to be missing, and was given up as lost; but while his friends were deploring his unfortunate fate, he and lieutenant Marks, who had been taken prisoner, were seen rushing through the enemy from opposite directions, towards the fort. They gained it safely, notwithstanding they were actively pursued, and many shots fired at them. Lieutenant Marks had got off by knocking down the Indian who held him prisoner; and lieutenant Michael had lost all of his party but three men."

The official letter of general Wayne giving an account of this action, places the loss of the whites at twenty-two killed and thirty wounded. "The enemy," continues the report, "were soon repulsed with great slaughter, but immediately rallied and reiterated the attack, keeping up a very heavy and constant fire, at a more respectable distance, for the remainder of the day, which was answered with spirit and effect by the garrison, and that part of major McMahon's command that had regained the fort. The savages were employed during the night (which was dark and foggy,) in carrying off their dead by torchlight, which occasionally drew a fire from the garrison. They nevertheless succeeded so well, that there were but eight or ten bodies left on the field, and those close under the influence of the fire from the fort. The enemy again renewed the attack on the morning of the first inst., but were ultimately compelled to retreat with loss and disgrace from that very field, where they had upon a former occasion, been proudly victorious."

Tecumseh fought in the decisive battle between the American troops under general Wayne, and the combined Indian forces, which occurred on the 20th of August, 1794, near the rapids of the Miami of the lakes. It is not known whether he attended the council, the evening previous to the engagement, in which the advice of Little Turtle, the Miami chief, was overruled by the influence of the Shawanoe chief, Blue Jacket. The former was opposed to giving battle on the following day; the latter in favor of it. As a *brave* of distinction, Tecumseh took the command of a party of Shawanoes in the engagement, but had no participation in the plan of the attack, or the mode of carrying it into execution. At the commencement of the action, he was in the advance guard with two of his brothers. After fighting for some time, in attempting to load his rifle, he put in a bullet before the powder, and was thus unable to use his gun. Being at this moment pressed in front by some infantry, he fell back with his party until they met another detachment of Indians.

Tecumseh urged them to stand fast and fight, saying if any one would lend him a gun, he would show them how to do it. A fowling-piece was handed to him, with which he fought for some time, until the Indians were again compelled to give ground. While falling back, he met another party of Shawanoes, and although the whites were pressing on them, he rallied the Indians, and induced them to make a stand in a thicket. When the infantry pressed close upon them, and had discharged their muskets into the bushes, Tecumseh and his party returned their fire, and then retreated, until they had joined the main body of the Indians below the rapids of the Miami.*

In this memorable action, which gave victory to the American arms, and humbled the north-western Indians, William Henry Harrison and Tecumseh were for the first time opposed to each other in battle. They were both young, and indeed nearly the same age, and both displayed that courage and gallantry which ever afterwards signalized their brilliant and eventful lives.

CHAPTER IV.

Tecumseh's skill as a hunter—declines attending the treaty of Greenville in 1795—in 1796 removed to Great Miami—in 1798 joined a party of Delawares on White river, Indiana—in 1799 attended a council between the whites and Indians near Urbana—another at Chillicothe in 1803—makes an able speech—removes with the Prophet to Greenville, in 1805—the latter commences prophecying—causes the death of Teteboxti, Patterson, Coltos, and Joshua—governor Harrison's speech to the Prophet to arrest these murderers—effort of Wells, the U. S. Indian agent, to prevent Tecumseh and the Prophet from assembling the Indians at Greenville—Tecumseh's speech in reply—he attends a council at Chillicothe—speech on that occasion—council at Springfield—Tecumseh principal speaker and actor.

In the spring of the year 1795, Tecumseh was established on Deer creek, near where Urbana now stands, and engaged in his favorite amusement of hunting. This was more as a pastime than a matter of business.

---

* Anthony Shane.

The love of property was not a distinguishing trait of his character; on the contrary, his generosity was proverbial among his tribe. If he accumulated furs, they, or the goods which he received in return for them, were dispensed with a liberal hand. He loved hunting because it was a manly exercise, fit for a *brave;* and, for the additional reason, that it gave him the means of furnishing the aged and infirm with wholesome and nourishing food. The skill of Tecumseh in the chase has already been adverted to. While residing on Deer creek, an incident occurred which greatly enhanced his reputation as a hunter. One of his brothers, and several other Shawanoes of his own age, proposed to bet with him, that they could each kill as many deer, in the space of three days, as he could. Tecumseh promptly accepted the overture. The parties took to the woods, and at the end of the stipulated time, returned with the evidences of their success. None of the party, except Tecumseh, had more than twelve deer skins; he brought n upwards of thirty—near three times as many as any of his competitors. From this time he was generally conceded to be the greatest hunter in the Shawanoe nation.

In the course of the summer of this year, 1795, he commenced raising a party of his own, and began to style himself a chief. He did not attend the treaty of Greenville, held by general Wayne, on the 3d of August, 1795, with the hostile Indians, but after its conclusion, Blue Jacket paid him a visit on Deer creek, and communicated to him the terms on which peace had been concluded.

Tecumseh remained at this place until the spring of 1796, when he removed with his party to the Great Miami, near to Piqua, where they raised a crop of corn. In the autumn he again changed his place of residence, and went over to the head branches of White Water, west of the Miami, where he and his party spent the winter; and in the spring and summer of 1797, raised another crop of corn.

In the year 1798, the Delawares, then residing in part, on White river, Indiana, invited Tecumseh and his followers, to remove to that neighborhood. Hav-

ing accepted this invitation, and made the removal, and
continued his head quarters in the vicinity of that nation for several years, occupied in the ordinary pursuits
of the hunter-life—gradually extending his influence
among the Indians, and adding to the number of his
party.

In 1799, there was a council held about six miles
north of the place where Urbana now stands, between
the Indians and some of the principal settlers on Mad
River, for the adjustment of difficulties which had grown
up between these parties. Tecumseh, with other Shawanoe chiefs, attended this council. He appears to have
been the most conspicuous orator of the conference,
and made a speech on the occasion, which was much
admired for its force and eloquence. The interpreter,
Dechouset, said that he found it very difficult to trans-
late the lofty flights of Tecumseh, although he was as
well acquainted with the Shawanoe language, as with
the French, which was his mother tongue.*

We next hear of Tecumseh, under circumstances
which show the confidence reposed in him by the
white settlers on the frontier.

In the month of April, 1803, Thomas Herrod, living
sixteen miles north-west of Chillicothe, was shot, tomahawked, and scalped, near his own house. The Indians were suspected of having committed this deed;
a wanton and cruel retaliation was made upon one of
them, (guiltless no doubt of that particular crime,) and
the settlement in the Scioto valley and north-west of it,
was thrown into a state of much excitement. The Indians fled in one direction and the whites in another.
For the purpose of ascertaining the facts in the case,
and preventing further hostilities, several patriotic citizens of Chillicothe mounted their horses, and rode into
the Indian country, where they found Tecumseh and a
body of Indians. They disavowed all knowledge of
the murder of Herrod, and stated, explicitly, that they
were peaceably inclined, and disposed to adhere to the
treaty of Greenville. Tecumseh finally agreed to return with the deputation from Chillicothe, that he

* James Galloway, of Xenia.

might in person, give similar assurances to the people of that place. He did so, and a day was fixed on, when he should make an address upon the subject. A white man, raised among the Indians, acted as interpreter. Governor Tiffin opened the conference. "When Tecumseh rose to speak," says an eyewitness, "as he cast his gaze over the vast multitude, which the interesting occasion had drawn together, he appeared one of the most dignified men I ever beheld. While this orator of nature was speaking, the vast crowd preserved the most profound silence. From the confident manner in which he spoke of the intention of the Indians to adhere to the treaty of Greenville, and live in peace and friendship with their white brethren, he dispelled, as if by magic, the apprehensions of the whites—the settlers returned to their deserted farms, and business generally was resumed throughout that region."* This incident is of value, in forming an estimate of the character of this chief: it exhibits the confidence reposed in him by the white inhabitants on the frontier. The declaration of no other Indian could thus have dissipated the fears of a border war, which then pervaded the settlement.

Some time during this year, a stout Kentuckian came to Ohio, for the purpose of exploring the lands on Mad River, and lodged one night at the house of captain Abner Barrett, residing on the head waters of Buck creek. In the course of the evening, he learned with apparent alarm, that there were some Indians encamped within a short distance of the house. Shortly after hearing this unwelcome intelligence, the door of captain Barrett's dwelling was suddenly opened, and Tecumseh entered with his usual stately air : he paused in silence, and looked around, until at length his eye was fixed upon the stranger, who was manifesting symptoms of alarm, and did not venture to look the stern savage in the face. Tecumseh turned to his host, and pointing to the agitated Kentuckian, exclaimed, "a big baby! a big baby!" He then stepped up to him, and gently slapping him on the shoulder several times, repeated with a contemptuous manner, the phrase "big

* Colonel John M'Donald.

H

baby! big baby!" to the great alarm cf the astonished man, and to the amusement of all present.*

In the early part of the year 1805, a portion of the Shawanoe nation, residing at the Tawa towns on the head waters of the Auglaize river, wishing to re-assemble their scattered people, sent a deputation to Tecumseh and his party, (then living on White river,) and also to a body of the same tribe upon the Mississiniway, another tributary of the Wabash, inviting them to remove to the Tawa towns, and join their brethren at that place. To this proposition both parties assented; and the two bands met at Greenville, on their way thither. There, through the influence of Laulewasikaw, they concluded to establish themselves; and accordingly the project of going to the Auglaize was abandoned. Very soon afterwards, Laulewasikaw assumed the office of a prophet; and forthwith commenced that career of cunning and pretended sorcery, which enabled him to sway the Indian mind in a wonderful degree, and win for himself a name on the page of history. A concise notice of his prophetical achievements is subjoined. While it serves to display his individual character and endowments, it also presents an interesting and instructive phase of aboriginal character.

It happened about this time that an old Shawanoe, named Penagashega, or the Change of Feathers, who had for some years been engaged in the respectable calling of a prophet, fell sick and died. Laulewasikaw, who had marked the old man's influence with the Indians, adroitly caught up the mantle of the dying prophet, and assumed his sacred office. He changed his name from Laulewasikaw, to Tenskwautawau,† meaning the Open Door, because he undertook to point out to the Indians the new modes of life which they should pursue. In the month of November, of this year, he assembled a considerable number of Shawanoes, Wyandots, Ottaways and Senecas, at Wapakonatta, on the Auglaize river, when he unfolded to them

---

* James Galloway.
† In the remaining pages of this work this person will be called the Prophet, the name by which he is most generally known.

the new character with which he was clothed, and made his first public effort in that career of religious imposition, which, in a few years, was felt by the remote tribes of the upper lakes, and on the broad plains which stretch beyond the Mississippi. At this time nothing, it is believed, was said by him in regard to the grand confederacy of the tribes, for the recovery of their lands, which shortly afterwards became an object of ambition with his brother; and, in the furtherance of which he successfully exerted his power and influence, as a prophet. In this assemblage he declaimed against witchcraft, which many of the Indians practised and still more believed. He pronounced that those who continued bewitched, or exerted their arts on others, would never go to heaven nor see the Great Spirit. He next took up the subject of drunkenness, against which he harangued with great force; and, as appeared subsequently, with much success. He told them that since he had become a prophet, he went up into the clouds; that the first place he came to was the dwelling of the Devil, and that all who had died drunkards were there, with flames issuing out of their mouths. He acknowledged that he had himself been a drunkard, but that this awful scene had reformed him. Such was the effect of his preaching against this pernicious vice, that many of his followers became alarmed, and ceased to drink the "fire-water," a name by which whiskey is significantly called among the Indians. He likewise declaimed against the custom of Indian women intermarrying with white men, and denounced it as one of the causes of their unhappiness. Among other doctrines of his new code, he insisted on a community of property—a very comfortable regulation for those, who like himself, were too indolent to labor for the acquisition of it. A more salutary and rational precept, and one which he enforced with considerable energy, was the duty of the young, at all times and under all circumstances, to support, cherish and respect the aged and infirm. He declaimed with vehemence against all innovations in the original dress and habits of the Indians—dwelt upon the high claims of the Shawanoes to superiority over other tribes, and prom-

ised to all his followers, who would believe his doctrines and practice his precepts, the comforts and happiness which their forefathers enjoyed before they were
debased by their connection with the whites. And
finally proclaimed, with much solemnity, that he had
received power from the Great Spirit, to cure all diseases, to confound his enemies, and stay the arm of
death, in sickness, or on the battle field.

Such is the superstitious credulity of the Indians, that
this crafty impostor not only succeeded for a time, in
correcting many of the vices of his followers, but likewise influenced them to the perpetration of outrages
upon each other, shocking to humanity. If an individual, and especially a chief, was supposed to be hostile
to his plans, or doubted the validity of his claim to the
character of a prophet, he was denounced as a witch,
and the loss of reputation, if not of life, speedily followed. Among the first of his victims were several Delawares,—Tatepocoshe (more generally known as Teteboxti,) Patterson, his nephew, Coltos, an old woman,
and an aged man called Joshua. These were successively marked by the Prophet, and doomed to be burnt
alive. The tragedy was commenced with the old woman. The Indians roasted her slowly over a fire for
four days, calling upon her frequently to deliver up her
charm and medicine bag. Just as she was dying, she
exclaimed that her grandson, who was then out hunting, had it in his possession. Messengers were sent
in pursuit of him, and when found he was tied and
brought into camp. He acknowledged that on one
occasion he had borrowed the charm of his grandmo-
ther, by means of which he had flown through the air,
over Kentucky, to the banks of the Mississippi, and
back again, between twilight and bed-time; but he insisted that he had returned the charm to its owner; and
after some consultation, he was set at liberty. The
following day, a council was held over the case of the
venerable chief Tatepocoshe, he being present. His
death was decided upon after full deliberation; and,
arrayed in his finest apparel, he calmly assisted in
building his own funeral pile, fully aware that there
was no escape from the judgment that had been passed

upon him   The respect due to his whitened locks, induced his executioners to treat him with mercy.   He
was deliberately tomahawked by a young man, and
his body was then placed upon the blazing faggots and
consumed.   The next day, the old preacher Joshua,
met a similar fate.   The wife of Tatepocoshe, and his
nephew Billy Patterson, were then brought into the
council house, and seated side by side.   The latter had
led an irreproachable life, and died like a christian,
singing and praying amid the flames which destroyed
his body.   While preparations were making for the
immolation of Tatepocoshe's wife, her brother, a youth
of twenty years of age, suddenly started up, took her
by the hand, and to the amazement of the council, led
her out of the house.   He soon returned, and exclaim-
ing, "the devil has come among us, (alluding to the
Prophet) and we are killing each other," he re-seated
himself in the midst of the crowd.   This bold step
checked the wild frenzy of the Indians, put an end to
these cruel scenes, and for a time greatly impaired the
impostor's influence among the Delawares.

The benevolent policy of the governor of Indiana
Territory (William Henry Harrison,) towards the Indian tribes, had given him much influence over them.
Early in the year 1806, and so soon as he had heard
of the movements of the Prophet, and the delusion of
the Delawares in regard to witchcraft, he sent a special
messenger to them with the following speech.   Had it
reached them a little earlier, it would probably have
saved the life of the aged Tatepocoshe.

" My Children:—My heart is filled with grief, and
my eyes are dissolved in tears, at the news which has
reached me.   You have been celebrated for your wisdom above all the tribes of red people who inhabit this
great island.   Your fame as warriors has extended to
the remotest nations, and the wisdom of your chiefs
has gained for you the appellation of grandfathers,
from all the neighboring tribes.   From what cause,
then, does it proceed, that you have departed from the
wise counsels of your fathers, and covered yourselves
with guilt?   My children, tread back the steps you
have taken, and endeavor to regain the straight road

which you have abandoned. The dark, crooked and thorny one which you are now pursuing, will certainly lead to endless woe and misery. But who is this pretended prophet, who dares to speak in the name of the Great Creator? Examine him. Is he more wise or virtuous than you are yourselves, that he should be selected to convey to you the orders of your God? Demand of him some proofs at least, of his being the messenger of the Deity. If God has really employed him, he has doubtless authorized him to perform miracles, that he may be known and received as a prophet. If he is really a prophet, ask of him to cause the sun to stand still—the moon to alter its course—the rivers to cease to flow—or the dead to rise from their graves. If he does these things, you may then believe that he has been sent from God. He tells you that the Great Spirit commands you to punish with death those who deal in magic; and that he is authorized to point them out. Wretched delusion! Is then the Master of Life obliged to employ mortal man to punish those who offend him? Has he not the thunder and all the powers of nature at his command?—and could he not sweep away from the earth a whole nation with one motion of his arm? My children: do not believe that the great and good Creator of mankind has directed you to destroy your own flesh; and do not doubt but that if you pursue this abominable wickedness, his vengeance will overtake and crush you.

"The above is addressed to you in the name of the Seventeen Fires. I now speak to you from myself, as a friend who wishes nothing more sincerely than to see you prosperous and happy. Clear your eyes, I beseech you, from the mist which surrounds them. No longer be imposed upon by the arts of an impostor. Drive him from your town, and let peace and harmony once more prevail amongst you. Let your poor old men and women sleep in quietness, and banish from their minds the dreadful idea of being burnt alive by their own friends and countrymen. I charge you to stop your bloody career; and if you value the friendship of your great father, the President—if you wish to preserve the good opinion of the Seventeen Fires,

let me hear by the return of the bearer, that you have
determined to follow my advice."*

Among the Miamis, the Prophet was less successful
in establishing an influence than with the Delawares;
while over the Kickapoos he gained, for a time, a remarkable ascendency,—greater, indeed, than he ever
established in his own tribe. Most of the Shawanoe
chiefs were opposed to him, and even complained to
the agent at fort Wayne, that his conduct was creating
difficulties among the Indians.

We have met with no evidence that Tecumseh favored the destruction of the Delawares, whose unhappy
fate has been detailed. On the contrary, it is stated
by a credible authority,† that he was opposed to it.

Throughout the year 1806, the brothers remained
at Greenville, and were visited by many Indians from
different tribes, not a few of whom became their followers. The Prophet dreamed many wonderful dreams;
and claimed to have had many supernatural revelations
made to him. The great eclipse of the sun which occurred in the summer of this year, a knowledge of
which he had by some means attained, enabled him to
carry conviction to the minds of many of his ignorant
followers, that he was really the earthly agent of the
Great Spirit. He boldly announced to the unbelievers,
that on a certain day, he would give them proof of his
supernatural powers, by bringing darkness over the
sun. When the day and hour of the eclipse arrived,
and the earth, even at mid-day, was shrouded in the
gloom of twilight, the Prophet, standing in the midst
of his party, significantly pointed to the heavens, and
cried out, "did I not prophecy truly? Behold! darkness has shrouded the sun!" It may readily be supposed that this striking phenomenon, thus adroitly
used, produced a strong impression on the Indians, and
greatly increased their belief in the sacred character of
their Prophet.

In April, 1807, Tecumseh and his brother had assembled at Greenville about four hundred Indians,
most of them highly excited by religious fanaticism;

* Quoted from Dawson's Historical Narrative of the civil and military
services of William Henry Harrison.   † Anthony Shane.

and ready, it was feared, for any enterprise on which these brothers might be disposed to lead them. Considerable apprehension was entertained for the safety of the frontiers, and several fruitless efforts were made to ascertain the ulterior objects of the leaders. William Wells, then Indian agent at fort Wayne, despatched Anthony Shane, a half-blood Shawanoe, with a communication to Tecumseh and the Prophet, requesting them and two other of their chiefs, to visit him at fort Wayne, that he might read to them a letter which he had just received from their great father, the President of the United States.

A council being called, Shane made known the object of his mission. Tecumseh, without consulting with those around him, immediately arose and said to the messenger, "go back to fort Wayne, and tell captain Wells, that my fire is kindled on the spot appointed by the Great Spirit above; and, if he has any thing to communicate to me, *he* must come *here:*—I shall expect him in six days from this time." With this laconic, but dignified reply, the conference ended. The agent at fort Wayne declined waiting on Tecumseh, in person, but on the appointed day, sent Shane back to Greenville, with a copy of the President's communication, contained in a letter from the Secretary at War; the substance of which was, that Tecumseh and his party being established within the limits of the governor's purchase from the Indians, they were desired to remove to some point beyond the boundaries agreed upon by the treaty of Greenville; and, in case of their compliance, the government would afford them assistance, until they were properly established at their new post. A second council was assembled, and the communication fully interpreted to those present. Tecumseh felt indignant that captain Wells had not visited him in person. He arose deeply excited, and turning to his followers, addressed them in a long, glowing and impassioned speech, in which he dwelt upon the injuries the Indians had received from the whites, and especially the continued encroachments of the latter upon the lands of the red men: "These lands," said he in conclusion, "are ours: no one has a right to remove us, because we were the first owners; the Great Spirit above has appointed this place for us, on which to light our fires, and here we will remain. As to boundaries, the Great Spirit above knows no boundaries, nor will his red people acknowledge any."

Of this speech no copy has been preserved. Shane speaks of it as a masterpiece of Indian eloquence—bold, argumentative and powerful. It was delivered with great vehemence, and deep indignant feeling. After a moment's pause, Tecumseh turned to the messenger and said, with that stately indifference of manner, which he could so gracefully assume when in council, "if my great father, the President of the Seventeen Fires, has any thing more to say to me, he must send a man of note as his messenger. I will hold no further intercourse with captain Wells."

The Prophet, who seldom lost an opportunity of vaunting himself before his followers, then rose, and addressing captain Shane, said, "why does not the President send to us the greatest man in his nation? I can talk to him—I can bring darkness between him and me—nay more, I can bring the sun under my feet, and what white man can do this?" With this self-glorification, the council terminated.

The excitement continued to increase, and at the close of May, it was estimated by the agent at fort Wayne, that not less than fifteen hundred Indians, had within a short time, passed and repassed that fort, in making visits to the Prophet. Many of these were from distant points on the lakes. Councils were assembled, runners with pipes and belts of wampum, went from tribe to tribe, and strong evidence of some uncommon movement among the Indians became quite apparent. The British agents were active in fomenting this excitement, and in extending the influence of Tecumseh and his brother, whose ulterior objects were carefully concealed from the agents of the United States, and such Indian chiefs as were known to be friendly to our government.

In the month of August, on the testimony of several persons familiar with Indian affairs, then residing in the north-western portions of the state, the Indians at fort

Wayne and at Greenville, who were supposed to be under the influence of the Prophet, amounted to between seven and eight hundred, most of them equipped with new rifles. These facts being communicated to the governor of Ohio, he directed his attention to the subject, and, in the early part of September, despatched Thomas Worthington and Duncan McArthur, to Greenville, for the purpose of holding a conference with the Prophet and Tecumseh, and ascertaining the object of their assembling so large a body of Indians, within the limits of the cession of land made by them at the treaty of 1795. These commissioners left Chillicothe on the 8th of September, and reached Greenville on the 12th, where they were courteously received by the Indians. They were fortunate in securing the services of Stephen Ruddell, as their interpreter, who had resided for seventeen years among the Indians, and was familiar with the Shawanoe language. On the day of their arrival, the commissioners were invited to a general council of the Indians, at which the letter of the governor was read, and interpreted to the Shawanoes, Potawatamies and Chippewas. This was followed by an address from the commissioners, referring to the past relations between the United States and the Indians, the policy pursued towards the latter by Great Britain, and the importance of their remaining neutral, in case of a war between that country and the United States. On the following day, Blue Jacket, who, it was announced, had been authorized by all the Indians present, to speak for them, replied to the commissioners as follows:

"Brethren—We are seated who heard you yesterday. You will get a true relation, as far as we and our connections can give it, who are as follows: Shawanoes, Wyandots, Potawatamies, Tawas, Chippewas, Winnepaus, Malominese, Malockese, Secawgoes, and one more from the north of the Chippewas. *Brethren* —you see all these men sitting before you, who now speak to you.

"About eleven days ago we had a council, at which the tribe of Wyandots, (the elder brother of the red people) spoke and said God had kindled a fire and all

sat around it. In this council we talked over the treaties with the French and the Americans. The Wyandot said, the French formerly marked a line along the
Alleghany mountains, southerly, to Charleston, (S. C.)
No man was to pass it from either side. When the
Americans came to settle over the line, the English
told the Indians to unite and drive off the French, until
the war came on between the British and the Americans, when it was told them that king George, by his
officers, directed them to unite and drive the Americans
back.

"After the treaty of peace between the English and
Americans, the summer before Wayne's army came
out, the English held a council with the Indians, and
told them if they would turn out and unite as one man,
they might surround the Americans like deer in a ring
of fire and destroy them all. The Wyandot spoke further in the council. We see, said he, there is like to
be war between the English and our white brethren,
the Americans. Let us unite and consider the sufferings we have undergone, from interfering in the wars
of the English. They have often promised to help us,
and at last, when we could not withstand the army
that came against us, and went to the English fort for
refuge, the English told us, "I cannot let you in; you
are painted too much, my children." It was then we
saw the British dealt treacherously with us. We now
see them going to war again. We do not know what
they are going to fight for. Let us, my brethren, not
interfere, was the speech of the Wyandot.

"Further, the Wyandot said, I speak to you, my little brother, the Shawanoes at Greenville, and to you,
our little brothers all around. You appear to be at
Greenville to serve the *Supreme Ruler* of the universe. Now send forth your speeches to all our
brethren far around us, and let us unite to seek for that
which shall be for our eternal welfare, and unite ourselves in a band of perpetual brotherhood. These,
brethren, are the sentiments of all the men who sit
around you: they all adhere to what the elder brother,
the Wyandot, has said, and these are their sentiments.
It is not that they are afraid of their white brethren,

but that they desire peace and harmony, and not that their white brethren could put them to great necessity, for their former arms were bows and arrows, by which they got their living."

The commissioners made some explanations in reply, when they were told that the Prophet would assign the reasons why the Indians had settled at Greenville. "He then proceeded to inform us," says the report, "that about three years since, he became convinced of the error of his ways, and that he would be destroyed from the face of the earth, if he did not amend them; that it was soon after made known to him what he should do to be right; that from that time he constantly preached to his red brethren the miserable situation they were in by nature, and endeavored to convince them that they must change their lives, live honestly, and be just in all their dealings, kind towards one another, and their white brethren: affectionate towards their families, put away lying and slandering, and serve the Great Spirit in the way he had pointed out; never think of war again; that at first the Lord did not give them the tomahawk to go to war with one another. His red brethren, the chiefs of the Shawanoes at Tawa town, would not listen to him, but persecuted him. This produced a division in the nation; those who adhered to him, separated themselves from their brethren at Tawa town, removed with and settled where he now was, and where he had constantly preached the above doctrines to all the strangers who came to see them. They did not remove to this place because it was a pretty place, or very valuable, for it was neither; but because it was revealed to him that the place was a proper one to establish his doctrines; that he meant to adhere to them while he lived; they were not his own, nor were they taught him by man, but by the Supreme Ruler of the universe; that his future life should prove to his white brethren the sincerity of his professions. He then told us that six chiefs should go with us to Chillicothe."

The commissioners left Greenville entirely convinced of the sincerity of the Prophet in his declaration of pacific intentions towards the United

States.* Four chiefs, Tecumseh, Blue Jacket, Sti-aglı-
ta, (or Roundhead) and Panther, accompanied them
to the seat of government, for the purpose of holding a
conference with the governor; and giving him assurances that the Indians were not assembling at Greenville for the purpose of making war upon the frontiers.
These chiefs remained about a week in Chillicothe, in
the course of which a public council was held between
them and the governor. Stephen Ruddell acted as the
interpreter. Tecumseh was the principal speaker; and
in the course of the conference, made a speech which
occupied three hours in the delivery.

His great object was to prove the nullity of the treaties under which the whites claimed the country north
and west of the Ohio. He seemed to have a familiar
knowiedge of all the treaties made with the western
tribes; reviewed them in their order, and with the most
intense bitterness and scorn, denounced them as null
and void. This speech is described by one † who heard
it, as possessing all the characteristics of a high effort
of oratory. The utterance of the speaker was rapid
and vehement; his manner bold and commanding; his
gestures impassioned, quick and violent, and his countenance indicating that there was something more in
his mind, struggling for utterance, than he deemed it
prudent to express. While he fearlessly denied the
validity of these *pretended* treaties, and openly avowed his intention to resist the further extension of the
white settlements upon the Indian lands, he disclaimed
all intention of making war upon the United States.
The result was, a conviction on the part of the governor, that no immediate danger was to be apprehended
from the Indians, at Greenville and fort Wayne; and,
as a consequence, the militia which had been called into service were ordered to be disbanded, and the chiefs
returned to their head quarters.

In the autumn of this year, a white man by the
name of Myers, was killed a few miles west of where

the town of Urbana now stands, by some straggling Indians. This murder, taken in connection with the assemblage of the Indians under Tecumseh and the Prophet, created a great alarm on the frontier, and actually induced many families to remove back to Kentucky, from whence they had emigrated. A demand was made by the whites upon these two brothers for the Indians who had committed the murder. They denied that it was done by their party, or with their knowledge, and declared that they did not even know who the murderers were. The alarm continued, and some companies of militia were called out. It was finally agreed, that a council should be held on the subject in Springfield, for the purpose of quieting the settlements. General Whiteman, major Moore, captain Ward and one or two others, acted as commissioners on the part of the whites. Two parties of Indians attended the council; one from the north, in charge of McPherson; the other, consisting of sixty or seventy, came from the neighborhood of fort Wayne, under the charge of Tecumseh. Roundhead, Blackfish, and several other chiefs, were also present. There was no friendly feeling between these two parties, and each was willing that the blame of the murder should be fixed upon the other. The party under McPherson, in compliance with the wishes of the commissioners, left their arms a few miles from Springfield. Tecumseh and his party refused to attend the council, unless permitted to retain their arms. After the conference was opened, it being held in a maple grove, a little north of where Werden's hotel now stands, the commissioners, fearing some violence, made another effort to induce Tecumseh to lay aside his arms. This he again refused, saying, in reply, that his tomahawk was also his pipe, and that he might wish to use it in that capacity before their business was closed. At this moment, a tall, lank-sided Pennsylvanian, who was standing among the spectators, and who, perhaps, had no love for the shining tomahawk of the self-willed chief, cautiously approached, and handed him an old, long stemmed, dirty looking earthen pipe, intimating, that if Tecumseh would deliver up the fearful tomahawk, he might smoke the aforesaid pipe. The chief took it between his thumb and finger, held it up, looked at it for a moment, then at the owner, who was gradually receding from the point of danger, and immediately threw it, with an indignant sneer, over his head, into the bushes. The commissioners yielded the point, and proceeded to business.

After a full and patient enquiry into the facts of the case, it appeared that the murder of Myers, was the act of an individual, and not justly chargeable upon either party of the Indians. Several speeches were made by the chiefs, but Tecumseh was the principal speaker. He gave a full explanation of the views of the Prophet and himself, in calling around them a band of Indians—disavowed all hostile intentions towards the United States, and denied that he or those under his control had committed any aggressions upon the whites. His manner, when speaking, was animated, fluent and rapid, and made a strong impression upon those present. The council terminated. In the course of it, the two hostile parties became reconciled to each other, and quiet was restored to the frontier.

The Indians remained in Springfield for three days, and on several occasions amused themselves by engaging in various games and other athletic exercises, in which Tecumseh generally proved himself victorious. His strength, and power of muscular action, were remarkably great, and in the opinion of those who attended the council, corresponded with the high order of his moral and intellectual character.*

---

* Dr. Hunt.

CHAPTER V.

Governor Harrison's address to the Shawanoe chiefs at Greenville—the Prophet's reply—his influence felt among the remote tribes—he is visited in 1808 by great numbers of Indians—Tecumseh and the Prophet remove to Tippecanoe—the latter sends a speech to governor Harrison —makes him a visit at Vincennes.

THE alarm caused by the assembling of the Indians at Greenville, still continuing, governor Harrison, in the autumn of this year, sent to the head chiefs of the Shawanoe tribe, by John Conner, one of our Indian agents, the following address:—

" My Children—Listen to me, I speak in the name of your father, the great chief of the Seventeen Fires.

" My children, it is now twelve years since the tomahawk, which you had raised by the advice of your father, the king of Great Britain, was buried at Greenville, in the presence of that great warrior, general Wayne.

" My children, you then promised, and the Great Spirit heard it, that you would in future live in peace and friendship with your brothers, the Americans. You made a treaty with your father, and one that contained a number of good things, equally beneficial to all the tribes of red people, who were parties to it.

" My children, you promised in that treaty to acknowledge no other father than the chief of the Seventeen Fires; and never to listen to the proposition of any foreign nation. You promised never to lift up the tomahawk against any of your father's children, and to give him notice of any other tribe that intended it: your father also promised to do something for you, particularly to deliver to you, every year, a certain quantity of goods; to prevent any white man from settling on your lands without your consent, or to do you any personal injury. He promised to run a line between your land and his, so that you might know your own; and you were to be permitted to live and hunt upon your father's land, as long as you behaved yourselves well. My children, which of these articles has your father broken? You know that he has observed them all with the utmost good faith. But, my children, have you done so? Have you not always had your ears open to receive bad advice from the white people beyond the lakes?

" My children, let us look back to times that are past. It has been a long time since you called the king of Great Britain, father. You know that it is the duty of a father to watch over his children, to give them good advice, and to do every thing in his power to make them happy. What has this father of yours done for you, during the long time that you have looked up to him for protection and advice? Are you wiser and happier than you were before you knew him; or is your nation stronger or more respectable? No, my children, he took you by the hand when you were a powerful tribe; you held him fast, supposing he was your friend, and he conducted you through paths filled with thorns and briers, which tore your flesh and shed your blood. Your strength was exhausted, and you could no longer follow him. Did he stay by you in your distress, and assist and comfort you? No, he led you into danger, and then abandoned you. He saw your blood flowing and he would give you no bandage to tie up your wounds. This was the conduct of the man who called himself your father. The Great Spirit opened your eyes; you heard the voice of the chief of the Seventeen Fires, speaking the words of peace. He called to you to follow him; you came to him, and he once more put you on the right way, on the broad smooth road that would have led to happiness. But the voice of your deceiver is again heard; and forgetful of your former sufferings, you are again listening to him.

" My children, shut your ears, and mind him not, or he will lead you to ruin and misery.

" My children, I have heard bad news. The sacred spot where the great council fire was kindled, around which the Seventeen Fires and ten tribes of their children, smoked the pipe of peace—that very spot where the Great Spirit saw his red and white children encircle themselves with the chain of friendship—that place has been selected for dark and bloody councils.

" My children, this business must be stopped. You

I 2

have called in a number of men from the most distant tribes, to listen to a fool, who speaks not the words of the Great Spirit, but those of the devil, and of the British agents. My children, your conduct has much alarmed the white settlers near you. They desire that you will send away those people, and if they wish to have the impostor with them, they can carry him. Let him go to the lakes; he can hear the British more distinctly."

At the time of the delivery of this speech, the head chiefs of the Shawanoes were absent from Greenville The Prophet, after listening patiently to it, requested the interpreter to write down the following answer, which was transmitted to the governor.

"Father,—I am very sorry that you listen to the advice of bad birds. You have impeached me with having correspondence with the British; and with calling and sending for the Indians from the most distant part of the country, "to listen to a fool that speaks not the words of the Great Spirit, but the words of the devil." Father, those impeachments I deny, and say they are not true. I never had a word with the British, and I never sent for any Indians. They came here themselves to listen, and hear the words of the Great Spirit.

"Father, I wish you would not listen any more to the voice of bad birds; and you may rest assured that it is the least of our idea to make disturbance, and we will rather try to stop any such proceedings than to encourage them."

The appeal of the governor, as may be inferred from the evasive and cunning answer of the Prophet, produced no change in his measures, nor did it arrest the spread of the fanaticism among the Indians which his incantations had set afloat. The happiness of the Indians was the great idea which Tecumseh and his brother promulgated among their followers as being the object of their labors. This was to be attained by leading more virtuous lives, by retaining their lands, and in simply doing what the government of the United States had frequently urged upon them, effecting an extended and friendly union of the different tribes. These plausible reasons, backed by the superstitious belief of the Indians in the inspired character of the

Prophet, and the insidious efforts of the British agents, in fomenting discontent among them, were sufficient to keep alive the excitement, and even extend the circle of its influence. Thus ended the year 1807.

The reader may learn the extraordinary success of the Prophet in spreading his influence among the remote tribes, by a reference to the narrative of Mr. John Tanner. This man had been taken captive in Boone county, Kentucky, when a boy; had been raised by the Indians, and was at this time, living among the Ojibbeways, who reside far up the lakes.

News reached that remote tribe that a great man had arisen among the Shawanoes, who had been favored by a revelation of the mind and will of the Great Spirit. The messenger bearing this information to them, seemed deeply penetrated with the sacred character of his mission. Upon his arrival among them, he announced himself after a mysterious silence, as the forerunner of the great Prophet, who was shortly to shake hands with the Ojibbeways, and explain to them more fully his inspired character, and the new mode of life and conduct which they were hereafter to pursue. He then gravely repeated to them the Prophet's system of morals; and in a very solemn manner, enjoined its observance. So strong was the impression made upon the principal men of the Ojibbeways, that a time was appointed and a lodge prepared for the public espousal of these doctrines. When the Indians were assembled in the new lodge, "we saw something," says Mr. Tanner, "carefully concealed under a blanket, in figure and dimensions bearing some resemblance to a man. This was accompanied by two young men, who, it was understood, attended constantly upon it, made its bed at night, as for a man, and slept near it. But while we remained, no one went near to it, or raised the blanket which was spread over its unknown contents. Four strings of mouldy and discolored beads were all the visible insignia of this important mission.

"After a long harangue, in which the prominent features of the new revelation were stated, and urged upon the attention of all, the four strings of beads, which we were told were made of the flesh of the Prophet, were carried with much solemnity, to each man in the lodge, and he was expected to take hold of each string at the top, and draw them gently through his hand. This was called shaking hands with the Prophet, and was considered as solemnly engaging to obey his injunctions, and accept of his mission as from the Supreme. All the Indians who touched the beads had previously killed their dogs; they gave up their medicine bags, and showed a disposition to comply with all that should be required of them."

The excitement among the Ojibbeways continued for some time; they assembled in groups, their faces wearing an aspect of gloom and anxiety, while the active sunk into indolence, and the spirit of the bravest warriors was subdued. The influence of the Prophet, says Mr. Tanner, "was very sensibly and painfully felt by the remotest Ojibbeways of whom I had any knowledge; but it was not the common impression among them, that his doctrines had any tendency to unite them in the accomplishment of any human purpose. For two or three years drunkenness was much less frequent than formerly; war was less thought of; and the entire aspect of things among them was changed by the influence of this mission. But in time these new impressions were obliterated; medicine-bags, flints and steels, the use of which had been forbidden, were brought into use; dogs were reared, women and children beaten as before; and the Shawanoe Prophet was despised."

With the beginning of the year 1808, great numbers of Indians came down from the lakes, on a visit to the Prophet, where they remained until their means of subsistence were exhausted. The governor of Indiana, with the prudence and humanity which marked his administration, directed the agent at fort Wayne, to supply them with provisions from the public stores at that place. This was done, and from his intercourse with them he came to the conclusion that they had no hostile designs against the United States. About this time, Tecumseh made a visit to the Mississinaway towns, the immediate object of which could not be clearly ascertained. That it was connected with the grand scheme in which he was engaged, is probable from the fact that the Indians of that region agreed to meet him and the Prophet on the Wabash, in the following June, to which place he had at this time resolved to move his party. Mr. Jouett, one of the United States' Indian agents, apprehended that this meeting would result in some hostile action against the frontiers; and, as a means of preventing it, and putting an end to the influence of the Prophet, recommended to the governor that he should be seized and confined. The proposition, however, was not entertained.

In the spring of this year, 1808, Tecumseh and the Prophet removed to a tract of land granted them by the Potawatamies and Kickapoos, on Tippecanoe, one of the tributaries of the Wabash river. They had not been long at their new residence before it became apparent that the Prophet had established a strong influence over the minds of the surrounding Indians, and there was much reason for believing that his views were hostile to the United States. The governor still confided in the fidelity of the Delawares and the Miamis; but he apprehended, that although disbelievers in the Prophet's divine mission, they might be turned from the line of duty from a fear of his temporal power. When he had established himself upon the banks of the Tippecanoe, the Prophet drew around him a body of northern Indians, principally from the Potawatamies, Ottowas and Chippewas. To this, the Miamis and Delawares had strong objections; and a deputation of the latter was sent to the Prophet on the subject. He refused to see them himself, but Tecumseh met them; and after a solemn conference, they returned to their tribe with increased apprehensions of the combination at Tippecanoe, which was now uniting warlike sports with the performance of religious duties.* The Delawares decided in council to arrest the progress of this rising power, but in vain. Strong in the moral force with which they were armed, the two brothers were not to be driven from their purpose of planting the banner of union, which they were now

* Governor Harrison s Correspondence with the War Department.

holding out to the tribes, upon the waters of the Wabash. The sacred office which the Prophet had impiously assumed, enabled him to sway many minds, and in doing so, he was effectively sustained by the personal presence, tact and sagacity of his brother. From his youth, Tecumseh had been noted for the influence which he exercised over those by whom he was surrounded. Hence, when the chiefs of the Miamis and Delawares, who were disbelievers in the Prophet's holy character, set out to prevent his removal to the Wabash, Tecumseh boldly met them, and turned them from their purpose. This was done at a moment when the number of the Prophet's followers was greatly reduced, as we gather from the statement of the agent, John Conner, who in the month of June, of this year, visited his settlement on the Wabash to reclaim some horses which had been stolen from the whites. At this time, the Prophet had not more than forty of his own tribe with him; and less than a hundred from others, principally Potawatamies, Chippewas, Ottawas and Winebagoes. The Prophet announced his intention of making a visit to governor Harrison, for the purpose of explaining his conduct, and procuring a supply of provisions for his followers. This, he insisted, could not be consistently withheld from him, as the white people had always encouraged him to preach the word of God to the Indians; and in this holy work he was now engaged.

Some time in the month of July, the governor received a speech from the Prophet, sent to Vincennes by a special messenger. It was cautious, artful and pacific in its character. It deprecated in strong terms the misrepresentations which had been circulated in regard to the ulterior objects of the Prophet and his brother as to the whites; and renewed the promise of an early visit. This visit was made in the month following, and was continued for two weeks, during which time he and the governor had frequent interviews. In these, the Prophet, with his characteristic plausibility, denied that his course was the result of British influence. His sole object, he alleged, was a benevolent one towards his red brethren; to reclaim them from the

degrading vices to which they were addicted, and induce them to cultivate a spirit of peace and friendship,
not only with the white people, but their kindred
tribes. To this sacred office, he insisted, with much
earnestness, he had been specially called by the Great
Spirit. That he might the more successfully enforce
the sincerity of his views upon the mind of the governor, he took occasion several times during the visit, to
address the Indians who had accompanied him to Vincennes, and dwelt upon the great evils resulting to
them from wars, and the use of ardent spirits. It was
apparent to the governor that the Prophet was a man
of decided talents, of great tact, and admirably qualified to play successfully, the part he had assumed. In
order to test the extent of his influence over his followers, the governor held conversations with them, and
several times offered them whiskey, which they invariably refused. Looking to that amelioration of the
condition of the Indians, which had long engaged his
attention, the governor began to hope that the Prophet's power over them might be turned to advantage;
and that the cause of humanity would be benefited by
sustaining rather than trying to weaken the influence
of the preacher. This impression was much strengthened by the following speech which the Prophet delivered to him, before the close of the visit.

"Father :—It is three years since I first began with
that system of religion which I now practice. The
white people and some of the Indians were against
me; but I had no other intention but to introduce
among the Indians, those good principles of religion
which the white people profess. I was spoken badly
of by the white people, who reproached me with mis-
leading the Indians; but I defy them to say that I did
any thing amiss.

"Father, I was told that you intended to hang me.
When I heard this, I intended to remember it, and tell
my father, when I went to see him, and relate to him
the truth.

"I heard, when I settled on the Wabash, that my
father, the governor, had declared that all the land between Vincennes and fort Wayne, was the property of

the Seventeen Fires. I also heard that you wanted to know, my father, whether I was God or man; and that you said if I was the former, I should not steal horses. I heard this from Mr. Wells, but I believed it originated with himself.

"The Great Spirit told me to tell the Indians that he had made them, and made the world—that he had placed them on it to do good, and not evil.

"I told all the red skins, that the way they were in was not good, and that they ought to abandon it.

"That we ought to consider ourselves as one man; but we ought to live agreeably to our several customs, the red people after their mode, and the white people after theirs; particularly, that they should not drink whiskey; that it was not made for them, but the white people, who alone knew how to use it; and that it is the cause of all the mischiefs which the Indians suffer; and that they must always follow the directions of the Great Spirit, and we must listen to him, as it was he that made us: determine to listen to nothing that is bad: do not take up the tomahawk, should it be offered by the British, or by the long knives: do not meddle with any thing that does not belong to you, but mind your own business, and cultivate the ground, that your women and your children may have enough to live on.

"I now inform you, that it is our intention to live in peace with our father and his people forever.

"My father, I have informed you what we mean to do, and I call the Great Spirit to witness the truth of my declaration. The religion which I have established for the last three years, has been attended to by the different tribes of Indians in this part of the world. Those Indians were once different people; they are now but one: they are all determined to practice what I have communicated to them, that has come immediately from the Great Spirit through me.

"Brother, I speak to you as a warrior. You are one. But let us lay aside this character, and attend to the care of our children, that they may live in comfort and peace. We desire that you will join us for the preservation of both red and white people. Formerly, when we lived in ignorance, we were foolish; but now, since we listen to the voice of the Great Spirit, we are happy.

"I have listened to what you have said to us. You have promised to assist us: I now request you, in behalf of all the red people, to use your exertions to prevent the sale of liquor to us. We are all well pleased to hear you say that you will endeavor to promote our happiness. We give you every assurance that we will follow the dictates of the Great Spirit.

"We are all well pleased with the attention that you have showed us; also with the good intentions of our father, the President. If you give us a few articles, such as needles, flints, hoes, powder, &c., we will take the animals that afford us meat, with powder and ball."

Governor Harrison, if not deceived by the plausible pretences and apparently candid declarations of the Prophet, was left in doubt, whether he was really meditating hostile movements against the United States, or only laboring, with the energy of an enthusiast, in the good work of promoting the welfare of the Indians. Having received a supply of provisions, the Prophet and his followers, at the end of a fortnight, took leave of the governor and returned to their head quarters, on the banks of the Tippecanoe.

CHAPTER VI.

Tecumseh visits the Wyandots—governor Harrison's letter about the Prophet to the Secretary at War—British influence over the Indians—Tecumseh burns governor Harrison's letter to the chiefs—great alarm in Indiana, in consequence of the assemblage of the Indians at Tippecanoe—death of Leatherlips, a Wyandot chief, on a charge of witchcraft.

DURING the autumn of this year, 1808, nothing material occurred with the Prophet and his brother, calculated to throw light upon their conduct. The former continued his efforts to induce the Indians to forsake their vicious habits. The latter was occupied in visit-

K

ing the neighboring tribes, and quietly strengthening his own and the Prophet's influence over them.   Early in the succeeding year, Tecumseh attended a council of Indians, at Sandusky, when he endeavored to prevail upon the Wyandots and Senecas to remove and join his establishment at Tippecanoe.   Among other reasons presented in favor of this removal, he stated that the country on the Tippecanoe was better than that occupied by these tribes; that it was remote from the whites, and that in it they would have more game and be happier than where they now resided.   In this mission he appears not to have been successful.   The Crane, an old chief of the Wyandot tribe, replied, that he feared he, Tecumseh, was working for no good purpose at Tippecanoe; that they would wait a few years, and then, if they found their red brethren at that place contented and happy, they would probably join them.*   In this visit to Sandusky, Tecumseh was accompanied by captain Lewis, a Shawanoe chief of some note, who then engaged to go with him to the Creeks and Cherokees, on a mission which he was contemplating, and which was subsequently accomplished. Lewis, however, did not finally make the visit, but permitted Jim Blue Jacket to make the tour in his place.

In April of the year 1809, the agent of the United States at fort Wayne, informed governor Harrison, that it had been reported to him that the Chippewas, Potawatamies and Ottawas, were deserting the standard of the Prophet, because they had been required to take up arms against the whites, and to unite in an effort to exterminate all the inhabitants of Vincennes, and those living on the Ohio, between its mouth and Cincinnati— it being the order of the Great Spirit; and that their own destruction would be the consequence of a refusal. The agent did not think, however, that hostilities were likely to ensue, as he was informed there were not more than one hundred warriors remaining with the Prophet.   The governor, however, had information from other sources, that although there might be but that number of warriors at the Prophet's village,

---

* Anthony Shane.

there were, within fifty miles of his head-quarters, four or five times that number, who were devoted to him and to his cause. Under these circumstances, he decided to organize forthwith, under previous orders from the War department, two companies of volunteer militia, and with them to garrison fort Knox—a post about two miles from Vincennes—then the general depot of arms and ammunition, for the use of the neighboring militia. The agent at fort Wayne was accordingly directed by the governor to require the Delaware, Miami and Potawatamie tribes, to prevent any hostile parties of Indians from passing through their respective territories. This they were bound to do, by a stipulation in the treaty of Greenville. But no hostile movements, (if any had been meditated,) were made by the Prophet, and before the close of the month of May, most of his warriors had dispersed, and all apprehension of an attack from the Indians was dispelled.

In the month of July, in reply to a letter from the Secretary of War, on the subject of the defence of the north-western frontier, governor Harrison, in reference to the Prophet, says:

" The Shawanoe Prophet and about forty followers, arrived here about a week ago. He denies most strenuously, any participation in the late combination to attack our settlements, which he says was entirely confined to the tribes of the Mississippi and Illinois rivers; and he claims the merit of having prevailed upon them to relinquish their intentions.

" I must confess that my suspicions of his guilt have been rather strengthened than diminished at every interview I have had with him since his arrival. He acknowledges that he received an invitation to war against us, from the British, last fall; and that he was apprised of the intention of the Sacs and Foxes, &c. early in the spring, and was warmly solicited to join in their league. But he could give no satisfactory explanation of his neglecting to communicate to me, circumstances so extremely interesting to us; and towards which I had a few months before directed his attention, and received a solemn assurance of his cheerful compliance with the injunctions I had impressed upon him.

" The result of all my enquiries on the subject is, that the late combination was produced by British intrigue and influence, in anticipation of war between them and the United States. It was, however, premature and ill-judged, and the event sufficiently manifests a great decline in their influence, or in the talents and address, with which they have been accustomed to manage their Indian relations.

" The warlike and well armed tribes of the Potawatamies, Ottawas, Chippewas, Delawares, and Miamis, I believe, neither had, nor would have, joined in the combination; and although the Kickapoos, whose warriors are better than those of any other tribe, the remnant of the Wyandots excepted, are much under the influence of the Prophet, I am persuaded that they were never made acquainted with his intentions, if these were really hostile to the United States."

In the latter part of the year 1809, under instructions from the President of the United States, governor Harrison deemed the period a favorable one to extinguish the Indian title to the lands on the east of the Wabash, and adjoining south on the lines established by the former treaties of fort Wayne and Grousland. A council was accordingly held, in the latter part of September, at fort Wayne, with the Miami, Eel river, Delaware and Potawatamie tribes, which resulted in the purchase of the land above mentioned. A separate treaty was made with the Kickapoos, who confirmed the grants made at the above treaty, and also ceded another tract. In making these treaties, governor Harrison invited all those Indians to be present, who were considered as having any title to the lands embraced within them.

Throughout the remainder of the year 1809, things remained quiet with Tecumseh and the Prophet. The number of their followers was again on the increase; and, although no overt acts of hostility against the frontier settlements were committed, there was a prevalent suspicion in that quarter, that the Indians entertained sinister designs towards the whites. The events of the early part of the year 1810, were such as to leave little doubt of the hostile intentions of the broth ers. In the latter part of April, governor Harrison was informed, upon credible authority, that the Prophet was really instigating the Indians to acts of hostility against the United States; and that he had under his immediate control about four hundred warriors, chiefly composed of Kickapoos and Winnebagoes, but embracing also some Shawanoes, Potawatamies, Chippewas, and Ottawas. The traders among them attributed this hostile feeling to British influence. That the followers of the Prophet had received a supply of powder and ball from the English agents, was generally admitted. They refused to buy ammunition from our traders, alleging that they were plentifully supplied from a quarter where it cost them nothing. About the middle of May, it was ascertained that the number of warriors with the Prophet, amounted to more than six hundred men, and there were reasons to apprehend that his influence had kindled a hostile feeling among several of the tribes to the west and north of his head quarters. A meeting of Indians having been appointed to take place about this time, on the St. Joseph's river, governor Harrison made an appeal to them through the Delawares, in which he forcibly pointed out the unhappy results that would certainly follow any attack upon the United States; and cautioned the friendly tribes, upon the dangers to which they would be subjected, in consequence of the difficulty of discriminating between friends and enemies, in case a war should occur. In July the governor was authorized by the Secretary of War, to take such steps as he might deem necessary for the protection of the frontier; and, at the same time was informed that some troops had been ordered to Vincennes to keep in check the hostile Indians of that quarter.

Fresh apprehensions were now felt for the safety of the frontiers. The Prophet, it appears, had gained over to his cause the Wyandot tribe, whose councils had always exerted a strong influence among the Indians. To this tribe had been committed the preservation of the Great Belt, the symbol of union among the tribes in their late war with the United States; and also the original duplicate of the Greenville treaty of

1795. The Prophet sent a deputation to the Wyandots requesting permission to examine the provisions of that treaty, and artfully expressing his astonishment that they, who had ever directed the councils of the Indians, and who were alike renowned for their talents and bravery, should remain passive, and see the lands of the red men usurped by a part of that race. The Wyandots, pleased with these flattering speeches, replied, that they had carefully preserved the former symbol of union among the tribes; but it had remained so long in their hands without being called for, they supposed it was forgotten. They further replied, that weary of their present situation, they felt desirous of seeing all the tribes united in one great confederacy: that they would join such a union, and labor to arrest the encroachments of the whites upon their lands, and if possible recover those which had been unjustly taken from them. This reply of the Wyandots was exactly suited to the objects of the Prophet; and he lost no time in sending his heralds with it, in every direction. The Wyandots soon afterwards made a visit to Tippecanoe; and in passing thither, had a conference with some of the Miami chiefs, to whom they showed the great belt, and charged them with having joined the whites in opposition to their red brethren. The Miamis at length concluded to join in a visit to the Prophet, and also invited the Weas to join with them.

About this time, the governor was informed by an aged Piankishaw, friendly to the United States, that the Prophet had actually formed a plan for destroying the citizens of Vincennes by a general massacre; and that he boasted that he would walk in the footsteps of the great Pontiac. From another source the governor learned that there were probably three hundred Indians within thirty miles of the Prophet's quarters; and that although their proceedings were conducted with great secrecy, it had been discovered that they were determined to stop the United States' surveyors from running any lines west of the Wabash. Other evidences of approaching hostilities were not wanting. The Prophet, and the Kickapoos who were at his village, refused to accept the salt which had been sent up to them as a part of their annuities, and after it had been put upon the shore, the carriers were not only required to replace it in their boat, but whilst doing so, were treated with rudeness, and ordered to take the salt back to Vincennes. They were Frenchmen, or in all probability they would have been treated still more harshly *

In the early part of July, governor Harrison received a letter from John Johnston, Indian agent at fort Wayne, in which he says :

"A person just arrived, who it appears has lost himself in his route to Vincennes, affords me an opportunity of announcing to you my return to this fort. I was delayed on my journey in attending to the transportation of the public goods; and on my arrival in the state of Ohio, I had learned that the Prophet's brother had lately been at work among the Shawanoes, on the Auglaize; and, among other things, had burned your letter delivered to the chiefs at this place last fall. I accordingly took Wapakonetta in my route home, assembled the chiefs, and demanded the reason why they had suffered such an improper act to be committed at their door. They disavowed all agency in the transaction, and their entire disapprobation of the Prophet's conduct; and concurring circumstances satisfied me that they were sincere. The white persons at the town informed me that not one of the chiefs would go into council with the Prophet's brother, and that it was a preacher named Riddle, who took the letter to have it interpreted, and that the brother of the Prophet took it from his hand, and threw it into the fire, declaring, that if governor Harrison were there, he would serve *him* so. He told the Indians that the white people and the government were deceiving them, and that for his part, he never would believe them, or put any confidence in them; that he never would be quiet until he effected his purpose; and that if he was dead, *the cause* would not die with him. He urged the Indians to move off to the Mississippi with him, saying, that there he would assemble his forces. All his argu-

---

* Governor Harrison's letters to the War Department.

ments seemed to be bottomed on the prospect of hostilities against our people. He made no impression on the Shawanoes, and went away much dissatisfied at their not coming into his views. I consider them among our best friends. I indirectly encouraged their emigration westward, and told them their annuity should follow them. They appear determined to remain, and are much attached to the town and the improvements, which are considerable."

Notwithstanding the Prophet appears in all these recent transactions, to be the prominent individual, it is certain that a greater one was behind the scene. In the junction of the Wyandots with the Prophet, may be seen the result of Tecumseh's visit to that tribe, in the previous year, at Sandusky, an account of which has been already given. In regard to the salt annuity, the Prophet knew not what course to pursue, until he had consulted with his brother. Tecumseh, burning the governor's letter, and the threat, that if he were present he should meet the same fate, were acts in keeping with his bold character, and well calculated to maintain his ascendancy among the Indians. While the Prophet was nominally the head of the new party, and undoubtedly exercised much influence by means of his supposed supernatural power, he was but an agent, controlled and directed by a master spirit, whose energy, address and ceaseless activity, were all directed to the accomplishment of the grand plan to which he had solemnly devoted his life.

The information which flowed in upon governor Harrison, from different quarters, relative to the movements of Tecumseh and the Prophet, and the number of their followers, were such as to induce him to make the most active preparations to meet the impending storm. A meeting of the citizens of Vincennes was held on the subject, two companies of militia were called into active service, and the rest were directed to hold themselves in readiness for the field. Alarm-posts were established, and other measures adopted, especially for the preservation of Vincennes, which appeared to have been fixed upon as the first point of attack.

Toward the close of June, Winnemac, at the head

of a deputation of Potawatamies, visited the governor at Vincennes, for the purpose of informing him of the decision of a council, held at the St. Joseph's of lake Michigan, which had been attended by all the tribes of that quarter, and by a delegation from the Delawares. This deputation was present for the purpose of dissuading the Indians from joining the Prophet. The duty appears to have been faithfully performed by them. They protested in strong terms, against the schemes of the Prophet and his brother, and induced, it is believed, these tribes to give up all idea of joining them. Winnemac was directed to inform the governor, of the determination to which they had come, and also, to lay before him the plans of the Prophet. According to the information before the council, Detroit, St. Louis, fort Wayne, Chicago and Vincennes, were all to be surprised. Efforts were making to persuade the tribes residing on the Mississippi, to unite in the confederacy. It further appeared, that the followers of the Prophet, drawn as they were from all the tribes, embraced but few, if any of the peace chiefs, while not a few of the war chiefs, or the leaders of small parties, were enrolling themselves under his standard. Winnemac stated to the governor, that the Prophet had actually suggested to his young men, the expediency of murdering all the leading chiefs of the surrounding tribes, on the plea that their own hands would never be untied until this was done. They, he said, were the men who sold their lands, and invited the encroachments of the whites.

About the period of Winnemac's visit, an Indian belonging to the Iowa tribe, told general Harrison, that two years before, a British agent visited the Prophet, and delivered a message to him. The object was to induce the Prophet to persevere in uniting the tribes against the United States, but not to make any hostile movement, until the signal was given him by the British authorities. From this Iowa, and others of his tribe, the governor ascertained that the Prophet had been soliciting them and other tribes on the Mississippi to join the confederacy. To these the Prophet stated, in his plausible manner, that the Americans were ceaselessly and silently invading the Indians, until those

who had suffered most, had resolved to be driven back
no farther; and that it was the duty of the remote
tribes upon whose lands the march of civilization had
not yet pressed, to assist those who had already lost
theirs, or in turn a corresponding calamity would follow upon them.   This, the Prophet declared, he was
directed by the Great Spirit of the Indians to tell them,
adding, that this Great Spirit would utterly destroy
them, if they ventured to doubt the words of his chosen Prophet.*

On the first of June, a Wyandot chief, called Leatherlips, paid the forfeit of his life on a charge of witchcraft.   General Harrison entertained the opinion that
his death was the result of the Prophet's command,
and that the party who acted as executioners went
directly from Tippecanoe, to the banks of the Scioto,
where the tragedy was enacted.   Leatherlips was
found encamped upon that stream, twelve miles above
Columbus.   The six Wyandots who put him to death,
were headed, it is supposed, by the chief Roundhead.
An effort was made by some white men who were
present to save the life of the accused, but without success.   A council of two or three hours took place : the
accusing party spoke with warmth and bitterness of
feeling: Leatherlips was calm and dispassionate in his
replies.   The sentence of death, which had been previously passed upon him, was reaffirmed.   "The prisoner then walked slowly to his camp, partook of a
dinner of jerked venison, washed and arrayed himself
in his best apparel, and afterwards painted his face.
His dress was very rich—his hair gray, and his whole
appearance graceful and commanding."   When the
hour for the execution had arrived, Leatherlips shook
hands in silence with the spectators.   "He then turned from his wigwam, and with a voice of surpassing
strength and melody commenced the chant of the death
song.   He was followed closely by the Wyandot warriors, all timing with their slow and measured march,
the music of his wild and melancholy dirge.   The

* General Harrison's official correspondence—Dawson's Historical Narrative.

white men were likewise all silent followers in that strange procession. At the distance of seventy or eighty yards from the camp, they came to a shallow grave, which, unknown to the white men, had been previously prepared by the Indians. Here the old man knelt down, and in an elevated but solemn tone of voice, addressed his prayer to the Great Spirit. As soon as he had finished, the captain of the Indians knelt beside him, and prayed in a similar manner. Their prayers of course were spoken in the Wyandot tongue. * * * * "After a few moments delay, the prisoner again sank down upon his knees and prayed as he had done before. When he had ceased, he still continued in a kneeling position. All the rifles belonging to the party had been left at the wigwam. There was not a weapon of any kind to be seen at the place of execution, and the spectators were consequently unable to form any conjecture as to the mode of procedure, which the executioners had determined on, for the fulfilment of their purpose. Suddenly one of the warriors drew from beneath the skirts of his capote, a keen, bright tomahawk—walked rapidly up behind the chieftain— brandished the weapon on high, for a single moment, and then struck with his whole strength. The blow descended directly upon the crown of the head, and the victim immediately fell prostrate. After he had lain awhile in the agonies of death, the Indian captain directed the attention of the white men to the drops of sweat which were gathering upon his neck and face; remarked with much apparent exultation, that it was conclusive proof of the sufferer's guilt. Again the executioner advanced, and with the same weapon, inflict- ed two or three additional and heavy blows. As soon as life was entirely extinct, the body was hastily buried, with all its apparel and decorations; and the assemblage dispersed."*

One of Mr. Heckewelder's correspondents, as quoted in his Historical Account of the Indian Nations, makes Tarhe, better known by the name of Crane, the leader of this party. This has been denied; and, the letter †

---

* Mr. Otway Curry, in the Hesperian for May, 1838.
† Published in the Hesperian for July, 1838.

of general Harrison on the subject, proves quite con-
clusively that this celebrated chief had nothing to do
with the execution of Leatherlips.   Mr. Heckewelder's
correspondent concurs in the opinion that the original
order for the death of this old man, was issued from
the head quarters of the Prophet and his brother.

CHAPTER VII.

*Governor Harrison makes another effort to ascertain the designs of Te-
cumseh and the Prophet—Tecumseh visits the governor at Vincennes,
attended by four hundred warriors—a council is held—Tecumseh becomes deeply excited, and charges governor Harrison with falsehood—
council broken up in disorder—renewed the next day.*

For the purpose of ascertaining more fully the designs of the Prophet and his brother, governor Harrison now despatched two confidential agents to their
head quarters at Tippecanoe.   One of these agents,
Mr. Dubois, was kindly received by the Prophet.   He
stated to him that he had been sent by governor Harrison to ascertain the reason of his hostile preparations,
and of his enmity to the United States; that his conduct had created so much alarm, that warriors both in
Kentucky and Indiana were arming for service, and
that a detachment of regular troops was then actually
on its way to Vincennes: that he was further authorized by the governor to say, that these preparations
were only for defence; that no attempt would be made
against him, until *his* intention to commence hostilities
could be doubted no longer.   The Prophet denied that
he intended to make war, and declared that on this
point he had been unjustly accused: that it was by the
express commands of the Great Spirit that he had fixed himself there; and that he was ordered to assemble
the Indians at that spot.   When urged by the agent to
state the grounds of his complaints against the United
States, he replied, the Indians had been cheated of their
lands; that no sale was valid unless sanctioned by all
the tribes.   He was assured that the government would

listen to any complaints he might have to urge; and
that it was expedient for him to go to Vincennes and
see governor Harrison on the subject. This he declined doing, giving as a reason, that on his former visit to
him, he had been badly treated. Mr. Dubois met at
the Prophet's town with some Kickapoos, with whom
he was acquainted. They seemed to regret having
joined the Prophet, and admitted that they had long
suspected that it was his wish to go to war with the
United States. War was undoubtedly his intention,
but whether against the United States or the Osage
nation, they were unable to say with certainty. Mr.
Dubois, on this trip, visited the Wea and Eel river
tribes, and found them apprehensive that war would
ensue, and that they would find themselves involved
in it.

The letter of general Harrison to the Secretary of
War, detailing the results of this mission, concludes
with the following remarks upon the principles long
and stoutly contended for by Tecumseh, that the Indian lands were the common property of all the tribes,
and could not be sold without the consent of all.

" The subject of allowing the Indians of this country to consider all their lands as common property, has
been frequently and largely discussed, in my communications with your predecessor, and in a personal
interview with the late President. The treaties made
by me last fall were concluded on principles as liberal
towards the Indians, as my knowledge of the views
and opinions of the government would allow. For
although great latitude of discretion has always been
given to me, I knew that the opinion of Mr. Jefferson
on the subject went so far as to assert a claim of the
United States, as lords paramount, to the lands of all
extinguished or decayed tribes, to the exclusion of all
recent settlers. Upon this principle, the Miami nation
are the only rightful claimants of all the unpurchased
lands from the Ohio to the Illinois and Mississippi rivers. But, sir, the President may rest assured that the
complaint of injury, with regard to the sale of lands,
is a mere pretence suggested to the Prophet by British
partisans and emissaries."

L

Early in July, some of the Prophet's followers descended the Wabash to a point below Terre Haute, and stole several horses. A few days afterwards, governor Harrison ascertained from a party of Indians who were on a visit to Vincennes, that the Sacs and Foxes had taken up the hatchet, and declared themselves ready to act with the Prophet, whenever it should be required. It was further stated, that a Miami chief, who had just returned from his annual visit to Malden, after receiving his usual stipend of goods, was addressed by the British agent, Elliot, in these words : " My son, keep your eyes fixed on me— my tomahawk is now up—be you ready, but do not strike till I give the signal."

About the same time, the governor, in the hope of staying the movements of the Prophet, or at least of ascertaining the amount of his forces, forwarded to him by a confidential interpreter, the following speech:

"William Henry Harrison, governor and commander-in-chief of the territory of Indiana, to the Shawanoe chief, and the Indians assembled at Tippecanoe:

" Notwithstanding the improper language which you have used towards me, I will endeavor to open your eyes to your true interests. Notwithstanding what white bad men have told you, I am not your personal enemy. You ought to know this from the manner in which I received and treated you, on your visit to this place.

" Although I must say, that you are an enemy to the Seventeen Fires, and that you have used the greatest exertions with other tribes to lead them astray. In this, you have been in some measure successful; as I am told they are ready to raise the tomahawk against their father ; yet their father, notwithstanding his anger at their folly, is full of goodness, and is always ready to receive into his arms those of his children who are willing to repent, acknowledge their fault, and ask for his forgiveness.

" There is yet but little harm done, which may be easily repaired. The chain of friendship which united the whites with the Indians, may be renewed, and be as strong as ever. A great deal of that work depends on you—the destiny of those who are under your direction, depends upon the choice you may make of the two roads which are before you. The one is large, open and pleasant, and leads to peace, security and happiness; the other, on the contrary, is narrow and crooked, and leads to misery and ruin. Don't deceive yourselves; do not believe that all the nations of Indians united, are able to resist the force of the Seventeen Fires. I know your warriors are brave, but ours are not less so; but what can a few brave warriors do, against the innumerable warriors of the Seventeen Fires? Our blue coats are more numerous than you can count; our hunters are like the leaves of the forest, or the grains of sand on the Wabash.

"Do not think that the red coats can protect you; they are not able to protect themselves. They do not think of going to war with us. If they did, you would in a few moons see our flag wave over all the forts of Canada.

"What reason have you to complain of the Seventeen Fires? have they taken any thing from you—have they ever violated the treaties made with the red men? You say that they purchased lands from them who had no right to sell them: show that this is true, and the land will be instantly restored. Show us the rightful owners of those lands which have been purchased—let them present themselves. The ears of your father will be opened to your complaints, and if the lands have been purchased of those who did not own them, they will be restored to the rightful owners. I have full power to arrange this business; but if you would rather carry your complaints before your great father, the President, you shall be indulged. I will immediately take means to send you with those chiefs which you may choose, to the city where your father lives. Every thing necessary shall be prepared for your journey, and means taken for your safe return."

Tecumseh was present when the interpreter delivered this speech. The Prophet made no reply to it, but promised to send one by his brother, who intended, in a few weeks, to make a visit to governor Harrison. In conversation, however, with the interpreter, the

Prophet strongly disavowed the idea that he had any hostile intentions; but at the same time declared, that it would not be practicable long to maintain peace with the United States, unless the government would recognize the principle, that the lands were the common property of *all* the Indians; and cease to make any further settlement to the north and west. "The Great Spirit" continued he, "gave this great island to his red children; he placed the whites on the other side of the big water; they were not contented with their own, but came to take ours from us. They have driven us from the sea to the lakes: we can go no further. They have taken upon them to say, this tract belongs to the Miamis, this to the Delawares, and so on; but the Great Spirit intended it as the common property of us all. Our father tells us, that we have no business upon the Wabash, the land belongs to other tribes; but the Great Spirit ordered us to come here, and here we will stay." He expressed himself, in the course of the conversation, gratified with the speech which the governor had sent him; saying, he recollected to have seen him, when a very young man, sitting by the side of general Wayne.

Some of the Indians, then at the Prophet's town, appeared to be alarmed at the arrival of the interpreter, and professed themselves dissatisfied with the conduct of their leaders. Tecumseh told him, that in making his promised visit to the governor, he should bring with him about thirty of his principal warriors; and as the young men were fond of attending on such occasions, the whole number might probably be one hundred. The Prophet added, that the governor might expect to see a still larger number than that named by his brother.

Upon the return of the interpreter to Vincennes, the governor, not wishing to be burthened with so large a body of Indians, despatched a messenger to Tecumseh, requesting that he would bring with him but a few of his followers. This request, however, was wholly disregarded; and on the 12th of August, the chief, attended by four hundred warriors, fully armed with tomahawks and war-clubs, descended the Wabash to Vincennes, for the purpose of holding the proposed conference. From a family letter written by captain Floyd, then commanding at fort Knox, three miles above Vincennes, under date of 14th of August, 1810, the following extract is made, referring to this visit of the chieftain and his war-like retinue.

"Nothing new has transpired since my last letter to you, except that the Shawanoe Indians have come; they passed this garrison, which is three miles above Vincennes, on Sunday last, in eighty canoes; they were all painted in the most terrific manner: they were stopped at the garrison by me, for a short time: I examined their canoes and found them well prepared for war, in case of an attack. They were headed by the brother of the Prophet, (Tecumseh) who, perhaps, is one of the finest looking men I ever saw—about six feet high, straight, with large, fine features, and altogether a daring, bold looking fellow. The governor's council with them will commence to-morrow morning. He has directed me to attend."

Governor Harrison had made arrangements for holding the council on the portico of his own house, which had been fitted up with seats for the occasion. Here, on the morning of the fifteenth, he awaited the arrival of the chief, being attended by the judges of the Supreme Court, some officers of the army, a sergeant and twelve men, from fort Knox, and a large number of citizens. At the appointed hour Tecumseh, supported by forty of his principal warriors, made his appearance, the remainder of his followers being encamped in the village and its environs. When the chief had approached within thirty or forty yards of the house, he suddenly stopped, as if awaiting some advances from the governor. An interpreter was sent requesting him and his followers to take seats on the portico. To this Tecumseh objected—he did not think the place a suitable one for holding the conference, but preferred that it should take place in a grove of trees,—to which he pointed,—standing a short distance from the house. The governor said he had no objection to the grove, except that there were no seats in it for their accommodation. Tecumseh replied, that constituted no ob-

jection to the grove, the earth being the most suitable
place for the Indians, who loved to repose upon the bo-
som of their mother. The governor yielded the point,
and the benches and chairs having been removed to
the spot, the conference was begun, the Indians being
seated on the grass.

Tecumseh opened the meeting by stating, at length,
his objections to the treaty of fort Wayne, made by governor Harrison in the previous year; and in the course
of his speech, boldly avowed the principle of his party
to be, that of resistance to every cession of land, unless
made by all the tribes, who, he contended, formed but
one nation. He admitted that he had threatened to
kill the chiefs who signed the treaty of fort Wayne;
and that it was his fixed determination not to permit
the *village* chiefs, in future, to manage their affairs, but
to place the power with which *they* had been hereto-
fore invested, in the hands of the war chiefs. The
Americans, he said, had driven the Indians from the
sea coast, and would soon push them into the lakes;
and, while he disclaimed all intention of making war
upon the United States, he declared it to be his unal-
terable resolution to take a stand, and resolutely oppose
the further intrusion of the whites upon the Indian
lands. He concluded, by making a brief but impassioned recital of the various wrongs and aggressions
inflicted by the white men upon the Indians, from the
commencement of the Revolutionary war down to the
period of that council; all of which was calculated to
arouse and inflame the minds of such of his followers
as were present.

The governor rose in reply, and in examining the
right of Tecumseh and his party to make objections to
the treaty of fort Wayne, took occasion to say, that the
Indians were not one nation, having a common property in the lands. The Miamis, he contended, were
the real owners of the tract on the Wabash, ceded by
the late treaty, and the Shawanoes had no right to interfere in the case; that upon the arrival of the whites
on this continent, they had found the Miamis in possession of this land, the Shawanoes being then residents
of Georgia, from which they had been driven by the

Creeks, and that it was ridiculous to assert that the red
men constituted but one nation; for, if such had been
the intention of the Great Spirit, he would not have
put different tongues in their heads, but have taught
them all to speak the same language.

The governor having taken his seat, the interpreter commenced explaining the speech to Tecumseh,
who, after listening to a portion of it, sprung to his
feet and began to speak with great vehemence of
manner.

The governor was surprised at his violent gestures,
but as he did not understand him, thought he was making some explanation, and suffered his attention to be
drawn towards Winnemac, a friendly Indian lying on
the grass before him, who was renewing the priming
of his pistol, which he had kept concealed from the
other Indians, but in full view of the governor. His
attention, however, was again directed towards Tecumseh, by hearing general Gibson, who was intimately acquainted with the Shawanoe language, say to lieutenant Jennings, "those fellows intend mischief; you
had better bring up the guard."   At that moment, the
followers of Tecumseh seized their tomahawks and
war clubs, and sprung upon their feet, their eyes turned
upon the governor.   As soon as he could disengage
himself from the armed chair in which he sat, he rose,
drew a small sword which he had by his side, and
stood on the defensive.   Captain G. R. Floyd, of the army, who stood near him, drew a dirk, and the chief Winnemac cocked his pistol.   The citizens present, were
more numerous than the Indians, but were unarmed;
some of them procured clubs and brick-bats, and also
stood on the defensive.   The Rev. Mr. Winans, of the
Methodist church, ran to the governor's house, got a
gun, and posted himself at the door to defend the family.   During this singular scene, no one spoke, until the
guard came running up, and appearing to be in the act
of firing, the governor ordered them not to do so.   He
then demanded of the interpreter, an explanation of
what had happened, who replied that Tecumseh had
interrupted him, declaring that all the governor had

said was *false;* and that he and the **Seventeen Fires** had cheated and imposed on the Indians.*

The governor then told Tecumseh that he was a bad man, and that he would hold no further communication with him; that as he had come to Vincennes under the protection of a council-fire, he might return in safety, but that he must immediately leave the village. Here the council terminated. During the night, two companies of militia were brought in from the country, and that belonging to the town was also embodied. Next morning Tecumseh requested the governor to afford him an opportunity of explaining his conduct on the previous day—declaring, that he did not intend to attack the governor, and that he had acted under the advice of some of the white people. The governor consented to another interview, it being understood that each party should have the same armed force as on the previous day. On this occasion, the deportment of Tecumseh was respectful and dignified. He again denied having had any intention to make an attack upon the governor, and declared that he had been stimulated to the course he had taken, by two white men, who assured him that one half of the citizens were opposed to the governor, and willing to restore the land in question; that the governor would soon be put out of office, and a good man sent to fill his place, who would give up the land to the Indians. When asked by the governor whether he intended to resist the survey of these lands, Tecumseh replied that he and his followers were resolutely determined to insist upon the old boundary. When he had taken his seat, chiefs from the Wyandots, Kickapoos, Potawatamies, Ottawas, and Winnebagoes, spoke in succession, and distinctly avowed that they had entered into the Shawanoe confederacy, and were determined to support the principles laid down by their leader. The governor, in conclusion, stated that he would make known to the President, the claims of Tecumseh and his party, to the land in question; but that he was satisfied the government

---

* Dawson's Historical Narrative.

would never admit that the lands on the Wabash were the property of any other tribes than those who occupied them, when the white people first arrived in America; and, as the title to these lands had been derived by purchase from those tribes, he might rest assured that the right of the United States would be sustained by the sword. Here the council adjourned.

On the following day, governor Harrison visited Tecumseh in his camp, attended only by the interpreter, and was very politely received. A long conversation ensued, in which Tecumseh again declared that his intentions were really such as he had avowed them to be in the council; that the policy which the United States pursued, of purchasing lands from the Indians, he viewed as a mighty water, ready to overflow his people; and that the confederacy which he was forming among the tribes to prevent any individual tribe from selling without the consent of the others, was the dam he was erecting to resist this mighty water. He stated further, that he should be reluctantly drawn into a war with the United States; and that if he, the governor, would induce the President to give up the lands lately purchased, and agree never to make another treaty without the consent of all the tribes, he would be their faithful ally and assist them in the war, which he knew was about to take place with England; that he preferred being the ally of the Seventeen Fires, but if they did not comply with his request, he would be compelled to unite with the British. The governor replied, that he would make known his views to the President, but that there was no probability of their being agreed to. "Well," said Tecumseh, "as the great chief is to determine the matter, I hope the Great Spirit will put sense enough into his head to induce him to give up this land: it is true, he is so far off he will not be injured by the war; he may sit still in his town and drink his wine, whilst you and I will have to fight it out." This prophecy, it will be seen, was literally fulfilled; and the great chieftain who uttered it, attested that fulfilment with his blood. The governor, in conclusion, proposed to Tecumseh, that in the event of hostilities between the Indians and the United

States, he should use his influence to put an end to the cruel mode of warfare which the Indians were accustomed to wage upon women and children, or upon prisoners. To this he cheerfully assented; and, it is due to the memory of Tecumseh to add, that he faithfully kept his promise down to the period of his death.*

Whether in this council Tecumseh really meditated treachery or only intended to intimidate the governor, must remain a matter of conjecture. If the former, his force of four hundred well armed warriors was sufficient to have murdered the inhabitants and sacked the town, which at that time did not contain more than one thousand persons, including women and children.

When in the progress of the conference, he and his forty followers sprung to their arms, there would have been, in all probability, a corresponding movement with the remainder of his warriors encamped in and around the village, had he seriously contemplated an attack upon the governor and the inhabitants. But this does not appear to have been the case. It is probable, therefore, that Tecumseh, in visiting Vincennes with so large a body of followers, expected to make a strong impression upon the whites as to the extent of his influence among the Indians, and the strength of his party. His movement in the council may have been concerted for the purpose of intimidating the governor; but the more probable supposition is, that in the excitement of the moment, produced by the speech of the governor, he lost his self-possession, and involuntarily placed his hand upon his war-club, in which movement he was followed by the warriors around him, without any previous intention of proceeding to extremities. Whatever may have been the fact, the bold chieftain found in governor Harrison a firmness of purpose and an intrepidity of manner which must have convinced him that nothing was to be gained by an effort at intimidation, however daring.

Soon after the close of this memorable council, go-

* In Marshall's History of Kentucky, vol. 2. p. 482, there is a speech quoted as having been delivered by Tecumseh at this council. We are authorised, on the best authority, to say that it is a sheer fabrication. No such speech was delivered by him at the council.

vernor Harrison made arrangements for the survey of the land purchased at the treaty of fort Wayne, under the protection of a detachment of soldiers. About the same time, "a young Iowa chief, whom the governor had employed to go to the Prophet's town to gain information, reported, on his return, that he had been told by an old Winnebago chief, who was his relation, that the great Belt which had been sent round to all the tribes, for the purpose of uniting them, was returned; and he mentioned a considerable number who had acceded to the confederacy, the object of which was "to confine the great water and prevent it from overflowing them." That the belt since its return had been sent to the British agent, who danced for joy at seeing so many tribes had joined against the United States. That the Prophet had sent a speech to his confedrates not to be discouraged at the apparent defection of some of the tribes near him; for that it was all a sham, intended to deceive the white people; that these tribes hated the Seventeen Fires; and that though they gave them sweet words, they were like grass plucked up by the roots, they would soon wither and come to nothing. The old Winnebago chief told him with tears in his eyes, that he himself and all the village chiefs, had been divested of their power, and that everything was managed by the warriors, who breathed nothing but war against the United States.*"

Governor Harrison, in his address to the legislature of Indiana, in the month of November of this year, refers to the difficulties with the Indians at Tippecanoe; and bears testimony to the fact, that the Prophet and Tecumseh were instigated to assume a hostile attitude towards the United States, by British influence. He says,

"It is with regret that I have to inform you that the harmony and good understanding which it is so much our interest to cultivate with our neighbors, the aborigines, have for some time past experienced considerable interruption, and that we have indeed been threatened with hostilities, by a combination formed under

---

* Dawson's Historical Narrative.

the auspices of a bold adventurer, who pretends to act under the immediate inspiration of the Deity. His character as a Prophet would not, however, have given him any very dangerous influence, if he had not been assisted by the intrigues and advice of foreign agents, and other disaffected persons, who have for many years omitted no opportunity of counteracting the measures of the government with regard to the Indians, and filling their naturally jealous minds with suspicions of the justice and integrity of our views towards them."

That our government was sincerely desirous of preserving peace with these disaffected Indians, appears from the following extract of a letter from the Secretary of War, to governor Harrison, written in the autumn of this year. "It has occurred to me," said the Secretary, "that the surest means of securing good behavior from this conspicuous personage and his brother, [the Prophet and Tecumseh] would be to make them prisoners; but at this time, more particularly, it is desirable that peace with all the Indian tribes should be preserved; and I am instructed by the President to express to your excellency his expectations and confidence, that in all your arrangements, this may be considered, (as I am confident it ever has been) a primary object with you."

During the autumn, a Kickapoo chief visited Vincennes, and informed the governor that the pacific professions of the Prophet and Tecumseh were not to be relied on,—that their ultimate designs were hostile to the United States. At the same time governor Clark, of Missouri, forwarded to the governor of Indiana information that the Prophet had sent belts to the tribes west of the Mississippi, inviting them to join in a war against the United States; and, stating that he would commence the contest by an attack on Vincennes Governor Clark further said, that the Sacs had at length joined the Tippecanoe confederacy, and that a party of them had gone to Malden for arms and ammunition. The Indian interpreter, at Chicago, also stated to governor Harrison, that the tribes in that quarter were disaffected towards the United States, and seemed de-

termined upon war.   One of the surveyors, engaged
to run the lines of the new purchase, was driven off the
lands by a party of the Wea tribe, who took two of his
men prisoners: thus closed the year 1810.

CHAPTER VIII.

Alarm on the frontier continues—a Muskoe Indian killed at Vincennes—
governor Harrison sends a pacific speech to Tecumseh and the Prophet
—the former replies to it—in July Tecumseh visits governor Harrison at
Vincennes—disavows any intention of making war upon the whites—
explains his object in forming a union among the tribes—governor Harrison's opinion of Tecumseh and the Prophet—murder of the Deaf Chief
—Tecumseh visits the southern Indians.

THE spring of 1811 brought with it no abatement of
these border difficulties.   Early in the season, governor
Harrison sent a boat up the Wabash, loaded with salt
for the Indians,—that article constituting a part of their
annuity.   Five barrels were to be left with the Prophet, for the Kickapoos and Shawanoes.   Upon the
arrival of the boat at Tippecanoe, the Prophet called a
council, by which it was decided to seize the whole of
the salt, which was promptly done—word being sent
back to the governor, not to be angry at this measure,
as the Prophet had two thousand men to feed; and,
had not received any salt for two years past.   There
were at this time about six hundred men at Tippecanoe; and, Tecumseh, who had been absent for some
time, on a visit to the lakes, was expected daily, with
large reinforcements.   From appearances, it seemed probable that an attack was meditated on Vincennes by
these brothers, with a force of eight hundred or one
thousand warriors; a number far greater than the governor could collect, even if he embodied all the militia
for some miles around that place.   He accordingly
wrote to the Secretary of War, recommending that the
4th regiment of U. S. troops, then at Pittsburg, under
the command of colonel Boyd, should be ordered to
Vincennes; at the same time asking for authority to

M

act offensively against the Indians, so soon as it was found that the intentions of their leaders were decidedly hostile towards the United States.

Under date of June 6th, governor Harrison, in a letter to the war department, expresses the opinion that the disposition of the Indians is far from being pacific. Wells, the agent at fort Wayne, had visited the Prophet's town, relative to some stolen horses, and certain Potawatamies who had committed the murders on the Mississippi. Four of the horses were recovered, but Tecumseh disclaimed all agency in taking them, although he acknowledged that it was done by some of his party. Tecumseh openly avowed to the agent his resolute determination to resist the further encroachments of the white people. In this letter the governor remarks, " I wish I could say the Indians were treated with justice and propriety on all occasions by our citizens; but it is far otherwise. They are often abused and maltreated; and it is very rare that they obtain any satisfaction for the most unprovoked wrongs." He proceeds to relate the circumstance of a Muskoe Indian having been killed by an Italian innkeeper, in Vincennes, without any just cause. The murderer, under the orders of the governor, was apprehended, tried, but acquitted by the jury almost without deliberation. About the same time, within twenty miles of Vincennes, two Weas were badly wounded by a white man without the smallest provocation. Such aggressions tended greatly to exasperate the Indians, and to prevent them from delivering up such of their people as committed offences against the citizens of the United States. Such was the fact with the Delawares, upon a demand from the governor for White Turkey, who had robbed the house of a Mr. Vawter. The chiefs refused to surrender him, declaring that they would never deliver up another man until some of the whites were punished, who had murdered their people. They, however, punished White Turkey themselves, by putting him to death.

On the 24th of June, soon after the return of Tecumseh from his visit to the Iroquois and Wyandots, for the purpose of increasing his confederacy, governor

Harrison transmitted to him and the Prophet, together with the other chiefs at Tippecanoe, the following speech:

"Brothers,—Listen to me. I speak to you about matters of importance, both to the white people and yourselves; open your ears, therefore, and attend to what I shall say.

"Brothers, this is the third year that all the white people in this country have been alarmed at your proceedings; you threaten us with war, you invite all the tribes to the north and west of you to join against us.

"Brothers, your warriors who have lately been here, deny this; but I have received the information from every direction; the tribes on the Mississippi have sent me word that you intended to murder me, and then to commence a war upon our people. I have also received the speech you sent to the Potawatamies and others, to join you for that purpose; but if I had no other evidence of your hostility to us, your seizing the salt I lately sent up the Wabash, is sufficient.

"Brothers, our citizens are alarmed, and my warriors are preparing themselves; not to strike you, but to defend themselves and their women and children. You shall not surprise us as you expect to do; you are about to undertake a very rash act; as a friend, I advise you to consider well of it; a little reflection may save us a great deal of trouble and prevent much mischief; it is not yet too late.

"Brothers, what can be the inducement for you to undertake an enterprise when there is so little probability of success; do you really think that the handful of men that you have about you, are able to contend with the Seventeen Fires, or even that the whole of the tribes united, could contend against the Kentucky Fire alone?

"Brothers, I am myself of the long knife fire; as soon as they hear my voice, you will see them pouring forth their swarms of hunting shirt men, as numerous as the musquetoes on the shores of the Wabash; brothers, take care of their stings.

"Brothers, it is not our wish to hurt you: if we did, we certainly have power to do it; look at the number of our warriors to the east of you, above and below the Great Miami,—to the south, on both sides of the Ohio, and below you also. You are brave men; but what could you do against such a multitude?—but we wish you to live in peace and happiness.

"Brothers, the citizens of this country are alarmed; they must be satisfied that you have no design to do them mischief, or they will not lay aside their arms. You have also insulted the government of the United States by seizing the salt that was intended for other tribes; satisfaction must be given for that also.

"Brothers, you talk of coming to see me, attended by all your young men; this, however, must not be so; if your intentions are good, you have no need to bring but a few of your young men with you. I must be plain with you; I will not suffer you to come into our settlements with such a force.

"Brothers, if you wish to satisfy us that your intentions are good, follow the advice that I have given you before; that is, that one or both of you should visit the President of the United States, and lay your grievances before him. He will treat you well, will listen to what you say, and if you can show him that you have been injured, you will receive justice. If you will follow my advice in this respect, it will convince the citizens of this country and myself that you have no design to attack them.

"Brothers, with respect to the lands that were purchased last fall, I can enter into no negociations with you on that subject; the affair is in the hands of the President, if you wish to go and see him, I will supply you with the means.

"Brothers, the person who delivers this, is one of my war officers; he is a man in whom I have entire confidence: whatever he says to you, although it may not be contained in this paper, you may believe comes from me.

"My friend Tecumseh! the bearer is a good man and a brave warrior; I hope you will treat him well; you are yourself a warrior, and all such should have esteem for each other."

Tecumseh to the governor of Indiana, in reply:

"Brother; I give you a few words until I will be with you myself.

"Brother, at Vincennes, I wish you to listen to me whilst I send you a few words, and I hope they will ease your heart; I know you look on your young men and young women and children with pity, to see them so much alarmed.

"Brother, I wish you now to examine what you have from me; I hope that it will be a satisfaction to you, if your intentions are like mine, to wash away all these bad stories that have been circulated. I will be with you myself in eighteen days from this day.

"Brother, we cannot say what will become of us, as the Great Spirit has the management of us all at his will. I may be there before the time, and may not be there until the day. I hope that when we come together, all these bad tales will be settled; by this I hope your young men, women and children, will be easy. I wish you, brother, to let them know when I come to Vincennes and see you, all will be settled in peace and happiness.

"Brother, these are only a few words to let you know that I will be with you myself, and when I am with you I can inform you better.

"Brother, if I find that I can be with you in less time than eighteen days, I will send one of my young men before me, to let you know what time I will be with you."

On the second of July, governor Harrison received information from the executive of Illinois, that several murders had been committed in that territory; and that there were good grounds for believing these crimes had been perpetrated by a party of Shawanoes. The governor had been previously informed that it was the design of the Prophet to commence hostilities in Illinois, in order to cover his main object—the attack on Vincennes. Both territories were in a state of great alarm; and the Secretary of War was officially notified, that if the general government did not take measures to protect the inhabitants, they were determined to protect themselves.

In a letter under date of Vincennes, 10th July, 1811,

governor Harrison writes as follows to the Secretary of War.

"Captain Wilson, the officer whom I sent to the Prophet's town, returned on Sunday last. He was well received, and treated with particular friendship by Tecumseh. He obtained, however, no satisfaction. The only answer given was, that in eighteen days Tecumseh would pay me a visit for the purpose of explaining his conduct. Upon being told that I would not suffer him to come with so large a force, he promised to bring with him a few men only. I shall not, however, depend upon this promise, but shall have the river well watched by a party of scouts after the descent of the chief, lest he should be followed by his warriors. I do not think that this will be the case. The detection of the hostile designs of an Indian, is generally (for that time) to defeat them. The hopes of an expedition, conducted through many hundred miles of toil and difficulty, are abandoned frequently, upon the slightest suspicion; their painful steps retraced, and a more favorable moment expected. With them the surprise of an enemy bestows more eclat upon a warrior than the most brilliant success obtained by other means. Tecumseh has taken for his model the celebrated Pontiac, and I am persuaded he will bear a favorable comparison, in every respect, with that far famed warrior. If it is his object to begin with the surprise of this place, it is impossible that a more favorable situation could have been chosen, than the one he occupies: it is just so far off as to be removed from immediate observation, and yet so near as to enable him to strike us, when the water is high, in twenty-four hours, and even when it is low, their light canoes will come fully as fast as the journey could be performed on horseback. The situation is in other respects admirable for the purposes for which he has chosen it. It is nearly central with regard to the tribes which he wishes to unite. The water communication with lake Erie, by means of the Wabash and Miami—with lake Michigan and the Illinois, by the Tippecanoe, is a great convenience. It is immediately in the centre of the back line of that fine country which he wishes to prevent us from settling—and above all, he has immediately in his rear a country that has been but little explored, consisting principally of barren thickets, interspersed with swamps and lakes, into which our cavalry could not penetrate, and our infantry, only by slow, laborious efforts."

The promised visit of Tecumseh took place in the latter part of July. He reached Vincennes on the 27th, attended by about three hundred of his party, of whom thirty were women and children. The council was opened on the 30th, in an arbor erected for the purpose, and at the appointed time the chief made his appearance, attended by about one hundred and seventy warriors, without guns, but all of them having knives and tomahawks, or war clubs, and some armed with bows and arrows. The governor, in opening the council, made reference to the late murders in Illinois, and the alarm which the appearance of Tecumseh, with so large an armed force, had created among the people on the Wabash. He further informed Tecumseh that, whilst he listened to whatever himself or any of the chiefs had to say in regard to the late purchase of land, he would enter into no negociation on that subject, as it was now in the hands of the President. The governor, after telling Tecumseh that he was at liberty to visit the President, and hear his decision from his own mouth, adverted to the late seizure of the salt, and demanded an explanation of it. In reply, the chief admitted the seizure, but said he was not at home, either this spring or the year before, when the salt boats arrived; that it seemed impossible to please the governor: last year he was angry, because the salt was refused, and this year equally so, because it was taken. The council was then adjourned until the following day. When it was again opened, a Wea chief made a long speech, giving the history of all the treaties which had been made by the governor and the Indian tribes; and concluded with the remark, that he had been told that the Miami chiefs had been forced by the Potawatamies to accede to the treaty of fort Wayne; and that it would be proper to institute enquiries to find out the person who had held the tomahawk over their heads, and punish him. This statement was immediately contradicted by the governor, and also by the Miami chiefs who were present. Anxious to bring the conference to a close, the governor then told Tecumseh that by delivering up the two Potawatamies who had murdered the four white men on the Missouri, last fall, he would at once attest the sincerity of his professions of friendship to the United States, and his desire to preserve peace. His reply was evasive, but developed very clearly his designs. After much trouble and difficulty he had induced, he said, all the northern tribes to unite, and place themselves under his direction; that the white people were unnecessarily alarmed at his measures, which really meant nothing but peace; that the United States had set him the example of forming a strict union amongst all the Fires that compose their confederacy; that the Indians did not complain of it, nor should his white brothers complain of him for doing the same thing in regard to the Indian tribes; that so soon as the council was over, he was to set out on a visit to the southern tribes, to prevail upon them to unite with those of the north. As to the murderers, they were not at his town, and if they were, he could not deliver them up; that they ought to be forgiven, as well as those who had committed some murders in Illinois; that he had set the whites an example of the forgiveness of injuries which they ought to follow. In reply to an enquiry on the subject, he said he hoped no attempt would be made to settle the new purchase, before his return next spring; that a great number of Indians were coming to settle at Tippecanoe in the autumn, and they would need that tract as a hunting ground, and if they did no further injury, they might kill the cattle and hogs of the white people, which would create disturbances; that he wished every thing to remain in its present situation until his return, when he would visit the President, and settle all difficulties with him. The governor made a brief reply, saying, that the moon which they beheld (it was then night) would sooner fall to the earth, than the President would suffer his people to be murdered with impunity; and that he would put his warriors in petticoats, sooner than he would give up a country which he had fairly acquired from the rightful owners. Here the council terminated. In a day or two afterwards, attended by twenty warriors, Tecumseh set off for the south, on a visit to the Creeks and Choctaws. The governor was at a loss to determine the object of Tecumseh, in taking with him to Vincennes, so large a body of his followers. The spies said that he intended to demand a retrocession of the late purchase, and if it was not obtained, to seize some of the chiefs who were active in making the treaty, in presence of the governor, and put them to death; and in case of his interference, to have subjected him to the same fate. Many of the neutral Indians entertained the opinion that he meditated an attack upon Vincennes. If such was the case, his plan was probably changed by observing the vigilance of governor Harrison and the display of seven or eight hundred men under arms. It is questionable, however, we think, whether Tecumseh really meditated violence at this time. He probably wished to impress the whites with an idea of his strength, and at the same time gratify his ambition of moving, as a great chieftain, at the head of a numerous retinue of warriors.

The day after the close of this council, the governor wrote to the War Department. The following is a part of his communication.

" My letter of yesterday will inform you of the arrival and departure of Tecumseh from this place, and of the route which he has taken. There can be no doubt his object is to excite the southern Indians to war against us. His mother was of the Creek nation, and he builds much upon that circumstance towards forwarding his views. I do not think there is any danger of further hostility until he returns: and his absence affords a most favorable opportunity for breaking up his confederacy, and I have some expectations of being able to accomplish it without a recourse to actual hostility. Tecumseh assigned the next spring as the period of his return. I am informed, however, that he will be back in three months. There is a Potawatamie chief here, who says he was present when the message from the British agent was delivered to the

Prophet, telling him that the time had arrived for taking up arms, and inviting him to send a party to Malden, to receive the necessary supplies. This man is one of the few who preserve their independence.

"The implicit obedience and respect which the followers of Tecumseh pay to him, is really astonishing, and more than any other circumstance bespeaks him one of those uncommon geniuses which spring up occasionally to produce revolutions, and overturn the established order of things. If it were not for the vicinity of the United States, he would, perhaps, be the founder of an empire that would rival in glory Mexico or Peru. No difficulties deter him. For four years he has been in constant motion. You see him to-day on the Wabash, and in a short time hear of him on the shores of lake Erie or Michigan, or on the banks of the Mississippi; and wherever he goes he makes an impression favorable to his purposes. He is now upon the last round to put a finishing stroke to his work. I hope, however, before his return that that part of the fabric which he considered complete, will be demolished, and even its foundations rooted up. Although the greater part of his followers are attached to him from principle and affection, there are many others who follow him through fear; and he was scarcely a mile from town, before they indulged in the most virulent invectives against him. The Prophet is impudent and audacious, but is deficient in judgment, talents and firmness."

The following anecdote illustrates the coolness and self-possession of Tecumseh, not less than the implicit obedience that was paid to his commands by his followers.

A Potawatamie, called the Deaf Chief, was present at the late council. After it was closed, he stated to the governor, that had he been called upon during the conference he would have confronted Tecumseh, when he denied that his intentions towards the United States were hostile. This declaration having been repeated to Tecumseh, he calmly intimated to the Prophet, that upon their return to Tippecanoe, the Deaf Chief must be disposed of. A friend of the latter informed him of

his danger, but the chief, not at all intimidated, returned to his camp, put on his war-dress, and equipping
himself with his rifle, tomahawk and scalping knife,
returned and presented himself before Tecumseh, who
was then in company with Mr. Baron, the governor's
interpreter.   The Deaf Chief there reproached Tecumseh for having ordered him to be killed, declaring that
it was an act unworthy of a warrior.   "But here I am
now," said he, "come and kill me."   Tecumseh making no answer, the Potawatamie heaped upon him
every term of abuse and contumely, and finally charged him with being the slave of the red-coats, (the British.)   Tecumseh, perfectly unmoved, made no reply,
but continued his conversation with Mr. Baron, until
the Deaf Chief, wearied with the effort to provoke his
antagonist to action, returned to his camp.   There is
some reason for believing that the Prophet did not disobey his orders: the Deaf Chief was never seen again
at Vincennes.

Of the result of the mission of Tecumseh to the
southern tribes, we have no detailed information.
Hodgson, who subsequently travelled through this
country, in his "Letters from North America," says:

"Our host told me that he was living with his Indian wife among the Creeks, when the celebrated Indian warrior Tecumseh, came more than one thousand
miles, from the borders of Canada, to induce the lower
Creeks, to promise to take up the hatchet in behalf of
the British, against the Americans, and the upper
Creeks whenever he should require it: that he was
present at the midnight convocation of the chiefs,
which was held on that occasion, and which terminated after a most impressive speech from Tecumseh
with a unanimous determination to take up the hatchet
whenever he should call upon them.   This was at least
a year before the declaration of the last war."

In the "History of the Tribes of North America,"
there is an interesting notice of this visit of Tecumseh.

"The following remarkable circumstance may serve
to illustrate the penetration, decision and boldness of
this warrior chief.   He had been south, to Florida, and

succeeded in instigating the Seminoles in particular, and portions of other tribes, to unite in the war on the side of the British. He gave out that a vessel, on a certain day, commanded by red-coats, would be off Florida, filled with guns and ammunition, and supplies for the use of the Indians. That no mistake might happen in regard to the day on which the Indians were to strike, he prepared bundles of sticks, each bundle containing the number of sticks corresponding to the number of days that were to intervene between the day on which they were received, and the day of the general onset. The Indian practice is to throw away a stick every morning; they make, therefore, no mistake in the time. These sticks Tecumseh caused to be painted red. It was from this circumstance that in the former Seminole war, these Indians were called " Red Sticks." In all this business of mustering the tribes, he used great caution; he supposed enquiry would be made as to the object of his visit; that his plans might not be suspected, he directed the Indians to reply to any questions that might be asked about him, by saying, that he had counselled them to cultivate the ground, abstain from ardent spirits, and live in peace with the white people. On his return from Florida, he went among the Creeks in Alabama, urging them to unite with the Seminoles. Arriving at Tuckhabatchee, a Creek town on the Tallapoosa river, he made his way to the lodge of the chief called the Big Warrior. He explained his object, delivered his war-talk, presented a bundle of sticks, gave a piece of wampum and a hatchet; all which the Big Warrior took. When Tecumseh, reading the intentions and spirit of the Big Warrior, looked him in the eye, and pointing his finger towards his face, said : " Your blood is white : you have taken my talk, and the sticks, and the wampum, and the hatchet, but you do not mean to fight : I know the reason : you do not believe the Great Spirit has sent me : you shall know : I leave Tuckhabatchee directly, and shall go straight to Detroit : when I arrive there, I will stamp on the ground with my foot, and shake down every house in Tuckhabatchee." So saying, he turned and left the Big Warrior in utter amazement, at both his manner and his threat, and pursued his journey. The Indians were struck no less with his conduct than was the Big Warrior, and began to dread the arrival of the day when the threatened calamity would befal them. They met often and talked over this matter, and counted the days carefully, to know the time when Tecumseh would reach Detroit. The morning they had fixed upon, as the period of his arrival, at last came. A mighty rumbling was heard—the Indians all ran out of their houses—the earth began to shake; when at last, sure enough, every house in Tuckhabatchee was shaken down! The exclamation was in every mouth, "Tecumseh has got to Detroit!" The effect was electrical. The message he had delivered to the Big Warrior was believed, and many of the Indians took their rifles and prepared for the war.

"The reader will not be surprised to learn, that an earthquake had produced all this; but he will be, doubtless, that it should happen on the very day on which Tecumseh arrived at Detroit; and, in exact fulfilment of his threat. It was the famous earthquake of New Madrid, on the Mississippi. We received the foregoing from the lips of the Indians, when we were at Tuckhabatchee, in 1827, and near the residence of the Big Warrior. The anecdote may therefore be relied on. Tecumseh's object, doubtless, was, on seeing that he had failed, by the usual appeal to the passions, and hopes, and war spirit of the Indians, to alarm their fears, little dreaming, himself, that on the day named, his threat would be executed with such punctuality and terrible fidelity."

CHAPTER IX.

Governor Harrison applies to the War Department for troops to maintain peace on the frontiers—battle of Tippecanoe on the 7th of November—its influence on the Prophet and his followers.

THE late council at Vincennes having failed in producing any satisfactory results, and Tecumseh having gone to the south for the avowed purpose of extending his confederacy, the alarm among the inhabitants of Indiana continued to increase. Public meetings were held, and memorials forwarded to the President, invoking protection, and requesting the removal of the Indians from the Prophet's town; the memorialists being "fully convinced that the formation of this combination, headed by the Shawanoe Prophet, was a British scheme, and that the agents of that power were constantly exciting the Indians to hostility against the United States." The President accordingly placed the 4th regiment U. S. infantry, commanded by colonel Boyd, and a company of riflemen, at the disposal of governor Harrison. The Secretary of War, under date of 20th October, 1811, in a letter to him, says: "I have been particularly instructed by the President to communicate to your excellency, his earnest desire that peace may, if possible, be preserved with the Indians; and that to this end, every proper means may be adopted. By this, it is not intended that murder or robberies committed by them, should not meet with the punishment due to those crimes; that the settlements should be unprotected, or that any hostile combination should avail itself of success, in consequence of a neglect to provide the means of resisting and defeating it; or that the banditti under the Prophet should not be attacked and vanquished, provided such a measure should be rendered absolutely necessary. Circumstances conspire, at this particular juncture, to render it peculiarly desirable that hostilities of any kind, or to any degree, not indispensably required, should be avoided."

On the seventh of August the governor informed the secretary that he should call, in a peremptory manner, on all the tribes, to deliver up such of their people as had been concerned in the murder of our citizens; that from the Miamis he should require an absolute disavowal of all connection with the Prophet; and that to all the tribes he would repeat the declaration, that the United States have manifested through a series of years, the utmost justice and generosity towards their Indian neighbors; and have not only fulfilled all the engagements which they entered into with them, but have spent considerable sums to civilize them and promote their happiness; but if, under those circumstances, any tribe should dare to take up the tomahawk against their fathers, they must not expect the same lenity that had been shown them at the close of the former war, but that they would either be exterminated or driven beyond the Mississippi.

In furtherance of this plan, the governor forwarded speeches to the different tribes, and instructed the Indian agents to use all possible means to recall them to a sense of duty. He also wrote to the governors of Illinois and Missouri, on the subject of the border difficulties, in the hope that a general and simultaneous effort might avert an appeal to arms.

In the month of September, the Prophet sent assurances to governor Harrison of his pacific intentions, and that his demands should be complied with; but about the same time some horses were stolen in the neighborhood of his town, and the whites who went in pursuit of them were fired upon by the Indians. Early in October the governor moved, with a considerable body of troops, towards the Prophet's town, with the expectation that a show of hostile measures would bring about an accommodation with the Indians of that place. On the 10th of October, one of the sentinels around his camp was fired on by the Indians, and severely wounded. About the same time the Prophet sent a messenger to the chiefs of the Delaware tribe, who were friendly to the United States, requiring them to say whether they would or would not join him in the war against them; that he had taken up the tomahawk and would not lay it down but with his life, unless their wrongs were redressed. The Delaware chiefs immediately visited the Prophet, for the purpose of dissuading him from commencing hostilities. Under these circumstances there seemed to be no alternative for governor Harrison, but to break up the Prophet's establishment. On the 27th, the Delaware chiefs returned to the camp of the governor, and reported that the Prophet would not listen to their council, and had grossly insulted them. While at the Prophet's town, the Indians who had wounded the sentinel, returned. They were Shawanoes and near friends of the Prophet, who was daily practising certain pretended rites, by means of which he played upon the superstitious feelings of his followers, and kept them in a state of feverish excitement. On the 29th, a body of twenty-four Miami chiefs were sent by governor Harrison, to make another effort with the Prophet. They were instructed to require that the Winnebagoes, Potawatamies and Kickapoos, should leave him and return to their respective tribes; that all the stolen horses in their possession should be delivered up; that the murderers of the whites should either be surrendered or satisfactory proof offered that they were not under his control. These chiefs, however, did not return, and there is reason to believe that they were induced to join the confederacy at Tippecanoe.

On the 5th of November, 1811, governor Harrison, with about nine hundred effective troops, composed of two hundred and fifty of the 4th regiment U. S. infantry, one hundred and thirty volunteers, and a body of militia, encamped within ten miles of the Prophet's town. On the next day, when the army was within five miles of the village, reconnoitering parties of the Indians were seen, but they refused to hold any conversation with the interpreters sent forward by the governor to open a communication with them. When within a mile and a half of the town a halt was made, for the purpose of encamping for the night. Several of the field officers urged the governor to make an immediate assault on the village; but this he declined, as his instructions from the President were positive, not to attack the Indians, as long as there was a probability of their complying with the demands of government. Upon ascertaining however, that the ground continued favorable for the disposition of his troops, quite up to the town, he determined to approach still nearer to it.   In the mean time, captain Dubois, with an interpreter, was sent forward to ascertain whether the Prophet would comply with the terms proposed by the governor.   The Indians, however, would make no reply to these enquiries, but endeavored to cut off the messengers from the army.   When this fact was reported to the governor, he determined to consider the Indians as enemies, and at once march upon their town.   He had proceeded but a short distance, however, before he was met by three Indians, one of them a principal counsellor to the Prophet, who stated that they were sent to know why the army was marching upon their town—that the Prophet was desirous of avoiding hostilities—that he had sent a pacific message to governor Harrison by the Miami and Potawatamie chiefs, but that those chiefs had unfortunately gone down on the south side of the Wabash, and had thus failed to meet him.   Accordingly, a suspension of hostilities was agreed upon, and the terms of peace were to be settled on the following morning by the governor and the chiefs.   In moving the army towards the Wabash, to encamp for the night, the Indians became again alarmed, supposing that an attack was about to be made on the town, notwithstanding the armistice which had just been concluded. They accordingly began to prepare for defence, and some of them sallied out, calling upon the advanced corps, to halt.   The governor immediately rode forward, and assured the Indians that it was not his intention to attack them, but that he was only in search of a suitable piece of ground on which to encamp his troops.   He enquired if there was any other water convenient besides that which the river afforded; and an Indian, with whom he was well acquainted, answered, that the creek which had been crossed two miles back, ran through the prairie to the north of the village.   A halt was then ordered, and majors Piatt, Clark and Taylor, were sent to examine this creek, as well as the river above the town, to ascertain the correctness of the information, and decide on the best

N 2

ground for an encampment. In the course of half an hour, the two latter reported that they had found on the creek, every thing that could be desirable in an encampment—an elevated spot, nearly surrounded by an open prairie, with water convenient, and a sufficiency of wood for fuel."* The army was now marched to this spot, and encamped "on a dry piece of ground, which rose about ten feet above the level of a marshy prairie in front towards the town; and, about twice as high above a similar prairie in the rear; through which, near the foot of the hill, ran a small stream clothed with willows and brush-wood. On the left of the encampment, this bench of land became wider; on the right, it gradually narrowed, and terminated in an abrupt point, about one hundred and fifty yards from the right bank."†

The encampment was about three-fourths of a mile from the Prophet's town; and orders were given, in the event of a night attack, for each corps to maintain its position, at all hazards, until relieved or further orders were given to it. The whole army was kept during the night, in the military position which is called, lying on their arms. The regular troops lay in their tents, with their accoutrements on, and their arms by their sides. The militia had no tents, but slept with their clothes and pouches on, and their guns under them, to keep them dry. The order of the encampment was the order of battle, for a night attack; and as every man slept opposite to his post in the line, there was nothing for the troops to do, in case of an assault, but to rise and take their position a few steps in the rear of the fires around which they had reposed. The guard of the night consisted of two captain's commands of forty-two men, and four non-commissioned officers each; and two subaltern's guards of twenty men and non-commissioned officers each—the whole amounting to about one hundred and thirty men, under the command of a field officer of the day. The night was dark and cloudy, and after midnight there was a drizzling rain. It was not anticipated by the governor or his of-

---

* M'Afee's History of the Late War.   † Ibid.

ficers, that an attack would be made during the night: it was supposed that if the Indians had intended to act offensively, it would have been done on the march of the army, where situations presented themselves that would have given the Indians a great advantage. Indeed, within three miles of the town, the army had passed over ground so broken and unfavorable to its march, that the position of the troops was necessarily changed, several times, in the course of a mile. The enemy, moreover, had fortified their town with care and great labor, as if they intended to act alone on the defensive. It was a favorite spot with the Indians, having long been the scene of those mysterious rites, performed by their Prophet, and by which they had been taught to believe that it was impregnable to the assaults of the white man.

At four o'clock in the morning of the 7th, governor Harrison, according to his practice, had risen, preparatory to the calling up the troops; and was engaged, while drawing on his boots by the fire, in conversation with general Wells, colonel Owen, and majors Taylor and Hurst. The orderly-drum had been roused for the purpose of giving the signal for the troops to turn out, when the attack of the Indians suddenly commenced upon the left flank of the camp. The whole army was instantly on its feet; the camp-fires were extinguished; the governor mounted his horse and proceeded to the point of attack. Several of the companies had taken their places in the line within forty seconds from the report of the first gun ; and the whole of the troops were prepared for action in the course of two minutes; a fact as creditable to their own activity and bravery, as to the skill and energy of their officers. The battle soon became general, and was maintained on both sides with signal and even desperate valor. The Indians advanced and retreated by the aid of a rattling noise, made with deer hoofs, and persevered in their treacherous attack with an apparent determination to conquer or die upon the spot. The battle raged with unabated fury and mutual slaughter, until daylight, when a gallant and successful charge by our troops, drove the enemy into the swamp, and put an end to the conflict.

Prior to the assault, the Prophet had given assurances to his followers, that in the coming contest, the
Great Spirit would render the arms of the Americans
unavailing; that their bullets would fall harmless at
the feet of the Indians; that the latter should have light
in abundance, while the former would be involved in
thick darkness. Availing himself of the privilege conferred by his peculiar office, and, perhaps, unwilling in
his own person to attest at once the rival powers of a
sham prophecy and a real American bullet, he pru-
dently took a position on an adjacent eminence; and,
when the action began, he entered upon the performance of certain mystic rites, at the same time singing a
war-song. In the course of the engagement, he was
informed that his men were falling: he told them to
fight on,—it would soon be as he had predicted; and
then, in louder and wilder strains, his inspiring battle-
song was heard commingling with the sharp crack of
the rifle and the shrill war-whoop of his brave but de-
luded followers.

Throughout the action, the Indians manifested more
boldness and perseverance than had, perhaps, ever
been exhibited by them on any former occasion. This
was owing, it is supposd, to the influence of the Prophet, who by the aid of his incantations had inspired
them with a belief that they would certainly overcome
their enemy : the supposition, likewise, that they had
taken the governor's army by surprise, doubtless contributed to the desperate character of their assaults.
They were commanded by some daring chiefs, and although their spiritual leader was not actually in the
battle, he did much to encourage his followers in their
gallant attack. Of the force of the Indians engaged,
there is no certain account. The ordinary number at
the Prophet's town during the preceding summer, was
four hundred and fifty; but a few days before the
action, they had been joined by all the Kickapoos of
the prairie, and by several bands of the Potawatamies,
from the Illinois river, and the St. Joseph's of lake
Michigan. Their number on the night of the engagement was probably between eight hundred and one
thousand. Some of the Indians who were in the ac-

tion, subsequently informed the agent at fort Wayne, that there were more than a thousand warriors in the battle, and that the number of wounded was unusually great. In the precipitation of their retreat, they left thirty-eight on the field; some were buried during the engagement in their town, others no doubt died subsequently of their wounds. The whole number of their killed, was probably not less than fifty.

Of the army under governor Harrison, thirty-five were killed in the action, and twenty-five died subsequently of their wounds: the total number of killed and wounded was one hundred and eighty-eight. Among the former were the lamented colonel Abraham Owen and major Joseph Hamilton Davies, of Kentucky.

Both officers and men behaved with much coolness and bravery,—qualities which, in an eminent degree, marked the conduct of governor Harrison throughout the engagement. The peril to which he was subjected may be inferred from the fact that a ball passed through his stock, slightly bruising his neck; another struck his saddle, and glancing hit his thigh; and a third wounded the horse on which he was riding.

Peace on the frontiers was one of the happy results of this severe and brilliant action. The tribes which had already joined in the confederacy were dismayed; and those which had remained neutral now decided against it.

CHAPTER X.

Tecumseh returns from the south—proposes to visit the President, but declines, because not permitted to go to Washington at the head of a party—attends a council at fort Wayne—proceeds to Malden and joins the British—governor Harrison's letter to the War Department relative to the north-west tribes.

DURING the two succeeding days, the victorious army remained in camp, for the purpose of burying the dead and taking care of the wounded. In the mean time, colonel Wells, with the mounted riflemen, visited the Prophet's town, and found it deserted by all the

Indians except one, whose leg had been broken in the action. The houses were mostly burnt, and the corn around the village destroyed. On the ninth the army commenced its return to Vincennes, having broken up or committed to the flames all their unnecessary baggage, in order that the wagons might be used for the transportation of the wounded.

The defeated Indians were greatly exasperated with the Prophet: they reproached him in bitter terms for the calamity he had brought upon them, and accused him of the murder of their friends who had fallen in the action. It seems, that after pronouncing some incantations over a certain composition, which he had prepared on the night preceding the action, he assured his followers, that by the power of his art, half of the invading army was already dead, and the other half in a state of distraction; and that the Indians would have little to do but rush into their camp, and complete the work of destruction with their tomahawks. "You are a liar," said one of the surviving Winnebagoes to him, after the action, "for you told us that the white people were dead or crazy, when they were all in their senses and fought like the devil." The Prophet appeared dejected, and sought to excuse himself on the plea that the virtue of his composition had been lost by a circumstance of which he had no knowledge until after the battle was over. His sacred character, however, was so far forfeited, that the Indians actually bound him with cords, and threatened to put him to death. After leaving the Prophet's town, they marched about twenty miles and encamped on the bank of Wild Cat creek.

In a letter to the war department, dated fourth of December, governor Harrison writes:

"I have the honor to inform you that two principal chiefs of the Kickapoos of the prairie, arrived here, bearing a flag, on the evening before last. The account which they give of the late confederacy under the Prophet, is as follows: The Prophet, with his Shawanoes, is at a small Huron village, about twelve miles from his former residence, on this side of the Wabash, where also were twelve or fifteen Hurons. The Kickapoos are encamped near the Tippecanoe, the Pota-

watamies have scattered and gone to different villages
of that tribe. The Winnebagoes had all set out on
their return to their own country, excepting one chief
and nine men, who remained at their former villages.
The Prophet had sent a messenger to the Kickapoos of
the prairie to request that he might be permitted to retire to their town. This was positively refused, and a
warning sent to him not to come there. These chiefs
say that the whole of the tribes who lost warriors in
the late action, attribute their misfortune to the Prophet alone; that they constantly reproach him with their
misfortunes, and threaten him with death; that they
are all desirous of making their peace with the United
States, and will send deputations to me for that purpose, as soon as they are informed that they will be
well received. They further say, that the Prophet's
followers were fully impressed with a belief that they
could defeat us with ease; that it was their intention
to have attacked us at fort Harrison, if we had gone no
higher; that Racoon creek was then fixed on, and
finally Pine creek, and that the latter would probably
have been the place, if the usual route had not been
abandoned, and a crossing made higher up; that the
attack made on our sentinels at fort Harrison was intended to shut the door against accommodation; that
the Winnebagoes had forty warriors killed in the action, and the Kickapoos eleven, and ten wounded.
They have never heard how many of the Potawatamies and other tribes were killed."

With the battle of Tippecanoe, the Prophet lost his
popularity and power among the Indians. His magic
wand was broken, and the mysterious charm by means
of which he had for years, played upon the superstitious minds of this wild people, scattered through a
vast extent of country, was dissipated forever. It was
not alone to the character of his prophetic office that he
was indebted for his influence over his followers. The
position which he maintained in regard to the Indian
lands, and the encroachments of the white people upon
their hunting grounds, increased his popularity, which
was likewise greatly strengthened by the respect and
deference with which the politic Tecumseh—the mas-

ter spirit of his day—uniformly treated him. He had, moreover, nimble wit, quickness of apprehension, much cunning and a captivating eloquence of speech. These qualities fitted him for playing his part with great suc cess; and sustaining for a series of years, the character of one inspired by the Great Spirit. He was, however, rash, presumptuous and deficient in judgment. And no sooner was he left without the sagacious counsel and positive control of Tecumseh, than he foolishly annihilated his own power, and suddenly crushed the grand confederacy upon which he and his brother had expended years of labor, and in the organization of which they had incurred much personal peril and endured great privation.

Tecumseh returned from the south through Missouri, visited the tribes on the Des Moins, and crossing the head waters of the Illinois, reached the Wabash a few days after the disastrous battle of Tippecanoe. It is believed that he made a strong impression upon all the tribes visited by him in his extended mission; and that he had laid the foundation of numerous accessions to his confederacy. He reached the banks of the Tippecanoe, just in time to witness the dispersion of his followers, the disgrace of his brother, and the final overthrow of the great object of his ambition, a union of all the Indian tribes against the United States : and all this, the result of a disregard to his positive commands. His mortification was extreme; and it is related on good authority, that when he first met the Prophet, he reproached him in bitter terms for having departed from his instructions to preserve peace with the United States at all hazards. The attempt of the Prophet to palliate his own conduct, excited the haughty chieftain still more, and seizing him by the hair and shaking him violently, he threatened to take his life.

During the ensuing winter, there was peace on the frontiers. In the month of January, 1812, Little Turtle, the celebrated Miami chief, wrote to governor Harrison, that all the Prophet's. followers had left him, except two camps of his own tribe, and that Tecumseh had just joined him with only eight men; from which he concluded there was no present danger to be apprehended from them. Shortly afterwards, Tecumseh sent a message to governor Harrison informing him of his return from the south; and that he was now ready to make the promised visit to the President. The governor replied, giving his permission for Tecumseh to go to Washington, but not as the leader of any party of Indians. The chieftain, who had been accustomed to make his visits to Vincennes, attended by three or four hundred warriors, all completely armed, did not choose to present himself to his great father, the President, shorn of his power and without his retinue. The visit was declined, and here terminated the intercourse between him and governor Harrison.

Early in March, the peace of the frontiers was again disturbed by Indian depredations; and in the course of this and the following month, several families were murdered on the Wabash and Ohio rivers. On the 15th of May, there was a grand council held at Mississiniway, which was attended by twelve tribes of Indians. They all professed to be in favor of peace, and condemned the disturbances which had occurred between the Indians and the settlers, since the battle of Tippecanoe. Tecumseh was present at this council and spoke several times. He defied any living creature to say that he had ever advised any one, directly or indirectly, to make war upon the whites: it had constantly been his misfortune, he said, to have his views misrepresented to his white brethren; and this had been done by pretended chiefs of the Potawatamies, who had been in the habit of selling land to the white people, which did not belong to them. "Governor Harrison," he continued, "made war on my people in my absence: it was the will of God that he should do so. We hope it will please God that the white people will let us live in peace. We will not disturb them, neither have we done it, except when they came to our village with the intention of destroying us. We are happy to state to our brothers present, that the unfortunate transaction that took place between the white people and a few of our young men at our village, has been settled between us and governor Harrison; and I will further state, that had I been

O

at home, there would have been no bloodshed at that time."

In the month of June, following this council, Tecumseh made a visit to fort Wayne, and sought an interview with the Indian agent at that place. Misfortune had not subdued his haughty spirit nor silenced the fearless expression of his feelings and opinions. He still maintained the justice of his position in regard to the ownership of the Indian lands, disavowed any intention of making war upon the United States, and reproached governor Harrison for having marched against his people during his absence. The agent made a long speech to him, presenting reasons why he should now become the friend and ally of the United States. To this harangue, Tecumseh listened with frigid indifference, made a few general remarks in reply, and then with a haughty air, left the council-house, and took his departure for Malden, where he joined the British standard.

In taking leave of that part of our subject which relates to the confederacy of Tecumseh and the Prophet, and the principle on which it was established, we quote, as relevant to the case, and as an interesting piece of general history, the following letter from governor Harrison to the Secretary of War :

" *Cincinnati, March* 22, 1814.

" Sir,—The tribes of Indians on this frontier and east of the Mississippi, with whom the United States have been connected by treaty, are the Wyandots, Delawares, Shawanoes, Miamis, Potawatamies, Ottawas, Chippewas, Piankashaws, Kaskaskias and Sacs. All but the two last were in the confederacy which carried on the former Indian war against the United States, that was terminated by the treaty of Greenville. The Kaskaskias were parties to the treaty, but they had not been in the war. The Wyandots are admitted by the others to be the leading tribe. They hold the grand *calumet* which unites them and kindles the council fire. This tribe is nearly equally divided between the *Crane*, at Sandusky, who is the grand sachem of the nation, and Walk-in-the-Water, at Brownstown, near

Detroit. They claim the lands bounded by the settlements of this state, southwardly and eastwardly; and by lake Erie, the Miami river, and the claim of the Shawanoes upon the Auglaize, a branch of the latter. They also claim the lands they live on near Detroit, but I am ignorant to what extent.

"The Wyandots of Sandusky have adhered to us through the war. Their chief, the Crane, is a venerable, intelligent and upright man. Within the tract of land claimed by the Wyandots, a number of Senecas are settled. They broke off from their own tribe six or eight years ago, but received a part of the annuity granted that tribe by the United States, by sending a deputation for it to Buffalo. The claim of the Wyandots to the lands they occupy, is not disputed, that I know of, by any other tribe. Their residence on it, however, is not of long standing, and the country was certainly once the property of the Miamis.

"Passing westwardly from the Wyandots, we meet with the Shawanoe settlement at Stony creek, a branch of the Great Miami, and at Wapauckanata, on the Auglaize. These settlements were made immediately after the treaty of Greenville, and with the consent of the Miamis, whom I consider the real owners of these lands. The chiefs of this band of Shawanoes, Blackhoof, Wolf and Lewis, are attached to us from principle as well as interest—they are all honest men.

"The Miamis have their principal settlement at the forks of the Wabash, thirty miles from fort Wayne; and at Mississinaway, thirty miles lower down. A band of them under the name of Weas, have resided on the Wabash, sixty miles above Vincennes; and another under the Turtle on Eel river, a branch of the Wabash, twenty miles north-west of fort Wayne. By an artifice of Little Turtle, these three bands were passed on general Wayne as distinct tribes, and an annuity granted to each. The Eel river and Weas, however, to this day call themselves Miamis, and are recognized as such by the Mississinaway band. The Miamis, Maumees or Tewicktowes, are the undoubted proprietors of all that beautiful country which is watered by the Wabash and its branches; and there is as little doubt that their claim extended at least as far east as the Scioto. They have no tradition of removing from any other quarter of the country; whereas all the neighboring tribes, the Piankishaws excepted, who are a branch of the Miamis, are either intruders upon them, or have been permitted to settle in their country. The Wyandots emigrated first from lake Ontario, and subsequently from lake Huron—the Delawares from Pennsylvania and Maryland—the Shawanoes from Georgia —the Kickapoos and Potawatamies from the country between lake Michigan and the Mississippi—and the Ottawas and Chippewas from the peninsula formed by lakes Michigan, Huron and St. Clair, and the strait connecting the latter with Erie. The claims of the Miamis were bounded on the north and west by those of the Illinois confederacy, consisting originally of five tribes, called Kaskaskias, Cahokias, Peorians, Michiganians, and Temorais, speaking the Miami language, and no doubt branches of that nation.

"When I was first appointed governor of Indiana territory, these once powerful tribes were reduced to about thirty warriors, of whom twenty-five were Kaskaskias, four Peorians, and a single Michiganian. There was an individual lately alive at St. Louis, who saw the enumeration made of them by the Jesuits in the year 1745, making the number of their warriors four thousand. A furious war between them and the Sacs and Kickapoos, reduced them to that miserable remnant, which had taken refuge amongst the white people of the towns of Kaskaskias and St. Genevieve. The Kickapoos had fixed their principal village at Peoria, upon the south bank of the Illinois river, while the Sacs remained masters of the country to the north.

"During the war of our Revolution, the Miamis had invited the Kickapoos into their country to assist them against the whites, and a considerable village was formed by that tribe on Vermillion river, near its junction with the Wabash. After the treaty of Greenville, the Delawares had, with the approbation of the Miamis, removed from the mouth of the Auglaize to the head waters of White river, a large branch of the Wabash —and the Potawatamies, without their consent, had formed two villages upon the latter river, one at Tippecanoe, and the other at Chippoy, twenty-five miles below.

"The Piankishaws lived in the neighborhood of Vincennes, which was their ancient village, and claimed the lands to the mouth of the Wabash, and to the north and west as far as the Kaskaskias claimed. Such was the situation of the tribes, when I received instructions from President Jefferson, shortly after his first election, to make efforts for extinguishing the Indian claims upon the Ohio, below the mouth of the Kentucky river, and to such other tracts as were necessary to connect and consolidate our settlements. It was at once determined, that the community of interests in the lands amongst the Indian tribes, which seemed to be recognized by the treaty of Greenville, should be objected to; and that each individual tribe should be protected in every claim that should appear to be founded in reason and justice. But it was also determined, that as a measure of policy and liberality, such tribes as lived upon any tract of land which it would be desirable to purchase, should receive a portion of the compensation, although the title might be exclusively in another tribe. Upon this principle the Delawares, Shawanoes, Potawatamies, and Kickapoos, were admitted as parties to several of the treaties. Care was taken, however, to place the title to such tracts as might be desirable to purchase hereafter, upon a footing that would facilitate the procuring of them, by getting the tribes who had no claim themselves, and who might probably interfere, to recognize the titles of those who were ascertained to possess them.

"This was particularly the case with regard to the lands watered by the Wabash, which were declared to be the property of the Miamis, with the exception of the tract occupied by the Delawares on White river, which was to be considered the joint property of them and the Miamis. This arrangement was very much disliked by Tecumseh, and the banditti that he had assembled at Tippecanoe. He complained loudly, as well of the sales that had been made, as of the principle of considering a particular tribe as the exclusive

o 2

proprietors of any part of the country, which he said the Great Spirit had given to all his red children. Besides the disaffected amongst the neighboring tribes, he had brought together a considerable number of Winnebagoes and Folsovoins, from the neighborhood of Green Bay, Sacs from the Mississippi, and some Ottawas and Chippewas from Abercrosh on lake Michigan. These people were better pleased with the climate and country of the Wabash, than with that they had left.

"The Miamis resisted the pretensions of Tecumseh and his followers for some time; but a system of terror was adopted, and the young men were seduced by eternally placing before them a picture of labor, and restriction as to hunting, to which the system adopted would inevitably lead. The Potawatamies and other tribes inhabiting the Illinois river and south of lake Michigan, had been for a long time approaching gradually towards the Wabash. Their country, which was never abundantly stocked with game, was latterly almost exhausted of it. The fertile regions of the Wabash still afforded it. It was represented, that the progressive settlements of the whites upon that river, would soon deprive them of their only resource, and indeed would force the Indians of that river upon them who were already half starved.

"It is a fact, that for many years the current of emigration, as to the tribes east of the Mississippi, has been from north to south. This is owing to two causes; the diminution of those animals from which the Indians procure their support; and the pressure of the two great tribes, the Chippewas and Sioux, to the north and west. So long ago as the treaty of Greenville, the Potawatamies gave notice to the Miamis, that they intended to settle upon the Wabash. They made no pretensions to the country, and their only excuse for the intended aggression was, that they were "tired of eating fish and wanted meat." It has already been observed that the Sacs had extended themselves to the Illinois river, and that the settlements of the Kickapoos at the Peorias was of modern date. Previously to the commencement of the present war, a considerable number had joined their brethren on the Wabash. The

Tawas from the Des Moins river, have twice made attempts to get a footing there.

*   *   *   *   *   *

"The question of the title to the lands south of the Wabash, has been thoroughly examined; every opportunity was afforded to Tecumseh and his party to exhibit their pretensions, and they were found to rest upon no other basis than that of their being the common property of all the Indians. The Potawatamies and Kickapoos have unequivocally acknowledged the Miami and Delaware titles."

CHAPTER XI.

Tecumseh participates in the battle of Brownstown—commands the Indians in the action near Maguaga—present at Hull's surrender—general Brock presents him his military sash—attack on Chicago brought about by Tecumseh.

On the 18th of June, 1812, the congress of the United States made a formal declaration of war against Great Britain. This gave a new aspect to affairs on the north-western frontier; and at the first commencement of hostilities between these two powers, Tecumseh was in the field, prepared for the conflict. In the month of July, when general Hull crossed over from Detroit into Canada, this chief, with a party of thirty Potawatamies and Shawanoes, was at Malden. About the same time there was an assemblage at Brownstown, opposite to Malden, of those Indians who were inclined to neutrality in the war. A deputation was sent to the latter place, inviting Tecumseh to attend this council. "No," said he, indignantly, "I have taken sides with the King, my father, and I will suffer my bones to bleach upon this shore, before I will recross that stream to join in any council of neutrality." In a few days he gave evidence of the sincerity of this declaration, by personally commanding the Indians in the first action that ensued after the declaration of war.*

* Anthony Shane.

Early in August, general Hull, then in Detroit, was notified by express that a company of Ohio volunteers, under the command of captain Henry Brush, with provisions for the army, were near the river Raisin, and needed an escort, as it had been ascertained that some British and a considerable body of Indians, under the command of Tecumseh, had crossed from Malden to Brownstown, with a view to intercept this convoy. General Hull, after some delay, gave a reluctant consent to the colonels of the Ohio militia, that a detachment of troops might march to the relief of colonel Brush. Major Van Horne, with a small body of men, started as an escort to the mail, with orders to join captain Brush at the river Raisin. He set off on the fourth of August, marching that evening as far as the river De Corce. On the next day, captain McCullough of the spies, was killed by some Indians. In the course of the succeeding one, near Brownstown, the detachment under major Van Horne was suddenly attacked by the Indians, who were lying in ambush. Apprehensive of being surrounded and entirely cut off, the major ordered a retreat, which was continued to the river De Corce, the enemy pursuing them to that point. Our loss was seventeen killed, besides several wounded, who were left behind. Among the former were captains Ulry, Gilchrist, Boersler, lieutenant Pents, and ensign Ruby. The loss of so many officers resulted from their attempts to rally the men. The loss of the enemy was supposed to be equal to that sustained by major Van Horne. There were about forty British soldiers and seventy Indians in this engagement, the latter being commanded by Tecumseh in person.

After general Hull had ingloriously retreated from Canada, he detached colonel Miller, with majors Van Horne and Morrison, and a body of troops, amounting to six hundred, to make a second effort to reach captain Brush. They were attended by some artillerists with one six pounder and a howitzer. The detachment marched from Detroit on the eighth, and in the afternoon of the ninth the front guard, commanded by captain Snelling, was fired upon by a line of British and Indians, about two miles below the village of Maguaga. At the moment of the attack, the main body was marching in two lines, and captain Snelling maintained his position in a gallant manner, until the line was formed and marched to the ground he occupied, where the whole, except the rear guard, was brought into action. The British were entrenched behind a breast-work of logs, with the Indians on the left covered by a thick wood. Colonel Miller ordered his whole line to advance, and when within a short distance of the enemy, fired upon them, and immediately followed it up by a charge with fixed bayonets, when the whole British line and the Indians commenced a retreat. They were vigorously pursued for near two miles. The Indians on the left were commanded by Tecumseh, and fought with great bravery, but were forced to retreat. Our loss in this severe and well fought action was ten killed and thirty-two wounded of the regular troops, and eight killed and twenty-eight wounded of the Ohio and Michigan militia. The full extent of the force of the enemy is not known. There were four hundred regulars and Canadian militia, under command of major Muir, and a considerable body of Indians under Tecumseh. Forty of the latter were found dead on the field : fifteen of the British regulars were killed and wounded, and four taken prisoners. The loss of the Canadian militia and volunteers, was never ascertained, but is supposed, from the position which they occupied in the action, to have been considerable. Both major Muir and Tecumseh were wounded. The bravery and good conduct of the latter, in this engagement, are supposed to have led to his being shortly afterwards appointed a brigadier general, in the service of the British king.

When Detroit was captured, on the 16th of August, Tecumseh was at the head of the Indians. After the surrender, general Brock requested him not to allow his men to ill-treat the prisoners, to which he replied, "no! I despise them too much to meddle with them."*

"Tecumseh was an excellent judge of position; and not only knew, but could point out the localities of the

* Book of the Indians, by S. G. Drake.

whole country through which he passed. His facility of communicating the information he had acquired, was thus displayed before a concourse of spectators. Previously to general Brock's crossing over to Detroit, he asked him what sort of a country he should have to pass through, in case of his proceeding farther. Tecumseh, taking a roll of elm bark, and extending it on the ground by means of four stones, drew forth his scalping knife, and with the point presently etched upon the bark a plan of the country, its hills, rivers, woods, morasses and roads; a plan which, if not as neat, was for the purpose required, fully as intelligible as if Arrowsmith himself had prepared it. Pleased with this unexpected talent in Tecumseh, also by his having, with his characteristic boldness, induced the Indians, not of his immediate party, to cross the Detroit, prior to the embarkation of the regulars and militia, general Brock, as soon as the business was over, publicly took off his sash, and placed it round the body of the chief. Tecumseh received the honor with evident gratification; but was next day seen without his sash. General Brock fearing something had displeased the Indian, sent his interpreter for an explanation. The latter soon returned with an account, that Tecumseh, not wishing to wear such a mark of distinction, when an older, and as he said, abler warrior than himself, was present, had transferred the sash to the Wyandot chief, Roundhead."*

On the 15th of August, the garrison of Chicago, situated in the south-western bend of lake Michigan,—consisting of about seventy men, with some women and children,—were attacked by a large body of Indians, who had been lying around the fort for some time, professing neutrality. The whole were either murdered or taken prisoners. The garrison, under the direction of captains Heald and Wells, having destroyed the fort and distributed the public stores among the Indians, was about to retreat towards fort Wayne. As the Indians around Chicago had not yet taken sides in the war, the garrison would probably have escaped, had

---

* James' Military Occurrences of the Late War.

not Tecumseh, immediately after the attack upon major Vanhorn, at Brownstown, sent a runner to these Indians, claiming the victory over that officer; and conveying to them information that general Hull had returned to Detroit; and that there was every prospect of success over him. This intelligence reached the Indians the night previous the evacuation of Chicago, and led them at once, as Tecumseh had anticipated, to become the allies of the British army.

At the period of colonel Campbell's expedition against the Mississinaway towns, in the month of December, Tecumseh was in that neighborhood, with about six hundred Indians, whose services he had engaged as allies of Great Britian. He was not in the battle of the river Raisin on the 22d of January. Had he been present on that occasion, the known magnanimity of his character, justifies the belief that the horrible massacre of prisoners, which followed that action, would not have taken place. Not only the savages, but their savage leaders, Proctor and Elliott, would have been held in check, by a chief who, however daring and dreadful in the hour of battle, was never known to illtreat or murder a prisoner.

CHAPTER XII.

Siege of fort Meigs—Tecumseh commands the Indians—acts with intrepidity—rescues the American prisoners from the tomahawk and scalping knife, after Dudley's defeat—reported agreement between Proctor and Tecumseh, that general Harrison, if taken prisoner, should be delivered to the latter to be burned.

FORT MEIGS, situated on the south-east side of the Miami of the lakes, and at the foot of the rapids of that stream, was an octagonal enclosure, with eight block houses, picketed with timber, and surrounded by ditches. It was two thousand five hundred yards in circumference, and required, to garrison it with efficiency, about two thousand men. It was constructed under the immediate superintendence of colonel E. D. Wood, of the corps of engineers, one of the most scientific and gallant officers of the late war. This post, which was established in the spring of 1813, was important not only for the protection of the frontiers, but as the depot for the artillery, military stores and provisions, necessary for the prosecution of the ensuing campaign. These circumstances could not fail to attract the attention of the enemy; and the commander of the American army was not disappointed in supposing that fort Meigs would be the first point of attack, upon the opening of the spring, by the combined forces of Proctor and Tecumseh.

In the latter part of March, intelligence reached this post that Proctor had issued a general order for assembling the Canadian militia at Sandwich, on the 7th of April, to unite in an expedition against fort Meigs. This information gave a fresh impulse to the efforts then making to render the fort, which was still in an unfinished state, as strong as possible. On the 8th of April, colonel Ball arrived with two hundred dragoons; and on the 12th general Harrison reached the fort with three hundred men from the posts on the Auglaize and St. Mary's. Vigorous preparations were now made for the anticipated siege. On the 19th, a scouting party returned from the river Raisin, with three Frenchmen, who stated that the British were still making arrangements for an attack on this post; and were assembling a very large Indian force. They informed general Harrison that Tecumseh and the Prophet had reached Sandwich, with about six hundred Indians, collected in the country between lake Michigan and the Wabash. This intelligence removed the apprehension entertained by the general, that the Indians intended to fall upon the posts in his rear, while Proctor should attack fort Meigs. On the 26th, the advance of the enemy was discovered at the mouth of the bay; and on the 28th, the British and Indian forces were found to be within a few miles of the fort. At this time, only a part of the troops destined for the defence of the place, had arrived; but the remainder, under the command of general Green Clay, of Kentucky, were daily expected. So soon as the fort was actually invested by the In dians, an express was sent by the commander-in-chief, to inform general Clay of the fact, and direct his subsequent movements. This dangerous enterprise—for the Indians were already in considerable numbers around the fort—was undertaken and successfully executed by captain William Oliver,* a, gallant young officer belonging to the commissary's department, who, to a familiar acquaintance with the geography of the country united much knowledge of Indian warfare. Attended by a white man and a Delaware Indian, Oliver traversed the country to fort Findlay, thence to fort Amanda, and finally met with general Clay at fort Winchester, on the 2d of May, and communicated to him general Harrison's instructions.

Soon after Oliver had started on this enterprise, the gunboats of the enemy approached the site of old fort Miami, on the opposite side of the river, about two miles below fort Meigs. In the course of the ensuing night they commenced the erection of three batteries, opposite the fort on a high bank, about three hundred yards from the river, the intermediate space of ground being open and partly covered with water. Two of them were gun batteries, with four embrasures, and were situated higher up the river than the fort; the third was a bomb battery, placed a short distance below. Early the next morning, a fire was opened upon them from the fort, which, to some extent, impeded the

---

* Now Major William Oliver, of Cincinnati. It is but an act of justice to this gentleman to state that, for the voluntary performance of this service, he refused all pecuniary compensation. General Harrison subsequently, in a letter to major Oliver, in relation to this service, says, "To prevent the possibility of these orders coming to the knowledge of the enemy, they could not be committed to writing, but must be communicated verbally, by a confidential officer. The selection of one suited to the performance of this important trust was a matter of no little difficulty. To the qualities of undoubted patriotism, moral firmness, as well as active courage, sagacity and prudence, it was necessary that he should unite a thorough knowledge of the country through which the troops were to pass, and of all the localities of the position upon which they were advancing. Without the latter, the possession of the former would be useless, and the absence of either of the former might render the 'atter not only useless, but in the highest degree mischievous. Although there was no coincidence between the performance of this duty and those which appertained to the department of the staff in which you held an appointment, [the commissariat] I did not long hesitate in fixing on you for this service."

P

progress of the works. On the morning of the 30th, the enemy, under a heavy and somewhat fatal fire from the guns of the fort, raised and adjusted their cannon, while at the same time, a number of boats filled with Indians were seen crossing to the south-eastern side of the river.

On the morning of the first of May, the British batteries were completed; and about ten o'clock, the enemy appeared to be adjusting their guns on certain objects in the fort. "By this time our troops had completed a grand traverse, about twelve feet high, upon a base of twenty feet, three hundred yards long, on the most elevated ground through the middle of the camp, calculated to ward off the shot of the enemy's batteries. Orders were given for all the tents in front to be instantly removed into its rear, which was effected in a few minutes, and that beautiful prospect of cannonading and bombarding our lines, which but a few moments before had excited the skill and energy of the British engineer, was now entirely fled; and in its place nothing was to be seen but an immense shield of earth, which entirely obscured the whole army. Not a tent nor a single person was to be seen. Those canvas houses, which had concealed the growth of the traverse from the view of the enemy, were now protected and hid in their turn. The prospect of *smoking us out*, was now at best but very faint. But as neither general Proctor nor his officers were yet convinced of the folly and futility of their laborious preparations, their batteries were opened, and five days were spent in arduous cannonading and bombarding, to bring them to this salutary conviction. A tremendous cannonading was kept up all the rest of the day, and shells were thrown until 11 o'clock at night. Very little damage, however, was done in the camp; one or two were killed, and three or four wounded; among the latter was major Amos Stoddard, of the first regiment of artillery, a survivor of the revolution, and an officer of much merit. He was wounded slightly with a piece of shell, and about ten days afterwards died with the lock-jaw.

"The fire of the enemy was returned from the fort with one eighteen pounder with some effect, though but sparingly, for the stock of eighteen pound shot was but small, there being but three hundred and sixty of that size in the fort when the siege commenced; and about the same number for the twelve pounders."*

Throughout the whole of the second day the firing was continued with great spirit, but without doing much damage on either side. General Harrison, in anticipation of a transfer of the enemy's guns to the other side of the river, and the establishment of batteries to play upon the centre or flanks of the camp, had directed the construction of works calculated to resist such an attack; and they were in a state of considerable forwardness on the morning of the third, when, from the the bushes on the left of the fort, three field pieces and a howitzer were suddenly opened upon the camp by the enemy. The fire was returned with such effect, that general Proctor was soon compelled to change his position. His batteries were again opened on the camp from another point, but without doing much injury. On the fourth, the fire of the enemy was renewed, but with less energy than on the previous days, the result, it is supposed, of a belief that their efforts to reduce the fort would fail. General Harrison was waiting the arrival of general Clay with his reinforcements. Late in the night of the fourth, captain Oliver, accompanied by majors David Trimble and —— Taylor, with fifteen Ohio militia, having left general Clay above the rapids, started in a boat for the fort, that the commanding general, by knowing the position of the reinforcements, might form his plans for the ensuing day. The effort to reach the fort under the existing circumstances was extremely dangerous. Captain Leslie Combs had already attempted it, and failed. He had been sent by colonel Dudley, upon his arrival at Defiance, to inform general Harrison of the fact. With five men, the captain approached within a mile of the fort, when he was attacked by the Indians, and compelled to retreat after a gallant resistance, in which nearly all his companions were killed. When Oliver drew near the fort, the night was extremely

* M'Affee.

dark, and he was only enabled to discover the spot by
the spreading branches of a solitary oak tree, standing
within the fortification.   The boat was fired upon by
the sentinels of the fort, but on their being hailed by
captain Oliver, no further alarm was given.   After
landing and wading over a ravine filled with water,
the party groped their way to one of the gates, and
were admitted. Tecumseh and his Indians were extremely vigilant, and, at night, usually came close to
the ramparts for the purpose of annoying our troops,
as opportunity might offer.   So soon as general Harrison had received the information brought by captain
Oliver and his companions, he made his arrangements
for the ensuing day.   Captain Hamilton, attended by a
subaltern, was immediately despatched up the river in
a canoe with orders to general Clay.   The captain met
him at daylight five miles above the fort, the boats
conveying the reinforcements having been delayed by
the darkness of the night.   Captain Hamilton delivered the following order to general Clay. " You must
detach about eight hundred men from your brigade,
and land them at a point I will show you about a mile
or a mile and a half above camp Meigs.   I will then
conduct the detachment to the British batteries on the
left bank of the river.   The batteries must be taken,
the cannon spiked, and the carriages cut down ; and
the troops must then return to their boats and cross
over to the fort.   The balance of your men must land
on the fort-side of the river, opposite the first landing,
and fight their way into the fort through the Indians.
The route they must take will be pointed out by a
subaltern officer now with me, who will land the canoe
on the right bank of the river to point out the landing for the boats."*   As soon as these orders were received by general Clay, who was in the thirteenth boat
from the front, he directed captain Hamilton to go to
colonel Dudley, with orders to take the twelve front
boats and execute the plan of the commanding general
on the left bank of the river; and to post the subaltern
with the canoe on the right bank, at the point where

* M'Affee.

the remainder of the reinforcement was directed to
land. It was the design of general Harrison while the
troops under Dudley were destroying the enemy's batteries on the north-west side of the river, and general
Clay was fighting the Indians above the fort on the
south-east side, to send out a detachment to take and
spike the British guns on the south side.

"General Clay ordered the five remaining boats to
fall behind the one occupied by him; but in attempting
to do so, they were driven on shore, and thus thrown
half a mile into the rear. The general kept close to
the right bank, intending to land opposite to the detachment under Dudley, but finding no guide there, and the
Indians having commenced a brisk fire on his boat, he
attempted to cross to the detachment. The current,
however, was so swift, that it soon carried him too far
down for that project; he therefore turned back, and
landed on the right bank further down. Captain Peter
Dudley, with a part of his company, was in this boat,
making in the whole upwards of fifty men, who now
marched into camp without loss, amidst a shower of
grape from the British batteries and the fire of some Indians. The boat with their baggage and four sick soldiers, was left, as the general supposed, in the care of
two men who met him at his landing, and by whom he
expected she would be brought down under the guns
of the fort. In a few minutes, however, she fell into
the hands of the Indians. The attempt which he had
made to cross the river, induced colonel Boswell, with
the rear boats, to land on the opposite side; but as soon
as captain Hamilton discovered the error under which
he was acting, he instructed him to cross over and fight
his way into camp. When he arrived at the south side,
he was annoyed on landing by the Indians; and as soon
as his men were on shore, he formed them and returned
the fire of the enemy; at the same time he was directed by captain Shaw, from the commanding general, to
march in open order, through the plain, to the fort. As
there was now a large body of Indians on his flank,
general Harrison determined to send out a reinforcement from the garrison to enable him to beat them.
Accordingly, Alexander's brigade, a part of Johnson's

battalion, and ᴠʜᴇ companies of captains Nearing and
Dudley, were ordered to prepare for this duty. When
the Kentuckians reached the gates of the fort, these
troops were ready to join them. Having formed in
order—colonel Boswell being on the right,—they marched against the Indians, who were superior to them in
numbers, and at the point of the bayonet, forced them
into the woods to the distance of half a mile or more.
Such was the ardor of our troops, in the pursuit, that
it was difficult, especially for the Kentucky officers, to
induce their men to return.

General Harrison had now taken a position on one
of the batteries of the fort, that he might see the various
movements which at this moment claimed his attention.
He soon perceived a detachment of British and Indians
passing along the edge of the woods, with a view to
reach the left and rear of the corps under Boswell: he
forthwith despatched his volunteer aid, John T. Johnston, to recall the troops under Boswell from the pursuit. Johnston's horse having been killed before he
delivered this order, it was repeated through major
Graham, and a retreat was commenced: the Indians
promptly rallied and boldly pursued them for some distance, killing and wounding a number of our troops.
So soon as the commanding general perceived that
colonel Dudley and his detachment had reached the
batteries on the northern bank of the river, and entered
successfully upon the execution of the duty assigned
them, he ordered colonel John Miller of the regulars to
make a sortie from the fort, against the batteries which
the enemy had erected on the south side of the river.
The detachment assigned to colonel Miller, amounted
to about three hundred and fifty men, composed of the
companies and parts of companies of captains Langham,
Croghan, Bradford, Nearing, Elliott, and lieutenants
Gwynne and Campbell of the regular troops; the volunteers of Alexander's battalion; and captain Sebree's
company of Kentucky militia. Colonel Miller and his
men charged upon the enemy, and drove them from
their position; spiked the cannon at their batteries, and
secured forty-one prisoners. The force of the enemy,
thus driven and defeated, consisted of two hundred

British regulars, one hundred and fifty Canadians and about five hundred Indians, under the immediate command of Tecumseh, in all more than double the force of the detachment under colonel Miller. In this sortie, captain Sebree's company of militia, was particularly distinguished. With the intrepid bravery and reckless ardor for which the Kentucky troops are noted, they plunged into the thickest ranks of the enemy, and were for a time surrounded by the Indians, who gallantly pressed upon them; but they maintained their ground, until lieutenant Gwynne,* of the 19th regiment, perceiving their imminent peril, boldly charged upon the Indians, with a portion of captain Elliott's company, and released captain Sebree and his men from their dangerous situation. Had the force of colonel Miller been something stronger, he would probably have captured the whole of the enemy, then on the south side of the river. The British and Indians suffered severely, being finally driven back and thrown into confusion. As colonel Miller commenced his return to the fort, the enemy rallied and pressed with great bravery upon his rear, until he arrived near the breast-works. A considerable number of our soldiers were left dead on the field, and several officers were wounded.

Colonel Dudley's movements on the north side of the river, are now to be noticed. A landing was effected by his detachment, which was immediately marched off, through an open plain, to a hill clothed with timber. Here the troops were formed into three columns, colonel Dudley placing himself at the head of the right, major Shelby leading the left, and captain Morrison, acting as major, the centre. The distance from the place where the detachment was formed in order, to the point to be attacked, was near two miles. The batteries were engaged in cannonading camp Meigs, when the column led by major Shelby, being a few hundred yards in advance of the others, rushed at full speed upon those having charge of the guns, and carried them without the loss of a single man. When the British flag was cut down, the garrison of fort Meigs shouted

* Major David Gwynne, now of Cincinnati.

for joy. The grand object of the enterprise having been achieved, the general, who was watching the movements of the detachment, made signs to them to retreat to their boats; but to his great surprise, and in express disobedience of the orders transmitted through colonel Hamilton, our troops remained at the batteries, quietly looking around, without spiking the cannon, cutting down the carriages or destroying the magazines. This delay proved fatal to them. The general, alarm ed for their safety, now offered a very high reward to any individual who would bear fresh orders to colonel Dudley and his men, to return to their boats and cross over the river to the fort. The service was undertaken by lieutenant Campbell. "About the time when the batteries were taken, a body of Indians, lying in ambush, had fired on a party of spies under captain Combs, who had marched down on the extreme left of the detachment. Presently colonel Dudley gave orders to reinforce the spies, and the greater part of the right and centre columns rushed into the woods in confusion, with their colonel among them—to fight the Indians, whom they routed and pursued near two miles. The left column remained in possession of the batteries, till the fugitive artillerists returned with a reinforcement from the main British camp, and attacked them. Some of them were then made prisoners, others fled to the boats, and a part, who were rallied by the exertions of their major, marched to the aid of colonel Dudley. The Indians had also been reinforced, and the confusion in which major Shelby found the men under Dudley, was so great as to amount to a cessation of resistance; while the savages, skulking around them, continued the work of destruction in safety. At last a retreat commenced in disorder, but the greater part of the men were captured by the Indians, or surrendered to the British at the batteries. The gallant but unfortunate colonel Dudley, after being wounded, was overtaken and despatched with the tomahawk. The number of those who escaped and got into the fort, out of the whole detachment, was considerably below two hundred. Had the orders which colonel Dudley recieved, been duly regarded, or a proper degree of judg ment exercised on the occasion, the day would certainly have been an important one for the country, and a glorious one for the army. Every thing might have been accomplished agreeably to the wishes and intentions of the general, with the loss of but few men. When the approach of the detachment under Dudley was reported to Proctor, he supposed it to be the main force of the American army, from which he was apprehensive that he might sustain a total defeat: he therefore recalled a large portion of his British and Indians from the opposite shore. They did not arrive, however, in time to partake in the contest on the north side."*

After the fighting had ceased on the fifth, the British general sent a flag to the fort by major Chambers, and his introduction to general Harrison was succeeded by the following significant dialogue:

"*Major Chambers.* General Proctor has directed me to demand the surrender of this post. He wishes to spare the effusion of blood.

"*General Harrison.* The demand, under present circumstances, is a most extraordinary one. As general Proctor did not send me a summons to surrender on his first arrival, I had supposed that he believed me determined to do my duty. His present message indicates an opinion of me that I am at a loss to account for.

"*Major Chambers.* General Proctor could never think of saying anything to wound your feelings, sir. The character of general Harrison, as an officer, is well known. General Proctor's force is very respectable, and there is with him a larger body of Indians than has ever before been embodied.

"*General Harrison.* I believe I have a very correct idea of general Proctor's force; it is not such as to create the least apprehension for the result of the contest, whatever shape he may be pleased hereafter to give it. Assure the general, however, that he will never have this post *surrendered* to him upon any terms. Should it fall into his hands, it will be in a manner calculated to do him more honor, and to give

---

* M'Affee.

him larger claims upon the gratitude of his government than any capitulation could possibly do "

The siege was continued, but without any very active efforts against the fort, until the morning of the 9th of May, when the enemy retreated down the bay, leaving behind them a quantity of cannon balls, and other valuable articles.

The force under general Proctor amounted, as nearly as could be ascertained, to six hundred regulars, eight hundred Canadian militia, and about eighteen hundred Indians. The number of troops under general Harrison, including those which arrived on the morning of the fifth, under general Clay, was about twelve hundred in all. The number fit for duty did not, perhaps, equal eleven hundred.

The number of the American troops killed and massacred on the north side of the river, was upwards of seventy. One hundred and eighty-nine were wounded, and eighty-one killed, in the two sorties from the fort. The loss of the British and Indians, in killed and wounded, could never be satisfactorily ascertained. That it was very considerable, there can be no doubt.

The enemy brought against fort Meigs a combined army of near three thousand men, under Proctor, Elliott and Tecumseh, and prepared, by a train of artillery, for vigorous operations. These were prosecuted with skill and energy. The Indians, led on by the daring Tecumseh, fought with uncommon bravery, and contributed largely to swell the list of our killed and wounded. It is said, that the sagacious leader of the Indian forces did not enter upon this siege with any strong hopes of ultimate success; but having embarked in it, he stood manfully in the post of danger, and took an active, if not a leading part, in planning and executing the various movements which were made against the fort. The spirit with which these were prosecuted may be in part inferred from the fact, that during the first five days of the siege, the enemy fired upon the fort with their cannon, fifteen hundred times,* many of their balls and bombs being red-hot, and directed spe-

---

* Brown's History of the Late War.

cially at the two block houses containing the ammunition. These shots made no decided impression upon the picketing of the fort, but killed or wounded about eighty of the garrison.

It has been already stated that the distinguished leader of the Indians, in this assault upon camp Meigs entered upon it with no sanguine hopes of success. His associate, general Proctor, however, is said to have entertained a different opinion, and flattered himself and his troops with the prospect of splendid success and rich rewards. In case of the reduction of the fort and the capture of its garrison, the British general intended to assign the Michigan territory to the Prophet and his followers, as a compensation for their services and general Harrison was to have been delivered into the hands of Tecumseh, to be disposed of at the pleasure of that chief.*

One of the public journals of the day† states that this proposition originated with Proctor, and was held out as an inducement to Tecumseh, to join in the siege General Harrison subsequently understood, that in case he had fallen into Proctor's hands, he was to have been delivered to Tecumseh, to be treated as that warrior might think proper : and in a note to Dawson's Historical Narrative, the author of that work says, " There is no doubt that when Proctor made the arrangement for the attack on fort Meigs with Tecumseh, the latter insisted and the former agreed, that general Harrison and all who fought at Tippecanoe, should be given up to the Indians to be burned. Major Ball of the dragoon ascertained this fact from prisoners, deserters and Indians, all of whom agreed to its truth." Whatever may have been the actual agreement between Proctor and Tecumseh in regard to general Harrison and those who fought with him at Tippecanoe, it is hardly credible that this chief had any intention of participating in an outrage of this kind, upon the prisoners. Tecumseh may possibly have made such an arrangement with Proctor, and announced it to the Indians, for the purpose of exciting them to activity and perseverance, in carrying on the siege ; but that this chief seriously meditated any such outrage, either against general Harrison

---

* M'Affee. † The Chillicothe Fredonian.

or his associates, is not to be credited but on the best authority.   It will be recollected that Tecumseh, when but a youth, succeeded by his personal influence, in putting an end to the custom of burning prisoners, then common among a branch of the Shawanoes.   In 1810, at a conference with general Harrison, in Vincennes, he made an agreement that prisoners and women and children, in the event of hostilities between the whites and the Indians, should be protected; and there is no evidence that this compact was ever violated by him; or indeed, that through the whole course of his eventful life, he ever committed violence upon a prisoner, or suffered others to do so without promptly interfering for the captive.   To suppose, then, that he really intended to permit general Harrison, or those who fought with him on the Wabash, to be burned, would have been at variance with the whole tenor of his life; and particularly with his manly and magnanimous conduct at the close of the assault upon fort Meigs.

The prisoners captured on the fifth, were taken down to Proctor's head-quarters and confined in fort Miami, where the Indians were permitted to amuse themselves by firing at the crowd, or at any particular individual.   Those whose taste led them to inflict a more cruel and savage death, led their victims to the gateway, where, under the eye of general Proctor and his officers, they were coolly tomahawked and scalped. Upwards of twenty prisoners were thus, in the course of two hours, massacred in cold blood, by those to whom they had voluntarily surrendered.   At the same time, the chiefs of the different tribes were holding a council to determine the fate of the remaining captives, when Tecumseh and colonel Elliott came down from the batteries to the scene of carnage.

A detailed account of the noble conduct of the former in regard to these captives is contained in the following extract from a letter,* upon the accuracy of which reliance may be placed.   The writer, after contrasting the brave and humane Tecumseh with the cruel and reckless Proctor, says:

---

* This letter is from Mr. Wm. G. Ewing, formerly of Piqua, O., and is addressed, under date of May 2d, 1818, to John H. James, Esq. now of Urbana.

"The most unfortunate event of that contest, I presume you will admit to have been the defeat of colonel Dudley. I will give you a statement made to me by a British officer who was present. He states, that when colonel Dudley landed his troops, Tecumseh, the brave but unfortunate commander, was on the south side of the river, annoying the American garrison with his Indians; and that Proctor, with a part of his troops and a few Indians, remained on the opposite side at the batteries. Dudley attacked him, and pursued him two miles. During this time, Harrison had sent out a detachment to engage Tecumseh; and that the contest with him continued a considerable length of time, before he was informed of what was doing on the opposite side. He immediately retreated, swam over the river and fell in the rear of Dudley, and attacked him with great fury. Being thus surrounded and their commander killed, the troops marched up to the British line and surrendered. Shortly afterwards, commenced the scene of horrors which I dare say is yet fresh in your memory; but I shall recall it to your recollection for reasons I will hereafter state. They (the American troops) were huddled together in an old British garrison, with the Indians around them, selecting such as their fancy dictated, to glut their savage thirst for murder. And although they had surrendered themselves prisoners of war, yet, in violation of the customs of war, the inhuman Proctor did not yield them the least protection, nor attempt to screen them from the tomahawk of the Indians. Whilst this blood-thirsty carnage was raging, a thundering voice was heard in the rear, in the Indian tongue, when, turning round, he saw Tecumseh coming with all the rapidity his horse could carry him, until he drew near to where two Indians had an American, and were in the act of killing him. He sprang from his horse, caught one by the throat and the other by the breast, and threw them to the ground; drawing his tomahawk and scalping knife, he ran in between the Americans and Indians, brandishing them with the fury of a mad man, and daring any one of the hundreds that surrounded him, to attempt to murder another American. They all appear

Q

ed confounded, and immediately desisted. His mind appeared rent with passion, and he exclaimed almost with tears in his eyes, "Oh! what will become of my Indians." He then demanded in an authoritative tone, where Proctor was; but casting his eye upon him at a small distance, sternly enquired why he had not put a stop to the inhuman massacre. "Sir," said Proctor, "your Indians cannot be commanded." "Begone!" retorted Tecumseh, with the greatest disdain, 'you are unfit to command; go and put on petticoats.'"

This was not the only occasion on which Tecumseh openly manifested the contempt which he felt for the character and conduct of general Proctor. Among other instances, it is stated by an officer of the United States' army, in a letter, under date of 28th September, 1813,* that in a conversation between these two commanders of the allied British army, Tecumseh said to Proctor, "I conquer to save, and you to murder;"—an expression founded in truth, and worthy of the magnanimous hero from whose lips it fell.

There is another incident connected with the defeat of Dudley, which justice to the character of Tecumseh requires should be recorded. Shortly after he had put a stop to the horrid massacre of the prisoners, his attention was called to a small group of Indians occupied in looking at some object in their midst. Colonel Elliott observed to him, "Yonder are four of your nation who have been taken prisoners; you may take charge of them, and dispose of them as you think proper." Tecumseh walked up to the crowd, where he found four Shawanoes, two brothers by the name of Perry, Big Jim, and the Soldier. "Friends," said he, "colonel Elliott has placed you under my charge, and I will send you back to your nation with a talk to our people." He accordingly took them on with the army as far as the river Raisin, from which point their return home would be less dangerous, and then appointed two of his followers to accompany them, with some friendly messages to the chiefs of the Shawanoe nation. They were thus discharged under their parole, not to fight against the British during the war.

* Niles' Register

CHAPTER XIII.

Tecumseh present at the second attack on fort Meigs—his stratagem of a sham-battle to draw out general Clay—is posted in the Black swamp with two thousand warriors at the time of the attack on fort Stephenson —from thence passes by land to Malden—compels general Proctor to release an American prisoner—threatens to desert the British cause— urges an attack upon the American fleet—opposes Proctor's retreat from Malden—delivers a speech to him on that occasion.

AFTER abandoning the siege of fort Meigs, general Proctor and Tecumseh returned to Malden, where the Canadian militia were disbanded, and the Indians, who had not already left the army, for their respective villages, were stationed at different cantonments. The Chippewas preferred going home; the Potawatamies were placed six miles up the river Rouge; the Miamis and Wyandots at Brownstown and up the Detroit river, as far as Maguaga. They were successively employ+ ed by the British commander as scouts, a party being sent regularly, once a week, to reconnoiter fort Meigs, and other points in that vicinity. They planted no corn and hunted but little, being regularly supplied with provisions from Detroit and Malden.

Early in July, the allies of the British again made their appearance in the vicinity of fort Meigs. Dickson, an influential Scotch trader among the Indians, having returned from the north-west with a large body of savages, general Proctor was urged to renew the attack on the fort, and it was accordingly done.

Late on the evening of the 20th of July, the garrison discovered the boats of the British army ascending the river. On the following morning general Clay, now in command of this post, despatched a picket guard of ten men to a point three hundred yards below the fort, where it was surprised by the Indians, and seven of the party either killed or captured. The combined army of British and Indians, were soon afterwards encamped on the north side of the river, below the old British fort Miami. For a short time, the Indians took a position in the woods, in the rear of the fort, from which they occasionally fired upon the garrison, but without doing any injury. In the night, captain William Oliver, accompanied by captain M'Cune, was sent express to general Harrison, then at Lower Sandusky, with information that fort Meigs was again invested; and, that the united force of the enemy did not fall far short of five thousand men. The general directed captain M'Cune to return to the fort, with information to the commander, that so soon as the necessary troops could be assembled, he would march to his relief. The general doubted, however, whether any serious attack was meditated against the place. He believed, and the result showed the accuracy of his judgment, that the enemy was making a feint at the Rapids, to call his attention in that direction, while Lower Sandusky or Cleveland, would be the real point of assault. On the 23d Tecumseh, with about eight hundred Indians, passed up the river, with the intention, as general Clay supposed, of attacking fort Winchester: this movement, as was subsequently ascertained, being also intended to deceive the commander of the fort. On the 25th the enemy removed to the south side of the river, and encamped behind a point of woods which partly concealed them from the view of the garrison. This, taken in connection with other circumstances, led general Clay to think that an effort would be made to carry the post by assault. Early on the morning of the 26th captain M'Cune reached the fort in safety. In the afternoon of that day, the enemy practised a well devised stratagem for the purpose of drawing general Clay and his troops from their fastness. On the Sandusky road, just before night, a heavy firing of rifles and muskets was heard: the Indian yell broke upon the ear, and the savages were seen attacking with great impetuosity a column of men, who were soon thrown into confusion; they, however, rallied, and in turn the Indians gave way. The idea flew through the fort that general Harrison was approaching with a body of reinforcements; and the troops under general Clay seized their arms, and with nearly all the officers in the garrison, demanded to be led to the support of their friends. General Clay was unable to explain the firing, but wisely concluded, from the information received in the morning by captain M'Cune, that there could be no reinforcements in the neighborhood of the fort. He had the prudent firmness to resist the earnest importunity of his officers and men, to be led to the scene of action. The enemy finding that the garrison could not be drawn out, and a heavy shower of rain beginning to fall, terminated their sham-battle. It was subsequently ascertained that this was a stratagem, devised by Tecumseh, for the purpose of decoying out a part of the force under general Clay, which was to have been attacked and cut off by the Indians; while the British troops were to carry the fort by storm. But for the opportune arrival of the express in the morning of this day, and the cool judgment of the commander, there is great reason to suppose that this admirably planned manœuvre would have succeeded; which must have resulted in the total destruction of the garrison, the combined force of the enemy, then investing fort Meigs, being about five thousand in number, while the troops under general Clay were but a few hundred strong. The enemy remained around the fort but one day after the failure of this ingenious stratagem, and on the 28th embarked with their stores, and proceeded down the lake.

As had been anticipated by general Harrison, immediately after the siege was raised, the British troops sailed round into Sandusky bay, while a portion of the Indians marched across the land, to aid in the meditated attack upon fort Stephenson, at lower Sandusky. Tecumseh, in the mean time, with about two thousand warriors, took a position in the great swamp, between that point and fort Meigs, ready to encounter any reinforcement that might have been started to the relief of general Clay, to fall upon the camp at Seneca, or upon Upper Sandusky, according to circumstances. The gallant defence of fort Stephenson by captain Croghan, put a sudden stop to the offensive operations of the army under Proctor and Tecumseh; and very shortly afterwards transferred the scene of action to a new theatre on the Canada shore, where these commanders were, in turn, thrown upon the defensive.

Immediately after the signal defeat of general Proc

tor at fort Stephenson, he returned with the British troops to Malden by water, while Tecumseh and his followers passed over land round the head of lake Erie and joined him at that point. At this time, an incident occurred which illustrates the character of Tecumseh, while it shows the contumely with which he was accustomed to treat general Proctor, who did not dare to disobey him. A citizen of the United States, captain Le Croix, had fallen into the hands of Proctor, and was secreted on board one of the British vessels, until he could be sent down to Montreal. Tecumseh had a particular regard for captain Le Croix, and suspected that he had been captured. He called upon general Proctor, and in a peremptory manner demanded if he knew any thing of his friend. He even ordered the British general to tell him the *truth*, adding, "If I ever detect you in a falsehood, I, with my Indians, will immediately abandon you." The general was obliged to acknowledge that Le Croix was in confinement. Tecumseh, in a very imperious tone, insisted upon his immediate release. General Proctor wrote a line stating, that the "king of the woods" desired the release of captain Le Croix, and that he must be set at liberty; which was done without delay."*

Discouraged by the want of success, and having lost all confidence in general Proctor, Tecumseh now seriously meditated a withdrawal from the contest. He assembled the Shawanoes, Wyandots and Ottawas, who were under his command, and declared his intention to them. He told them, that at the time they took up the tomahawk and agreed to join their father, the king, they were promised plenty of white men to fight with them; "but the number is not now greater," said he, "than at the commencement of the war; and we are treated by them like the dogs of snipe hunters; we are always sent ahead to *start the game:* it is better that we should return to our country, and let the Americans come on and fight the British." To this proposition his followers agreed; but the Sioux and Chippewas, discovering his intention, went to him and insisted that

* Alden Collection.

inasmuch as he had first united with the British, and had been instrumental in bringing their tribes into the alliance, he ought not to leave them; and through their influence he was finally induced to remain.*

Tecumseh was on the island of Bois Blanc, in the Detroit river, when commodore Perry made the first display of his fleet before Malden. He appeared much pleased at the appearance of these vessels, and assured the Indians by whom he was surrounded, that the British fleet would soon destroy them. The Indians hastened to the shore to witness the contest, but the harbour of Malden presented no evidence that commodore Barclay intended to meet the American commander. Tecumseh launched his canoe, and crossed over to Malden to make enquiries on the subject. He called on general Proctor, and adverting to the apparent unwillingness of commodore Barclay to attack the American fleet, he said " a few days since, you were boasting that you commanded the waters—why do you not go out and meet the Americans? See yonder, they are waiting for you, and daring you to meet them : you must and shall send out your fleet and fight them." Upon his return to the island, he stated to the Indians, with apparent chagrin, that " the big canoes of their great father were not yet ready, and that the destruction of the Americans must be delayed for a few days."†

When the battle was finally fought, it was witnessed by the Indians from the shore. On the day succeeding the engagement, general Proctor said to Tecumseh, " my fleet has whipped the Americans, but the vessels being much injured, have gone into Put-in Bay to refit, and will be here in a few days." This deception, however, upon the Indians, was not of long duration. The sagacious eye of Tecumseh soon perceived indications of a retreat from Malden, and he promptly enquired into the matter. General Proctor informed him that he was only going to send their valuable property up the Thames, where it would meet a reinforcement, and be safe. Tecumseh, however, was not to be deceived by this shallow device; and remonstrated most

---

* Anthony Shane.   † Ibid.

urgently against a retreat.   He finally demanded, in the name of all the Indians under his command, to be heard by the general, and, on the 18th of September, delivered to him, as the representative of their great father, the king, the following speech :

"Father, listen to your children! you have them now all before you.

"The war before this, our British father gave the hatchet to his red children, when our old chiefs were alive. They are now dead. In that war our father was thrown on his back by the Americans; and our father took them by the hand without our knowledge ; and we are afraid that our father will do so again at this time.

"Summer before last, when I came forward with my red brethren and was ready to take up the hatchet in favor of our British father, we were told not to be in a hurry, that he had not yet determined to fight the Americans.

"Listen! when war was declared, our father stood up and gave us the tomahawk, and told us that he was then ready to strike the Americans; that he wanted our assistance, and that he would certainly get our lands back, which the Americans had taken from us.

"Listen! you told us at that time, to bring forward our families to this place, and we did so; and you promised to take care of them, and they should want for nothing, while the men would go and fight the enemy ; that we need not trouble ourselves about the enemy's garrisons; that we knew nothing about them, and that our father would attend to that part of the business. You also told your red children that you would take good care of your garrison here, which made our hearts glad.

"Listen! when we were last at the Rapids, it is true we gave you little assistance. It is hard to fight people who live like ground-hogs.

"Father, listen! our fleet has gone out; we know they have fought; we have heard the great guns; but we know nothing of what has happened to our father with one arm.* Our ships have gone one way, and

_____

* Commodore Barclay, who had lost an arm in some previous battle.

we are much astonished to see our father tying up every thing and preparing to run away the other, without letting his red children know what his intentions are. You always told us to remain here and take care of our lands; it made our hearts glad to hear that was your wish. Our great father, the king, is the head, and you represent him. You always told us you would never draw your foot off British ground; but now, father, we see that you are drawing back, and we are sorry to see our father doing so without seeing the enemy. We must compare our father's conduct to a fat dog, that carries his tail on its back, but when affrighted, drops it between its legs and runs off.

" Father, listen! the Americans have not yet defeated us by land; neither are we sure that they have done so by water; *we, therefore, wish to remain here and fight our enemy, should they make their appearance.* If they defeat us, we will then retreat with our father.

" At the battle of the Rapids, last war, the Americans certainly defeated us; and when we returned to our father's fort at that place, the gates were shut against us. We were afraid that it would now be the case; but instead of that, we now see our British father preparing to march out of his garrison.

" Father, you have got the arms and ammunition which our great father sent for his red children. If you have an idea of going away, give them to us, and you may go and welcome, for us. Our lives are in the hands of the Great Spirit. We are determined to defend our lands, and if it be his will, we wish to leave our bones upon them."

General Proctor, in disregarding the advice of Tecumseh, lost his only opportunity of making an effective resistance to the American army. Had the troops under general Harrison been attacked by the British and Indians at the moment of their landing on the Canada shore, the result might have been far different from that which was shortly afterwards witnessed on the banks of the Thames. Of the authenticity of this able speech, there is no doubt. It has been the cause of some surprise that it should have been preserved by general Proctor, and translated into English, especially as it speaks of the commander of the allied army in terms the most disrespectful. We are enabled to state, on the authority of John Chambers, Esq. of Washington, Kentucky, who was one of the aids of general Harrison in the campaign of 1813, that the speech as given above, is truly translated; and was actually de-delivered to general Proctor under the circumstances above related. When the battle of the Thames had been fought, the British commander sought safety in flight. He was pursued by colonels Wood, Chambers, and Todd, and three or four privates. He escaped, but his baggage was captured. Colonel Chambers was present when his port-folio was opened, and among the papers, a translation of this speech was found. In remarking upon the fact subsequently, to some of the British officers, they stated to colonel Chambers that the speech was undoubtedly genuine; and that general Proctor had ordered it to be translated and exhibited to his officers, for the purpose of showing them the insolence with which he was treated by Tecumseh, and the necessity he was under of submitting to every species of indignity from him, to prevent that chief from withdrawing his forces from the contest or turning his army against the British troops.

CHAPTER XIV.

Retreat of the combined British and Indian army to the river Thames—skirmish at Chatham with the troops under general Harrison—Tecumseh slightly wounded in the arm—battle on the Thames on the 5th of October—Tecumseh's death.

SHORTLY after the delivery of the speech quoted in the foregoing chapter, a considerable body of Indians abandoned general Proctor, and crossed the strait to the American shore. Tecumseh himself again manifested a disposition to take his final leave of the British service. Embittered by the perfidy of Proctor, his men suffering from want of clothes and provisions, with the prospect of a disgraceful flight before them, he was

strongly inclined to withdraw with his followers; and
leave the American general to chastise in a summary
manner those who had so repeatedly deceived him
and his Indian followers. The Sioux and Chippewas,
however, again objected to this course. *They* could
not, they said, withdraw, and there was no other leader
but Tecumseh, in whom they placed confidence : they
insisted that he was the person who had originally induced them to join the British, and that he ought not
to desert them in the present extremity. Tecumseh, in
reply to this remonstrance emarked, that the battle-
field had no terrors for him; he feared not death, and
if they insisted upon it, he would remain with them.

General Proctor now proposed to the Indians to remove their women and children to McGee's, opposite
the river Rouge, where they would be furnished with
their winter's clothing and the necessary supplies of
food. To this proposition, Tecumseh yielded a reluctant assent; doubting, as he did, the truth of the statement. When they were about to start, he observed to
young Jim Blue-Jacket, " we are now going to follow
the British, and I feel well assured, that we shall never return." When they arrived at McGee's, Tecumseh
found that there were no stores provided for them, as
had been represented. Proctor made excuses; and
again pledged himself to the Indians, that if they would
go with him to the Thames, they would there find an
abundance of every thing needful to supply their
wants; besides a reinforcement of British troops, and a
fort ready for their reception.*

The retreat was continued towards the Thames. On
the second of October, when the army had reached
Dalson's farm, Proctor and Tecumseh, attended by a
small guard, returned to examine the ground at a place
called Chatham, where a deep, unfordable creek falls
into the Thames. They were riding together in a gig,
and after making the necessary examination, the ground
was approved of; and general Proctor remarked, upon
that spot they would either defeat general Harrison or
there lay their bones. With this determination Tecum-

* Anthony Shane.

seh was highly pleased, and said, "it was a good place, and when he should look at the two streams, they would remind him of the Wabash and the Tippecanoe." Perhaps no better position could have been chosen for meeting the American army than this place presented. The allied force of British and Indians, had they made a stand upon it, would have been protected in front by a deep unfordable stream, while their right flank would have been covered by the Thames, and their left by a swamp. But general Proctor changed his mind; and leaving Tecumseh with a body of Indians to defend the passage of the stream, moved forward with the main army. Tecumseh made a prompt and judicious arrangement of his forces; but it is said that his Indians, in the skirmish which ensued, did not sustain their previous reputation as warriors. It is probable, however, that their leader did not intend to make any deci ded resistance to the American troops at this point, not being willing that general Proctor and his army should escape a meeting with the enemy. In this action Tecumseh was slightly wounded in the arm by a ball General Harrison, in his official report of this affair says:

"Below a place called Chatham, and four miles above Dalson's, is the third unfordable branch of the Thames: the bridge over its mouth had been taken up by the Indians, as well as that at M'Gregor's mills, one mile above—several hundred of the Indians remained to dispute our passage, and upon the arrival of the advanced guard, commenced a heavy fire from the opposite bank of the creek, as well as that of the river Believing that the whole force of the enemy was there, I halted the army, formed in order of battle, and brought up our two six pounders, to cover the party that were ordered to repair the bridge. A few shot from these pieces soon drove off the Indians, and enabled us in two hours to repair the bridge and cross the troops. Colonel Johnson's mounted regiment being upon the right of the army, had seized the remains of the bridge at the mills, under a heavy fire from the Indians. Our loss upon this occasion was two killed, and three or four wounded; that of the enemy was ascertained

to be considerably greater. A house near the bridge, containing a very considerable number of muskets, had been set on fire; but it was extinguished by our troops and the arms saved."

Tecumseh and his party overtook the main army near the Moravian towns, situated on the north side of the Thames. Here he resolved that he would retreat no further; and the ground being favorable for forming the line of battle, he communicated his determination to general Proctor, and compelled him, as there is every reason for believing, to put an end to his retreat, and prepare for meeting the pursuing army. After the Indians were posted in the swamp, in the position occupied by them during the battle, Tecumseh remarked to the chiefs by whom he was surrounded, "brother warriors! we are now about to enter into an engagement from which I shall never come out—my body will remain on the field of battle." He then unbuckled his sword, and placing it in the hands of one of them, said, "when my son becomes a noted warrior, and able to wield a sword, give this to him." He then laid aside his British military dress, and took his place in the line, clothed only in the ordinary deer-skin hunting shirt.*

The position selected by the enemy was eminently judicious. The British troops, amounting to eight or nine hundred, were posted with their left upon the river, which was unfordable at that point; their right extended to and across a swamp, and united them with the Indians, under Tecumseh, amounting to near eighteen hundred. The British artillery was placed in the road along the margin of the river, near to the left of their line. At from two to three hundred yards from the river, a swamp extends nearly parallel to it, the intermediate ground being dry. This position of the enemy, with his flank protected on the left by the river and on the right by the swamp, filled with Indians, being such as to prevent the wings from being turned, general Harrison made arrangements to concentrate his forces against the British line. The first division, under

---

* Anthony Shane, and colonel Baubee of the British army.

R

major general Henry, was formed in three lines at one
hundred yards from each other; the front line consisting of Trotter's brigade, the second of Chiles', and the
reserve of King's brigade. These lines were in front
of, and parallel to, the British troops. The second division, under major general Desha, composed of Allen's
and Caldwell's brigades, was formed *en potence*, or at
right angles to the first division. Governor Shelby, as
senior major general of the Kentucky troops, was posted at this crotchet, formed between the first and second
divisions. Colonel Simrall's regiment of light infantry
was formed in reserve, obliquely to the first division,
and covering the rear of the front division; and, after
much reflection as to the disposition to be made of colonel Johnson's mounted troops, they were directed, as
soon as the front line advanced, to take ground to the
left, and forming upon that flank, to endeavor to turn
the right of the Indians. A detachment of regular
troops, of the 26th United States infantry, under colonel Paul, occupied the space between the road and the
river, for the purpose of seizing the enemy's artillery;
and, simultaneously with this movement, forty friendly
Indians were to pass under the bank of the stream to
the rear of the British line, and by their fire and war-
cry, induce the enemy to think their own Indians were
turning against them. At the same time, colonel Wood
had been instructed to make preparations for using the
enemy's artillery, and to rake their own line by a flank
fire. By refusing the left or second division, the Indians were kept *in the air*, that is, in a position in which
they would be useless. It will be seen, as the com
mander anticipated, that they waited in their position
the advance of the second division, while the British
left was contending with the American right. John
son's corps consisted of nine hundred men, and the
five brigades under governor Shelby amounted to near
eighteen hundred, in all, not exceeding two thousand
seven hundred men.

In the midst of these arrangements, and just as the
order was about to be given to the front line to advance, at the head of which general Harrison had pla
ced himself with his staff, colonel Wood approached

him with intelligence, that having reconnoitered the enemy, he had ascertained the singular fact, that the British lines, instead of the usual close order, were drawn up at *open order*. This fact at once induced general Harrison to adopt the novel expedient of charging the British lines with Johnson's mounted regiment. "I was within a few feet of him," says the gallant colonel John O'Fallon, " when the report of colonel Wood was made, and he instantly remarked, that he would make a novel movement by ordering colonel Johnson's mounted regiment to charge the British line of regulars, which, thus drawn up, contrary to the habits and usages of that description of troops, always accustomed to *the touch*, could be easily penetrated and thrown into confusion, by a spirited charge of colonel Johnson's regiment." This determination was presently made known to the colonel, who was directed to draw up his regiment in close column, with its right fifty yards from the road—that it might be partially protected by the trees from the artillery—its left upon the swamp, and to charge at full speed upon the enemy.

At this juncture, general Harrison, with his aids-de-camp, attended likewise by general Cass and commodore Perry, advanced from the right of the front line of infantry, to the right of the front column of mounted troops, led by colonel James Johnson. The general, personally, gave the direction for the charge to be made. " When the right battalion of the mounted men received the first fire of the British, the horses in the front column recoiled; another fire was given by the enemy, but our column getting in motion, broke through the enemy with irresistible force. In one minute the contest was over. The British officers seeing no prospect of reducing their disordered ranks to order, and seeing the advance of the infantry, and our mounted men wheeling upon them and pouring in a destructive fire, immediately surrendered."*

Colonel Richard M. Johnson, by the extension of his line, was brought in contact with the Indians, upon whom he gallantly charged, but was unfortunately se-

* Official Despatch.

verely wounded by the first fire of the enemy, and was immediately taken off the field, not, however, it has been stated, until he had despatched an Indian by a pistol shot. The fire of the Indians having made some impression upon Johnson's men, and upon the left of Trotter's brigade, general Harrison despatched an order to governor Shelby to bring up Simrall's regiment to reinforce the point pressed by the Indians; and then the general passed to the left, to superintend the operations in that quarter. The governor, however, had anticipated the wishes of his commander, being in the act of leading up the regiment, when the order reached him. He and the general met near the crochet, where after a severe contest of several minutes, the battle finally ceased. The particulars of the charge made by colonel Johnson on the Indians, are thus given by an intelligent officer* of his corps. In a letter to the late governor Wickliffe of Kentucky, under date of Frankfort, September 7, 1840, he says:

"I was at the head or right of my company, on horseback, waiting orders, at about fifty or sixty yards from the line of the enemy. Colonel Johnson rode up and explained to me the mode of attack, and said in substance, "captain Davidson, I am directed by general Harrison to charge and break through the Indian line, and form in the rear. My brother James will charge in like manner through the British line at the same time. The sound of the trumpet will be the signal for the charge." In a few minutes the trumpet sounded, and the word "charge" was given by colonel Johnson. The colonel charged within a few paces of me. We struck the Indian line obliquely, and when we approached within ten or fifteen yards of their line, the Indians poured in a heavy fire upon us, killing ten or fifteen of our men and several horses, and wounded colonel Johnson very severely. He immediately retired. Doctor Theobald, of Lexington, (I think) aided him off."

The loss of the Americans in this battle was about twenty killed and between thirty and forty wounded. The British had eighteen killed and twenty-six wound-

* Captain James Davidson, of Kentucky.—See Cincinnati Republican.

ed. The Indians left on the ground between fifty and sixty killed; and, estimating the usual proportion for the wounded, it was probably more than double that number.

The British official account of this action is not before us. In a general order under date of Montreal, November 21, 1813, the adjutant general of the English forces, bears testimony to the good conduct of the Indian warriors, who gallantly maintained the conflict under the brave chief Tecumseh. This tribute to the Indians and their leader is well merited. Had general Proctor and his troops fought with the same valor that marked the conduct of Tecumseh and his men, the results of the day would have been far more creditable to the British arms. It has already been stated that Tecumseh entered this battle with a strong conviction on his mind that he should not survive it. Further flight he deemed disgraceful, while the hope of victory in the impending action, was feeble and distant. He, however, heroically resolved to achieve the latter or die in the effort. With this determination, he took his stand among his followers, raised the war-cry and boldly met the enemy. From the commencement of the attack on the Indian line, his voice was distinctly heard by his followers, animating them to deeds worthy of the race to which they belonged. When that well known voice was heard no longer above the din of arms, the battle ceased. The British troops having already surrendered, and the gallant leader of the Indians having fallen, they gave up the contest and fled. A short distance from where Tecumseh fell, the body of his friend and brother-in-law, Wasegoboah, was found. They had often fought side by side, and now, in front of their men, bravely battling the enemy, they side by side closed their mortal career.[*]

James, a British historian,[†] in his account of the battle of the Thames, makes the following remarks upon the character and personal appearance of Tecumseh.

" Thus fell the Indian warrior Tecumseh, in the 44th year of his age. He was of the Shawanoe tribe, five

---

* Anthony Shane.   † Military Occurrences of the Late War.

R 2

feet ten inches high, and with more than the usual
stoutness, possessed all the agility and perseverance of
the Indian character. His carriage was dignified, his
eye penetrating, his countenance, which even in death,
betrayed the indications of a lofty spirit, rather of the
sterner cast. Had he not possessed a certain austerity
of manners, he could never have controlled the way-
ward passions of those who followed him to battle.
He was of a silent habit; but when his eloquence became roused into action by the reiterated encroachments of the Americans, his strong intellect could supply him with a flow of oratory that enabled him, as he
governed in the field, so to prescribe in the council.
Those who consider that in all territorial questions, the
ablest diplomatists of the United States are sent to
negociate with the Indians, will readily appreciate the
loss sustained by the latter in the death of their cham-
pion. ＊　＊　＊　＊　Such a man was the unlettered
savage, Tecumseh, and such a man have the Indians
lost forever. He has left a son, who, when his father
fell, was about seventeen years old, and fought by his
side. The prince regent, in 1814, out of respect to the
memory of the old, sent out as a present to the young,
Tecumseh, a handsome sword. Unfortunately, however, for the Indian cause and country, faint are the
prospects that Tecumseh the son, will ever equal, in
wisdom or prowess, Tecumseh the father."

Mr. James (p. 295,) asserts, that Tecumseh was not
only scalped, but that his body was actually *flayed*, and
the skin converted into razor-straps by the Kentuckians.
We fear there is too much truth in this statement. It
is confirmed by the testimony of several American
officers and privates, who were in the battle of the
Thames. It is painful to make an admission of this
kind, but truth forbids the suppression of a fact, when
fairly established, however revolting to the feelings of
humanity, or degrading to a people. That there was
any general participation of our troops in this inhuman
and revolting deed, is not for a moment to be supposed. That it was the act of a few vulgar and brutish
individuals, is, we think, just as certain, as that the
great mass of the army were shocked at its perpetra-

tion. It is to be regretted that the names of the persons who committed this outrage have not been preserved, that their conduct on this occasion might have been held up to universal condemnation.

CHAPTER XV.

Critical examination of the question "who killed Tecumseh?"—colonel R. M. Johnson's claim considered.

TECUMSEH was a determined and subtle enemy of the United States, and during the palmy days of his bold career, wielded an influence over the north-western Indians which belonged to no other chief. His death was consequently an important circumstance in relation to the peace and safety of the frontiers. But whether he fell by a pistol shot from a field officer, or a rifle ball from a private soldier, however interesting as a matter of personal history, is certainly not one of national importance. Nevertheless, the question by whose hands he fell, has engaged public attention to some considerable extent ever since the memorable battle of the Thames. Its discussion has not been confined to the immediate friends of the several aspirants for the honor of having slain this distinguished warrior; it has enlivened the political canvass, and the halls of legislation; occupied the columns of journals and magazines, and filled no inconsiderable space on the pages of American and British histories. Under such circumstances, and as directly connected with the present biography, a fair presentation of all the testimony bearing on the case will now be attempted. It may at least gratify the public curiosity, if it do not definitively settle the long pending question in relation to the actual *slayer of Tecumseh*.

M'Affee, in his History of the Late War, says, Tecumseh "was found among the dead, at the point where colonel Johnson had charged upon the enemy, in person, and it is generally believed, that this celebrated chief fell by the hand of the colonel. It is certain that the latter killed the Indian with his pistol, who shot him through his hand, at the very spot where Tecumseh lay; but another dead body lay at the same place, and Mr. King, a soldier in captain Davidson's company, had the honor of killing one of them."

Brown, in his history of the same war, says, that "colonel Johnson, after receiving four wounds, perceived the daring Tecumseh commanding and attempting to rally his savage force; when he instantly put his horse towards him, and was shot by Tecumseh in the hand, as he approached him. Tecumseh advanced with a drawn weapon, a sword or tomahawk, at which instant the colonel, having reserved his fire, shot his ferocious antagonist dead at his feet; and that too, at the moment he was almost fainting with the loss of blood and the anguish of five wounds."

The statement of Shawbeneh, a Potawatamie chief, lately published in the "Chicago Democrat," goes to prove that Tecumseh was wounded in the neck; and telling his warriors that he must die, rushed forward to kill colonel Johnson. Shawbeneh saw him fall, having been shot by the colonel, just as his arm had reached the necessary height to strike the fatal blow. Shawbeneh says that colonel Johnson was riding a large white horse, with occasionally a jet black spot. He further states that Tecumseh's body was not mutilated by the American troops.

The testimony of another Potawatamie chief, Chamblee, as furnished us by captain Robert Anderson, of the U. S. army, is to this effect:

He saw Tecumseh engaged in a personal rencontre with a soldier armed with a musket; that the latter made a thrust at the chief, who caught the bayonet under his arm, where he held it, and was in the act of striking his opponent with his tomahawk, when a horseman rode up, and shot Tecumseh dead with a pistol. The horseman had a red feather, (plume) in his hat, and was mounted on a spotted or red-roan horse; he further says, that he saw the body of Tecumseh a day or two after the battle, and that it was not mutilated.

In a work entitled "History of the Indian Tribes of North America," there is the following note:

"A Potawatamie chief was thus questioned: Were you at the battle of the Thames? Yes. Did you know Tecumseh? Yes. Were you near him in the fight? Yes. Did you see him fall? Yes. Who shot him? Don't know. Did you see the man that shot him? Yes. What sort of looking man was he? Short, thick man. What color was the horse he rode? Most white. How do you know this man shot Tecumseh? I saw the man ride up—saw his horse get tangled in some bushes—when the horse was most still, I saw Tecumseh level his rifle at the man and shoot—the man shook on his horse—soon the horse got out of the bushes, and the man spurred him up—horse came slow —Tecumseh right before him—man's left hand hung down—just as he got near, Tecumseh lifted his tomahawk and was going to throw it, when the man shot him with a short gun (pistol)—Tecumseh fell dead and we all ran."

Mr. Garrett Wall, of Kentucky, who participated in the battle of the Thames, says:

"—— The men by this time had collected in groups; and it was remarked that colonel R. M. Johnson was dead, but I contradicted the report; also, that the great Indian commander, Tecumseh, was slain; I asked by what authority? I was told that Anthony Shane, who had known him from a small boy, said so, and had seen him among the slain. In a short time I saw Shane with a small group of men, walking towards a dead Indian; as he approached the body, I asked him if he knew that Indian. He said it was, in his opinion, Tecumseh; but he could tell better if the blood was taken from his face. I examined the Indian. He was shot in the left side of the breast with several balls or buck shot, all entering near and above the left nipple. There was also a wound in his head, too small for a rifle ball to make."

Atwater, in his History of Ohio, remarks, that two Winnebago chiefs, Four-Legs and Carymaunee, told him, that Tecumseh, at the commencement of the battle of the Thames, lay with his warriors in a thicket of

underbrush on the left of the American army, and that
they were, at no period of the battle, out of their covert
—that no officer was seen between them and the American troops—that Tecumseh fell the very first fire of
the Kentucky dragoons, pierced by thirty bullets, and
was carried four or five miles into the thick woods and
there buried by the warriors, who told the story of his
fate.

In 1838, a writer in the Baltimore American published Black Hawk's account of the fall of Tecumseh.
It is as follows:

"——— Shortly after this, the Indian spies came in
and gave word of the near approach of the Americans.
Tecumseh immediately posted his men in the edge of a
swamp, which flanked the British line, placing himself
at their head. I was a little to his right with a small
party of Sauks. It was not long before the Americans
made their appearance; they did not perceive us at
first, hid as we were by the undergrowth, but we soon
let them know where we were, by pouring in one or
two vollies as they were forming into line to oppose
the British. They faltered a little; but very soon we
perceived a large body of horse (colonel Johnson's regiment of mounted Kentuckians) preparing to charge
upon us in the swamp. They came bravely on; yet
we never stirred until they were so close that we could
see the flints in their guns, when Tecumseh, springing
to his feet, gave the Shawanoe war-cry, and discharged
his rifle. This was the signal for us to commence the
battle, but it did not last long; the Americans answered
the shout, returning our fire, and at the first discharge
of their guns, I saw Tecumseh stagger forwards over a
fallen tree, near which he was standing, letting his rifle
drop at his feet. As soon as the Indians discovered
that he was killed, a sudden fear came over them, and
thinking the Great Spirit was angry, they fought no
longer, and were quickly put to flight. That night we
returned to bury our dead; and search for the body of
Tecumseh. He was found lying where he had first
fallen; a bullet had struck him above the hip, and his
skull had been broken by the butt end of the gun of
some soldier, who had found him, perhaps, when life

was not yet quite gone. With the exception of these wounds, his body was untouched: lying near him was a large fine looking Potawatamie, who had been killed, decked off in his plumes and war-paint, whom the Americans no doubt had taken for Tecumseh, for he was scalped and every particle of skin flayed from his body. Tecumseh himself had no ornaments about his person, save a British medal. During the night, we buried our dead, and brought off the body of Tecumseh, although we were in sight of the fires of the American camp."

James, a British historian,[*] after describing the battle of the Thames, remarks:

"It seems extraordinary that general Harrison should have omitted to mention in his letter, the death of a chief, whose fall contributed so largely to break down the Indian spirit, and to give peace and security to the whole north-western frontier of the United States. Tecumseh, although he had received a musket ball in the left arm, was still seeking the hottest of the fire, when ne encountered colonel Richard M. Johnson, member of congress from Kentucky. Just as the chief, having discharged his rifle, was rushing forward with his tomahawk, he received a ball in the head from the colonel's pistol. Thus fell the Indian warrior, Tecumseh, in the forty-fourth year of his age.* * * * * * The body of Tecumseh was recognized, not only by the British officers, who were prisoners, but by commodore Perry, and several American officers."

This writer adds, that Tecumseh was scalped and his body flayed by the Kentuckians.

In Butler's History of Kentucky, there is a letter from the reverend Obediah B. Brown, of Washington city, then a clerk in the general post-office, under date of 18th September, 1834, in which the writer says, in substance:

That colonel Johnson, while leading the advance upon the left wing of the Indians, saw an Indian commander, who appeared to be a rallying point for his

---

[*] "Military Occurrences of the Late War between Great Britain and the United States, by William James, 2 vols. London, 1818."

savage companions, and whose costume indicated the superiority of his rank; that colonel Johnson, sitting upon his horse, covered with wounds and very faint with the loss of blood, and having a pistol in his right hand loaded with a ball and three buck-shot, thought that the fate of the battle depended upon killing this formidable chief, and he accordingly rode round a fallen tree for this purpose; that the chief, perceiving his approach, levelled his rifle and shot the colonel in the left hand; that the colonel continued to advance upon him, and at the moment when the Indian was raising his tomahawk, shot him dead with his pistol; that this deed spread consternation among the savages, and with hideous yells, they began from that point their retreat; that as soon as the battle ended, the Indian killed by colonel Johnson was recognized as Tecumseh; and before the colonel had so far recovered from the effects of his wounds as to be able to speak, word ran through the army that he had killed Tecumseh; and finally, that a medal was taken from the body which was known to have been presented to this chief by the British government. Mr. Brown further states, that a conversation which he had with Anthony Shane, some years since, strengthened his belief that Tecumseh fell by the hand of colonel Johnson; that Shane told him he went, after the battle, to the spot where it was reported the colonel had killed an Indian, and there he saw the dead body of Tecumseh, and that he must have been killed by a horseman, as a ball and three buck-shot had entered the breast and passed downwards; that he could not be mistaken as to the body of Tecumseh, as he had a remarkable scar upon his thigh, which, upon examination, was found as he had described it.

By recurring to the foregoing statements, it will be seen that eight Indians have borne testimony in relation to the death of Tecumseh. Of these, four assert that he was killed by the first fire from the American line; and four that he fell by the hands of a horseman, some time after the commencement of the action. One of these witnesses states that Tecumseh was shot in the neck; another, that he was hit above or in the eyes two others that he was killed by a ball in the hip; and again two others, that he was pierced by thirty bullets on the first fire of our troops. Three of these witnesses testify that the body of the fallen chief was mutilated by taking the skin from off the thigh, and three that it was not. One of them saw the body the day after the action, lying on the battle ground; a second bears witness that it was buried on the spot the night of the battle; and a third, that it was carried four or five miles into the woods, and there interred. A further examination of the testimony will show that these eight witnesses concur but in one single point,—that Tecumseh was killed in the battle of the Thames. As to the nature of his wounds, the mutilation of his body, the time when, the spot where, and by whose hands, he fell, these various statements are wholly irreconcilable with each other, and leave the main question involved in additional doubt and obscurity.

As the claim of colonel Johnson to the honor of having killed Tecumseh, has been recently and earnestly urged upon the public consideration, we propose, even at the risk of some repetition, to examine in detail the testimony which bears upon this point.

It will be recollected that the Potawatamie chief, whose narrative is quoted from the "History of the Indian Tribes of North America," testifies that Tecumseh met his death by a wound above or in the eyes; and, that upon his fall the Indians ran. If these statements be true, Tecumseh could not have been killed by colonel Johnson, as will be satisfactorily established in the course of this examination.

Shawbeneh, another Potawatamie chief, states that Tecumseh was mortally wounded in the neck, before he rushed upon the individual who killed him. All the other witnesses, except one, say that Tecumseh remained stationary, and that the horseman who fired the fatal shot, advanced upon him.

Chamblee, the third Potawatamie who testifies in the case, states that Tecumseh was engaged in a personal conflict with a soldier armed with a musket, when a horseman, on a spotted horse, rode up and shot him

S

dead with a pistol. This account is not sustained by any other witness.

Captain M'Affee, who belonged to the mounted regiment, and who has written a history of the late war, says, it is *generally believed that Tecumseh fell by the hand of colonel Johnson;* but the historian candidly admits that there was another dead Indian at the spot where Tecumseh lay, and that Mr. King, of captain Davidson's company, killed one of them. It may be questioned whether there is or ever has been any *general belief,*—whatever vague reports may have been circulated,—that colonel Johnson killed this chief; but even if such were the case, it does not by any means establish the allegation.

Brown, another historian of the late war, says, in general terms, that Tecumseh advanced upon the colonel with a sword or tomahawk, and that the colonel shot him dead. Tecumseh wore no sword in that action, nor did he advance upon colonel Johnson. Mr. Brown cites no authorities for his loose and general statements.

Garrett Wall testifies that he went to the spot where he was told colonel Johnson had fought, and there questioned Anthony Shane about the dead Indian before them. Shane remarked that he could tell better whether it was Tecumseh, if the blood was washed from the face. It does not appear that this was done, nor that Shane became satisfied as to the identity of the dead Indian. Mr. Wall infers that Tecumseh fell by a shot from colonel Johnson, because it was so reported, and because they both led their warriors to the charge, and the desire of victory brought them together. Mr. Wall cites no evidence to prove that the body over which Shane was doubting, fell by the colonel—a link in the chain of testimony, altogether important in making out his case.

The Rev. Obediah B. Brown, however, at Washington, is by far the most precise in his statements, of all the witnesses. But it is proper, before entering upon the examination of his testimony, to state that he was not at the battle of the Thames; and that his letter, in regard to Tecumseh's death, was written in 1834, more than twenty years after the action was fought, and upon the eve of a political campaign, in which his friend, colonel Johnson, was an aspirant for a high and honorable office. Mr. Brown, it is further proper to add, derived his information from "several persons," but he has inadvertently omitted the names of all but one.

He commences by saying, that colonel Johnson saw an Indian known to be a chief by his costume. Now it has been already shown that Tecumseh entered the action dressed in the plain deer-skin garb of his tribe, having nothing about him which would indicate his rank. The colonel thought, continues Mr. B., that the fate of the day depended upon the fall of this chief. The question might be asked whether the thoughts of colonel Johnson, at this particular juncture, became known to the witness by a logical process of ratiocination, or by a direct personal communication from his distinguished friend? He states further, that the colonel rode up within a few feet of the chief, received his fire, and then shot him dead with his pistol. This act, says the witness, caused the savages to retreat in consternation: now, the fact is well established, that the Indians, at this very point, fought bravely for twenty or twenty-five minutes after colonel Johnson was compelled, by his wounds, to leave the scene of action: it is further stated by Mr. B. that before the colonel was so far recovered from his wounds, as to be able to speak, it ran through the army that he had killed Tecumseh. Mr. Wall, who was in the action, says, that after colonel Johnson had retired from the contest, and was lifted from his horse, he said to those around him, "my brave men, the battle continues, leave me, and do not return until you bring me an account of the victory." Thus it would seem that the colonel, within a few minutes after receiving his last wound, was giving orders to his men, and in the mean time, according to Mr. B., "word ran through the army that he had killed Tecumseh." This is more remarkable, when it is recollected, that the only person, except the commanding general, who could identify the fallen chief, was Anthony Shane, and he was in a different part of the field, (on the bank of the Thames) and did not visit this part of the line until the action was entirely over! The witness further states, that no other chief of high rank was killed in this part of the line, but Tecumseh. Anthony Shane says that Tecumseh's brother-in-law, and principal chief, Wasegoboah, was killed ten or fifteen steps from where Tecumseh fell. Black Hawk also testifies, that near Tecumseh, there was lying a large, fine looking Potawatamie, decked off in his plumes and war-paint, whom the Americans mistook for Tecumseh. Mr. B. says that a medal was taken from the body of the Indian killed by colonel Johnson, which was known to have been presented by the British government to Tecumseh. Where is the authority for this? When Shane was examining the body, and so much in doubt whether it was Tecumseh as to require the blood to be washed from the face, before he could decide with certainty, where was this medal, which of itself would have settled the question of identity? It is singular, that neither Shane nor Wall speaks of a medal. Mr. B. says that Tecumseh was killed by a ball and three buckshot, fired by a horseman, and as colonel Johnson was the only person in that part of the battle who fought on horseback, his pistols being loaded with a ball and three buckshot, settles the question, that the colonel killed Tecumseh. Again, the question may be asked, how Mr. B. knows the fact as to the manner in which these pistols were loaded? And if they were so loaded, who can say whether the chief was killed by this shot, the wound in the eyes, that in the neck, or the one in the hip? But again; colonel Johnson was not the only person who fought on horseback in this part of the battle. He led a "forlorn hope" of twenty men, all mounted; while on his left was Davidson's company of one hundred and forty men, also on horseback. Mr. Wall, who was one of the "forlorn hope," says, "the fighting became very severe, each party mingling with the other." Finally, Mr. B. closes his testimony with the remark, that it was well known and acknowledged, by the British and Indians, at the time, that Tecumseh received his death from the hand of colonel Johnson, as appears by James' History of the Late War. It is stated by the historian here cited, that colonel Johnson shot Tecumseh in the head—that the body was recognized not only by the British officers who were prisoners, but by commodore Perry and several other American officers: Mr. James also expresses his surprise that general Harrison should have omitted, in his official letter to the War Department, to mention the death of this chief. Now, we have the authority of several American officers, of high rank, for stating, that these British officers were not, on the evening of the day on which the action was fought, in that part of the line where Tecumseh fell; and that early on the ensuing morning, they were taken to a house two miles below the battle ground, and from thence to Detroit, without returning to the scene of their defeat. Mr. James is, therefore, incorrect on this point, as he certainly is, in saying that commodore Perry and other American officers recognized the body of Tecumseh. The commodore had never seen this chief prior to the afternoon of the battle in which he fell. General Harrison, it is believed, was the only American officer in the engagement, who had a personal knowledge of Tecumseh. The day after the battle, the general, attended by several of his officers, visited the battle ground. The body of the Indian, supposed to be that of Tecumseh, was pointed out to him, but owing to its swollen condition, he was unable to say whether it was Tecumseh, or a Potawatamie chief, who usually visited Vincennes in company with him: he felt confident it was one of the two, but further than this could not pronounce with certainty. Mr. James and Anthony Shane are Mr. Brown's chief witnesses. The first states that Tecumseh was shot with a musket ball in the arm, and finally killed by a ball in the head from colonel Johnson's pistol: the second testifies that he fell by a ball and three buckshot which entered his left breast, and that he was wounded in no other part: the former says that Tecumseh's body was literally flayed—the latter, that only a small piece of skin was cut from one of his thighs.* It re-

---

* See James'. Military Occurrences, and Anthony Shane's Narrative.

s 2

mains for Mr. Brown to reconcile these glaring dis-
crepancies in the testimony of his own witnesses.   If
this dissection of Mr. Brown's elaborated letter, presents him more in the light of the partizan advocate
than the faithful historian, we are not responsible for
it; and if he has failed to establish the fact that colonel
Johnson killed Tecumseh, he must probably look for
the reason of that failure in the weakness of his claims,
rather than in any lack of zeal in advocating the colonel's cause.

Our analysis of the testimony which has at different
times been brought before the public, tending to establish the supposition that Tecumseh fell by the hands of
colonel Johnson, is now closed; and we think it will
be admitted, in reviewing the case, that the claims of
the colonel have not been satisfactorily established,
either by direct or circumstantial evidence.   But we
have further testimony to offer on this point.

It is proved by a number of witnesses, and among
them several who are relied upon to establish the fact,
that colonel Johnson killed Tecumseh, that upon the
fall of this chief, the action ceased and the Indians fled.

Even the reverend Mr. Brown admits such to have
been the case.   Now, we propose to show that colonel
Johnson was wounded and retired from the scene of
action at its commencement; and that the contest lasted
for twenty or thirty minutes afterwards.   As to the
first point, captain Davidson, who was by the side of
colonel Johnson, says, "We struck the Indian line obliquely, and when we approached within ten or fifteen
yards of their line, the Indians poured in a heavy fire
upon us, killing ten or fifteen of our men and several
horses, and wounding colonel Johnson very severely.
He immediately retired."*   Colonel Ambrose Dudley
says, "As I passed to the left, near the crochet, after the
firing had ceased on the right, I met colonel R. M.
Johnson passing diagonally from the swamp towards
the line of infantry, and spoke with him.   He said he
was badly wounded, his gray mare bleeding profusely
in several places.   The battle continued with the In-

---

* Cincinnati Republican, 30th September, 1840.

dians on the left. The infantry, with some of colonel R. M. Johnson's troops mixed up promiscuously with them, continued the battle for half an hour after colonel Johnson was disabled and had ceased to command his men."* Doctor S. Theobald, of Lexington, Kentucky, one of the surgeons to the mounted regiment, says, "colonel Johnson was wounded in the onset of the battle. I had the honor to compose one of his " forlorn hope," and followed him in the charge. It is impossible, under such circumstances, to estimate time with precision; but I know the period was a very brief one from the firing of the first guns, which indeed was tremendously heavy, till colonel Johnson approached me covered with wounds, but still mounted. I think he said to me, I am severely wounded, which way shall I go? That I replied, follow me, which he did: and I conducted him directly across the swamp, on the margin of which we had charged, and to the point where doctor Mitchell, surgeon-general of Shelby's corps, was stationed. Some one hundred and fifty or two hundred yards in the rear, colonel Johnson was taken from his horse. He appeared faint and much exhausted. I asked him if he would have water, to which he answered, yes. I cast about immediately for some, but there was none at hand, nor any thing that I could see to bring it in, better than a common funnel, which I saw lying on the ground, and which I seized and ran to the river, (Thames) a distance probably of one hundred yards or more; and closing the extremity of the funnel with my finger, made use of it as a cup, from which I gave him drink. In a few minutes after this, Garret Wall, who also composed one of the "forlorn hope," and was thrown from his horse in the charge, came and solicited me to return with him to the ground on which we had charged, to aid him in recovering his lost saddle-bags. I assented. We crossed the narrow swamp, to which I have before alluded, and had not progressed far, before we came to the body of one of our men who had been killed, and who I recognized as Mansfield, of captain Stucker's company: a little fur-

* See Cincinnati Republican, 30th September, 1840.

ther, that of Scott, of Coleman's company; and pro-
gressing some forty or fifty steps (it may have been
more,) in advance of that, we found our venerable and
brave old comrade, colonel Whitley, who was also
of the "forlorn hope." Near him, in a moment, I well
remember to have noticed, with a feeling and exclamation of exultation, the body of an Indian; and some
twenty or thirty steps in advance of this, another Indian, which last was afterwards designated as the body
of Tecumseh. I distinctly recollect, that as we returned to make this search, the firing was still kept up some
distance off on our left."*

Testimony on these points might be multiplied, but
could add nothing to the force of that which is here
cited. The letter of Dr. Theobald is conclusive as to
the time when colonel Johnson was wounded, and the
period during which the action continued after he retired from the battle ground. It seems the colonel was
disabled at the beginning of the action with the Indians, and immediately rode from the field; that the action lasted for near half an hour; that Tecumseh fell
at or near the close of it: and that he could not, therefore, have fallen by the hand of colonel Johnson. Whether the leader of the "forlorn hope" can claim the
credit of having actually killed an Indian chief on this
memorable day, is not the immediate question before
us: that he acted with dauntless bravery, in promptly
charging the Indian line, during the brief period which
he remained unwounded, is universally admitted; but
that he is entitled to the honor, (if such it may be called,) of having personally slain the gifted "king of the
woods," will not be so readily conceded.

James, the British historian, from whose "Military
Occurrences" we have already quoted, having charged
general Harrison with designedly omitting, in his official report, all reference to the death of Tecumseh,
leaves the inference to be drawn by the reader, that the
omission was prompted by a feeling of envy towards
colonel Johnson, who had done the deed. It is due to
the cause of truth, not less than to the reputation of the

* Dr. Theobald's letter, dated 27th November, 1840, in possession of
the author of this work.

American commander, that this charge should be impartially examined. It is true, that the official account of the battle of the Thames does not mention the death of Tecumseh, and the propriety of this omission will be sufficiently obvious from the following narrative.

General Harrison and Anthony Shane, so far as it is known, were the only persons in the American army who were personally acquainted with Tecumseh. It is possible that some of the friendly Indians, commanded by Shane, may have known him; but it does not appear that any of them undertook to identify the body after the battle was over. Shane was under the impression, on the evening of the action, that he had found the body of Tecumseh among the slain; but, as Mr. Wall testifies, expressed himself with caution. General Harrison himself was not, on the following day, enabled to identify with certainty the body of this chief, as appears from the testimony of a member of the general's military family, which we here quote, as having a direct bearing on the question under consideration:

"I am authorised," says colonel Charles S. Todd,[*] "by several officers of general Harrison's staff, who were in the battle of the Thames, to state most unequivocally their belief, that the general neither knew nor could have known the fact of the death of Tecumseh, at the date of his letter to the war department. It was the uncertainty which prevailed, as to the fact of Tecumseh's being killed, that prevented any notice of it in his report. On the next day after the battle, general Harrison, in company with commodore Perry and other officers, examined the body of an Indian supposed to be Tecumseh; but from its swollen and mutilated condition, he was unable to decide whether it was that chief or a Potawatamie who usually visited him at Vincennes, in company with Tecumseh; and I repeat most unhesitatingly, that neither commodore Perry nor any officer in the American army, excepting general Harrison, had ever seen Tecumseh previously to the battle; and even though he had recognized the body which he

---

[*] One of the aids of general Harrison, and inspector-general of the United States army, during the late war.

examined to be that of the celebrated chief, it was manifestly impossible that he could have known whether he
was killed by Johnson's corps, or by that part of the
infantry which par icipated in the action. No official or
other satisfactory report of his death, was made to him
by those engaged on that part of the battle ground
where he fell. It was not until after the return of the
army to Detroit, and after the date of general Harrison's despatches,* that it was ascertained from the enemy, that Tecumseh was *certainly* killed; and even then
the opinion of the army was divided as to the person
by whose hands he fell. Some claimed the credit of
it for colonel Whitley, some for colonel Johnson; but
others, constituting a majority, including governor Shelby, entertained the opinion that he fell by a shot from
David King, a private in captain Davidson's company,
from Lincoln county, Kentucky. In this state of the
case, even had the fact of Tecumseh's death been fully ascertained, at the date of general Harrison's letter,
it would have been manifestly unjust, not to say im-
practicable, for the commander-in-chief to have expressed an opinion as to the particular individual to
whose personal prowess his death was to be attributed." †

In taking leave of this branch of our subject, it may
be remarked, that the strong terms of approbation in
which general Harrison, in his official account of the
battle of the Thames, speaks of the bravery and bearing of colonel Johnson in the conflict, should have
shielded him from the suspicion that any unkind feeling towards that officer was allowed to sway his judgment in the preparation of his report.

We now proceed to give some testimony in favor of
other individuals, whose friends have claimed for them
the credit of having slain Tecumseh. It has been already stated, that before our army left the field of battle, it was reported and believed by many of the troops,

---

* Early on the 7th, general Harrison left the army under the command
of governor Shelby, and returned to Detroit. His report of the battle, was
dated on the 9th. The army did not reach Sandwich, opposite Detroit,
until the 10th.

† See Louisville Journal.

that colonel Whitley, of Johnson's corps of mounted men, had killed the Indian commander in the action of the Thames. The only testimony, in confirmation of this report, which has fallen under our observation, is contained in the two following communications. The first is a letter from Mr. Abraham Scribner, now of Greenville, Ohio, under date of September 8th, 1840. The writer says—"I had never seen Tecumseh, until the body was shown to me on the battle ground on the river Thames: by whose hand he fell must always be a matter of uncertainty. My own opinion was, the day after the battle, and is yet, that Tecumseh fell by a ball from the rifle of colonel Whitley, an old Indian fighter: two balls passed through colonel Whitley's head, at the moment that Tecumseh fell; he (colonel Whitley,) was seen to take aim at the Indian said to be Tecumseh, and his rifle was found empty."

The second is from colonel Ambrose Dudley, of Cincinnati, under date of 24th February, 1841, and is in the following words :

"The morning after the battle of the Thames, in company with several other persons, I walked over the ground, to see the bodies of those who had been slain in the engagement. After passing from the river a considerable distance, and the latter part of the way along what was termed a swamp, viewing the slain of the British army, we came to a place where some half a dozen persons were standing, and three dead Indians were lying close together. One of the spectators remarked, that he had witnessed that part of the engagement which led to the death of these three Indians and two of our troops, whose bodies had been removed the evening before for burial. He proceeded to point out the position of the slain as they lay upon the ground, with that of our men. He said old colonel Whitley rode up to the body of a tree, which lay before him, and behind which lay an Indian : he (the Indian,) attempted to fire, but from some cause did not succeed, and then Whitley instantly shot him. This Indian was recognized by one of the persons present as Tecumseh : the next Indian was pointed out as having killed Whitley; then the position of another of our troops who killed that Indian, and the Indian who killed him, with the position of the man who shot the third Indian—making three Indians and two Americans who had fallen on a very small space of ground. From the manner of the narrator, and the facts related at the time, I did not doubt the truth of his statement, nor have I ever had any reason to doubt it since. The Indian pointed out as Tecumseh, was wearing a bandage over a wound in the arm, and as it was known that Tecumseh had been slightly wounded in the arm the day before, while defending the passage of a creek, my conviction was strengthened by this circumstance, that the body before us was that of Tecumseh."

The reader will decide for himself how far this testimony sustains the plea that has been raised for colonel Whitley. It is certainly clear and to the point, and presents a plausible case in support of his claim.

Mr. David King is the other individual to whom reference has been made as entitled to the credit of having killed the great Shawanoe chief. He was a private in captain James Davidson's company of mounted men, belonging to Johnson's corps. The statement given below in support of King's claim, was written by the editor of the Frankfort (Ky.) Commentator, and published in that journal in 1831. It is given on the authority of captain Davidson and his brother, two highly respectable citizens of Kentucky, both of whom belonged to colonel Johnson's mounted regiment, and were in the battle of the Thames. We have omitted the first part of this statement as irrelevant to the point in issue.

"While these things were acting in this part of the field, and towards the close of the action, which did not last long—for though much was done, it was done quickly—when the enemy was somewhat thinned and considerably scattered, and our men were scattered amongst them, Clark, one of the men mentioned above, suddenly called out to his comrade, David King, to "take care of the Indian that was near to him." The warrior turned upon Clark; at the same instant, King fired at him with Whitley's gun, and lodged the two ʂ which he knew it was loaded with, in the chief-

tain's breast—for when Whitley fell, King threw away
his own gun, and took the better one and the powder
horn of the old Indian fighter. The Indian droped
upon King's fire :—"Whoop—by G——" exclaimed
King, "he was every inch a soldier. I have killed one
d——d yellow bugger," and passed on. Giles saw this
occurrence as well as Clark, and so did Von Treece
—they were all together. From the commencement
of the fight, the voice of an Indian commander had
been distinctly heard and observed by our soldiers.
About this time it ceased, and was heard no more :
Tecumseh was dead. Presently a cry of *"how!
how!"* was raised among the Indians; upon which
they turned and fled, pursued by our soldiers.

"Upon the return of the volunteers from the pursuit, King proposed to Sam Davidson, his friend and
relative, and to other comrades, to go round with him
by the spot where he had killed the Indian, because he
wanted to get his fine leggins. They had noticed a
particular tree and a log, near to which the Indian fell.
They found the tree without difficulty, but the body
was not discovered quite so readily; but King insisted
that it must be somewhere thereabouts. Sam Davidson first discovered it. It was lying behind a tree, face
downward. *"Here he is,"* said Davidson, "but I see
no wound upon him." *"Roll him over,"* said King,
"and if it is my Indian, you will find two bullet holes
in his left breast." It was done ; and there were the
two bullet holes, an inch apart, just below the left pap
—the same, no doubt, where King's balls had entered.
The Indian, from his dress, was evidently a chief. His
fanciful leggins, (King's main object in hunting out the
body,) his party-colored worsted sash, his pistols, his
two dirks, all his dress and equipments, were the *undisputed* spoils of King. He kept one of the dirks, the
sash, and moccasins for himself; the rest he distributed
as presents among his messmates.

"Now, *it was this very Indian,* which was afterwards identified by those who had known him, as TE-
CUMSEH—*this and no other.*"

This testimony, coming as it does from a highly respectable quarter, would seem to be conclusive in favor

T

of the claim of King. It contains, however, statements which, if true, greatly weaken its force; and, indeed, in our opinion, dissipate at once the idea that the Indian killed by King was Tecumseh. The narrative states that "the Indian, from his dress, was evidently a chief. His fanciful leggins, his party-colored worsted sash, his pistols, his two dirks, all his dress and equipments, were the undisputed spoils of King." Now, if there be any one fact connected with the fall of Tecumseh which is fully and fairly established upon unimpeachable authority, it is, that he entered the battle of the Thames, dressed in the ordinary deer-skin garb of his tribe. There was nothing in his clothes, arms or ornaments, indicating him to have been a chief. On this point the testimony of Anthony Shane is explicit; and his statement is confirmed by colonel Baubee of the British army, who was familiarly acquainted with Tecumseh. This officer, the morning after the action, stated to one of the aids of general Harrison, that he saw Tecumseh just before the battle commenced, and that he was clothed in his usual plain deer-skin dress, and in that garb took his position in the Indian line, where he heroically met his fate. The testimony in favor of Mr. King's claim, while it proves very satisfactorily that he killed an Indian, is equally conclusive, we think, in establishing the fact that that Indian was not the renowned Tecumseh.

With the statement of one other person, upon this vexed question, we shall take our final leave of it. Major William Oliver, of Cincinnati, in a communication to the author, under date of 23d December, 1840, says:—

"In 1819, I lodged with Anthony Shane, at what was then called "the Second Crossing of the St. Mary's." I had known Shane intimately for a long time, indeed, from my first settlement at fort Wayne, in 1806. In speaking of the battle of the Thames, and the fall of Tecumseh, he said, the most authentic information he had obtained upon this point, was from two brothers of his wife, who were in the battle, and near the person of Tecumseh when he fell. They stated, in positive terms, that Tecumseh was shot by a private of the Kentucky troops; and Shane seemed so well satisfied with the truth of their statement, that he informed me it was entitled to belief."

To John Johnston, of Piqua, late Indian agent, and others, Shane, at this early period, expressed the opinion that Tecumseh did not fall by the hands of the commander of the mounted regiment. The reader of this volume will recollect, that long subsequent to the period when these opinions were expressed, and upon the eve of a political campaign, in which colonel R. M. Johnson was a candidate for a high and honorable office, Anthony Shane is represented by the reverend O. B. Brown, as having stated to him his belief, that Tecumseh did meet his death by a shot from the colonel. Shane, who, we believe, is now deceased, sustained, through life, a character for integrity. Whether, in his latter years, his memory had failed him, by which he was led to express these contradictory opinions, or whether Mr. Brown misunderstood the import of his language, when talking upon this matter, we shall not undertake to decide. The reader who feels an interest in the point at issue will settle the question for himself, whether, under the peculiar circumstances of the case, the early or late declarations of Shane were the genuine expression of his belief on this subject.

CHAPTER XVI.

Mr. Jefferson's opinion of the Prophet—brief sketch of his character—anecdotes of Tecumseh—a review of the great principles of his plan of union among the tribes—general summary of his life and character.

MR. JEFFERSON, in a letter to John Adams,* says: "The Wabash Prophet is more rogue than fool, if to be a rogue is not the greatest of all follies. He rose to notice while I was in the administration, and became, of course, a proper subject for me. The inquiry was

---

* Jefferson's Correspondence, vol. 10. p. 171.

made with diligence. His declared object was the re-formation of his red brethren, and their return to their pristine manner of living. He pretended to be in constant communication with the Great Spirit; that he was instructed by Him to make known to the Indians that they were created by Him distinct from the whites, of different natures, for different purposes, and placed under different circumstances, adapted to their nature and destinies; that they must return from all the ways of the whites to the habits and opinions of their forefathers; they must not eat the flesh of hogs, of bullocks, of sheep, &c., the deer and buffalo having been created for their food; they must not make bread of wheat, but of Indian corn; they must not wear linen nor woollen, but dress like their fathers, in the skins and furs of animals; they must not drink ardent spirits; and I do not remember whether he extended his inhibitions to the gun and gunpowder, in favor of the bow and arrow. I concluded, from all this, that he was a visionary, enveloped in their antiquities, and vainly endeavoring to lead back his brethren to the fancied beatitudes of their golden age. I thought there was little danger of his making many proselytes from the habits and comforts they had learned from the whites, to the hardships and privations of savagism, and no great harm if he did. We let him go on, therefore, unmolested. But his followers increased until the British thought him worth corrupting, and found him corruptible. I suppose his views were then changed; but his proceedings in consequence of them, were after I left the administration, and are, therefore, unknown to me; nor have I ever been informed what were the particular acts on his part, which produced an actual commencement of hostilities on ours. I have no doubt, however, that his subsequent proceedings are but a chapter apart, like that of Henry and Lord Liverpool, in the book of the Kings of England."

Mr. Jefferson's account of the Prophet's "budget of reform," is correct as far as it goes: it embraced, however, many other matters, looking to the amelioration of savage life. Whatever may have been his original object, in the promulgation of his new code of ethics, there is enough, we think, in the character and conduct of this individual to warrant the opinion, that he was really desirous of doing good to his race; and, that with many foibles, and some positive vices, he was not destitute of benevolent and generous feelings. That in assuming the character of a prophet, he had, in connection with his brother, ulterior objects in view, is not to be doubted. It so happened, that the adoption of his doctrines was calculated to promote harmony among the tribes; and this was the very foundation of the grand confederacy, to which he and Tecumseh were zealously devoting the energies of their minds.

After the premature and, to the Indians, disastrous battle of Tippecanoe, the Prophet began to fall into obscurity. The result of that action materially diminished the wide spread influence which he had attained over his countrymen. The incantations, by means of which he had played upon their imaginations, and swayed their conduct, lost their potency. The inspired messenger of the Great Spirit, as he openly proclaimed himself, had boldly promised his followers an easy victory over their enemies. A battle was fought—the Indians were defeated—and the gory form of many a gallant, but credulous "brave," attested that the renowned Prophet had lost, amid the carnage of that nocturnal conflict, his office and his power.

At the time when this battle was fought, Tecumseh was on a mission to the southern Indians, with the view of extending his warlike confederacy. He had left instructions with the Prophet, to avoid any hostile collision with the whites; and from the deference which the latter usually paid to the wishes of the former, it is not probable that the battle would have occurred, had not extraneous influence been brought to bear upon the leader. The reason assigned by the Prophet to his brother, for this attack upon the army under general Harrison, is not known; but some of the Indians who were in this engagement, subsequently stated that the Winnebagoes forced on the battle contrary to the wishes of the Prophet. This is not improbable; yet, admitting it to be true, if he had taken a bold and decided stand against the measure, it might, in all probability, have been prevented. The influence of the Prophet, however, even at this time, was manifestly on the wane, and some of his followers were beginning to leave his camp. He doubtless felt that it was necessary to do something to sustain himself: a signal victory over the whites would accomplish this end; and hence he consented the more readily, to the wishes of the Winnebagoes, that an attack should be made, in the hope that it would prove successful.

Within a few months after this battle, war was declared against England by the United States. Tecumseh and the Prophet, discouraged in regard to their union of the tribes, decided on joining the British standard. The love of fighting, however, was not a remarkable trait of the Prophet's character. He won no military laurels during the continuance of that war; and although in the vicinity of the Moravian town on the 5th of October, 1813, he did not choose to participate in the action at the Thames. After the return of peace, he resided in the neighborhood of Malden for some time, and finally returned to Ohio: from whence, with a band of Shawanoes, he removed west of the Mississippi, where he resided until the period of his death, which occurred in the year 1834. It is stated, in a foreign periodical,* that the British government allowed him a pension from the year 1813, to the close of his life.

In forming an estimate of the Prophet's character, it seems unjust to hold him responsible for all the numerous aggressions which were committed by his followers upon the property and persons of the whites. His first proselytes were from the most worthless and vicious portion of the tribes from which they were drawn. "The young men especially, who gathered about him, like the young men who brought on the war of King Philip, were wrought up until the master spirit himself, lost his control over them; and to make the matter worse, most of them were of such a character in the first instance, that horse stealing and house breaking were as easy to them as breathing. Like the refugees

* The United Service Journal—London.

of Romulus, they were outcasts, vagabonds and criminals; in a great degree brought together by the novelty of the preacher's reputation, by curiosity to hear his doctrines, by the fascination of extreme credulity, by restlessness, by resentment against the whites, and by poverty and unpopularity at home."* To preserve an influence over such a body of men, to use them successfully as propagandists of his new doctrines, and, at the same time, prevent their aggressions upon the whites, who were oftentimes themselves the aggressors, required no small degree of talent; and called into activity the utmost powers of the Prophet's mind. In addition to these adverse circumstances, he had to encounter the opposition of all the influential chiefs in the surrounding tribes; and a still more formidable adversary in the poverty and extreme want of provisions, which, on several occasions, threatened the total disruption of his party, and undoubtedly led to many of the thefts and murders on the frontiers, of which loud and frequent complaints were made by the agents of the United States. In a word, difficulties of various kinds were constantly recurring, which required the most ceaseless vigilance and the shrewdest sagacity on the part of the two brothers to obviate or overcome. The Prophet had a clear head, if not an honest heart; courteous and insinuating in his address, with a quick wit and a fluent tongue, he seldom came out of any conference without rising in the estimation of those who composed it. He was no warrior, and from the fact of his never having engaged in a battle, the presumption has been raised that he was wanting in physical courage. With that of cowardice, the charge of cruelty has been associated, from the cold-blooded and deliberate manner in which he put to death several of those who were suspected of having exercised an influence adverse to his plans, or calculated to lessen the value of the inspired character which he had assumed. Finally, it may be said of him, that he was a vain, loquacious and cunning man, of indolent habits and doubtful principles. Plausible but deceitful, prone to deal in the marvellous,

---

* North American Review.

quick of apprehension, affluent in pretexts, winning and eloquent, if not powerful in debate, the Prophet was peculiarly fitted to play the impostor, and to excite into strong action, the credulous fanaticism of the stern race to which he belonged. Few men, in any age of the world, have risen more rapidly into extended notoriety; wielded, for the time being, a more extraordinary degree of moral influence, or sunk more suddenly into obscurity, than the Prophet.

Tecumseh was near six feet in stature, with a compact, muscular frame, capable of great physical endurance. His head was of a moderate size, with a forehead full and high; his nose slightly aquiline, teeth large and regular, eyes black, penetrating and overhung with heavy arched brows, which increased the uniformly grave and severe expression of his countenance. He is represented by those who knew him, to have been a remarkably fine looking man, always plain but neat in his dress, and of a commanding personal presence. His portrait, it is believed, was never painted, owing probably to his strong prejudices against the whites.

In the private and social life of Tecumseh there were many things worthy of notice. He was opposed, on principle, to polygamy, a practice almost universal among his countrymen. He was married but once; and this union, which took place at the age of twenty-eight, is said to have been more in compliance with the wishes of others than in obedience to the unbiassed impulse of his feelings or the dictates of his judgment. Mamate, his wife, was older than himself, and possessed few personal or mental qualities calculated to excite admiration. A son, called Pugeshashenwa, (a panther in the act of seizing its prey,) was the only fruit of this union. The mother died soon after his birth, and he was left to the care of his aunt, Tecumapease.* This son is now residing with the Shawanoes west of the Mississippi, but is not distinguished for talents, or renowned as a warrior. The British government, however, since the death of Tecumseh, has recognized its

* Recollections of John Johnston, and Anthony Shane.

obligations to the father by the extension of an annual stipend to the son.

From his boyhood, Tecumseh was remarkable for temperance and the strictest integrity. He was hospitable, generous and humane; and these traits were acknowledged in his character long before he rose to distinction, or had conceived the project of that union of the tribes, on which the energies of his manhood were fruitlessly expended. He was, says an intelligent Shawanoe, who had known him from childhood, kind and attentive to the aged and infirm, looking personally to their comfort, repairing their frail wigwams when winter approached, giving them skins for moccasins and clothing, and sharing with them the choicest game which the woods and the seasons afforded. Nor were these acts of kindness bestowed exclusively on those of rank or reputation. On the contrary, he made it his business to search out the humblest objects of charity, and in a quick, unostentatious manner, relieve their wants.

The moral and intellectual qualities of Tecumseh place him above the age and the race in which his lot was cast. "From the earliest period of his life," says Mr. Johnston, the late Indian agent at Piqua, "Tecumseh was distinguished for virtue, for a strict adherence to truth, honor, and integrity. He was sober * and abstemious, never indulging in the use of liquor nor eating to excess." Another respectable individual,† who resided for near twenty years as a prisoner among the Shawanoes, and part of that time in the family of Tecumseh, writes to us, "I know of no *peculiarity* about him that gained him popularity. His talents, rectitude of deportment, and friendly disposition, commanded the respect and regard of all about him. In short, I consider him a very great as well as a very good man, who, had he enjoyed the advantages of a liberal education, would have done honor to any age or any nation."

Tecumseh had, however, no education, beyond that

---

* Major James Galloway, of Xenia, states, that on one occasion, while Tecumseh was quite young, he saw him intoxicated. This is the only aberration of the kind, which we have heard charged upon him.

† Mr. Stephen Ruddell.

which the traditions of his race, and his own power of observation and reflection, afforded him. He rarely mingled with the whites, and very seldom attempted to speak their language, of which his knowledge was ex-tremely limited and superficial.

When Burns, the poet, was suddenly transferred from his plough in Ayrshire to the polished circles of Edin-burg, his ease of manner, and nice observance of the rules of good-breeding, excited much surprise, and be-came the theme of frequent conversation. The same thing has been remarked of Tecumseh: whether seated at the tables of generals McArthur and Worthington, as he was during the council at Chillicothe in 1807, or brought in contact with British officers of the highest rank, his manners were entirely free from vulgarity and coarseness: he was uniformly self-possessed, and with the tact and ease of deportment which marked the poet of the heart, and which are falsely supposed to be the result of civilization and refinement only, he readily ac-commodated himself to the novelties of his new posi-tion, and seemed more amused than annoyed by them.

The humanity of his character has been already por-trayed in the pages of this work. His early efforts to abolish the practice of burning prisoners—then common among the Indians—and the merciful protection which he otherwise invariably showed to captives, whether ta-ken by himself or his companions, need no commenda-tion at our hands. Rising above the prejudices and customs of his people, even when those prejudices and customs were tacitly sanctioned by the officers and agents of Great Britain, Tecumseh was never known to offer violence to prisoners, nor to permit it in others. So strong was his sense of honor, and so sensitive his feelings of humanity, on this point, that even frontier women and children, throughout the wide space in which his character was known, felt secure from the tomahawk of the hostile Indians, if Tecumseh was in the camp. A striking instance of this confidence is presented in the following anecdote. The British and Indians were encamped near the river Raisin; and while holding a talk within eighty or one hundred yards of Mrs. Ruland's house, some Sauks and Winnebagoes entered her dwelling, and began to plunder it. She immediately sent her little daughter, eight or nine years old, requesting Tecumseh to come to her assistance. The child ran to the council house, and pulling Tecumseh (who was then speaking) by the skirt of his hunting-shirt, said to him, "Come to our house—there are bad Indians there." Without waiting to close his speech, the chief started for the house in a fast walk. On entering, he was met by two or three Indians dragging a trunk towards the door: he seized his tomahawk and levelled one of them at a blow: they prepared for resistance, but no sooner did they hear the cry, "dogs! I am Tecumseh!" than under the flash of his indignant eye, they fled from the house: and "you," said Tecumseh, turning to some British officers, "are *worse* than dogs, to break your faith with prisoners." The officers expressed their regrets to Mrs. Ruland, and offered to place a guard around the house: this she declined, observing, that so long as that man, pointing to Tecumseh, was near them, she felt safe.*

Tecumseh entertained a high and proper sense of personal character—was equally bold in defending his own conduct, and condemning that which was reprehensible in others. In 1811, he abandoned his intention of visiting the President, because he was not permitted to march to Washington at the head of a party of his warriors. As an officer in the British army, he never lost sight of the dignity of his rank, nor suffered any act of injustice towards those under his command to pass without resenting it. On one occasion, while the combined British and Indian forces were quartered at Malden, there was a scarcity of provisions, the commissary's department being supplied with salt beef only, which was issued to the British soldiers, while horse flesh was given to the Indians. Upon learning this fact, Tecumseh promptly called on general Proctor, remonstrated against the injustice of the measure, and complained, indignantly, of the insult thus offered to himself and his men. The British general appeared indifferent to what was said; whereupon, the chief

* On the authority of colonel John Ruland.

struck the hilt of Proctor's sword with his hand, then
touched the handle of his own tomahawk, and sternly remarked, "You are Proctor—I am Tecumseh;"
intimating, that if justice was not done to the Indians,
the affair must be settled by a personal rencontre between the two commanders. General Proctor prudent-
ly yielded the point.*

But few of the numerous speeches made by Tecumseh have been preserved. Tradition speaks in exalted
terms of several efforts of this kind, of which no record
was made. All bore evidence of the high order of
his intellectual powers. They were uniformly forcible,
sententious and argumentative; always dignified, frequently impassioned and powerful. He indulged neither in sophism nor circumlocution, but with bold and
manly frankness, gave utterance to his honest opinions.
Mr. Ruddell, who knew him long and intimately, says,
that "he was naturally eloquent, very fluent, graceful
in his gestures, but not in the habit of using many; that
there was neither vehemence nor violence in his style of
delivery, but that his eloquence always made a strong
impression on his hearers." Dr. Hunt, of Clark county, Ohio, has remarked, that the first time he heard
Henry Clay make a speech, his manner reminded him,
very forcibly, of that of Tecumseh, in the council at
Springfield, in the year 1807, on which occasion he
made one of his happiest efforts.

Our present minister to France, Mr. Cass, has said,
with his usual discrimination, that "the character of
Tecumseh, in whatever light it may be viewed, must
be regarded as remarkable in the highest degree. That
he proved himself worthy of his rank as a general officer in the army of his Britannic majesty, or even of his
reputation as a great warrior among all the Indians of
the north-west, is, indeed, a small title to distinction.
Bravery is a savage virtue, and the Shawanoes are a
brave people: too many of the American nation have
ascertained this fact by experience. His oratory speaks
more for his genius. It was the utterance of a great
mind roused by the strongest motives of which human

* On the authority of the Rev. Wm. H. Raper.

nature is susceptible; and developing a power and a labor of reason, which commanded the admiration of the
civilized, as justly as the confidence and pride of the
savage." There was one subject, far better calculated
than all others, to call forth his intellectual energies,
and exhibit the peculiar fascination of his oratory.
"When he spoke to his brethren on the glorious theme
that animated all his actions, his fine countenance light-
ed up, his firm and erect frame swelled with deep emo-
tion, which his own stern dignity could scarcely re-
press ; every feature and gesture had its meaning, and
language flowed tumultuously and swiftly, from the
fountains of his soul."

Another writer, Judge Hall, long resident in the west,
and devoted to the study of aboriginal history, has thus
summed up the character of this chief :

"At this period the celebrated Tecumseh appeared
upon the scene. He was called the Napoleon of the
west; and so far as that title was deserved by splendid genius, unwavering courage, untiring perseverance,
boldness of conception and promptitude of action, it was
fairly bestowed upon this accomplished savage. He
rose from obscurity to the command of a tribe to which
he was alien by birth. He was, by turns, the orator,
the warrior and the politician; and in each of these ca-
pacities, towered above all with whom he came in contact. As is often the case with great minds, one master
passion filled his heart, prompted all his designs, and
gave to his life its character. This was hatred to the
whites, and, like Hannibal, he had sworn that it should
be perpetual. He entertained the same vast project of
uniting the scattered tribes of the west into one grand
confederacy, which had been acted on by King Philip
and Little Turtle. He wished to extinguish all dis-
tinctions of tribe and language, to bury all feuds, and
to combine the power and the prejudices of all, in defence of the rights and possessions of the whole, as the
aboriginal occupants of the country."

It may be truly said, that what Hannibal was to the
Romans, Tecumseh became to the people of the United
States. From his boyhood to the hour when he fell,
nobly battling for the rights of his people, he fostered

U

an invincible hatred to the whites. On one occasion, he was heard to declare, that he could not look upon the face of a white man, without feeling the flesh crawl upon his bones. This hatred was not confined, how-ever, to the Americans. Circumstances made him the ally of the British, and induced him to fight under their standard, but he neither loved nor respected them. He well understood their policy; they could not deceive his sagacious mind; he knew that their professions of regard for the Indians were hollow, and that when in-stigating him and his people to hostilities against the United States, the agents of Britain had far less anxiety about the rights of the Indians, than the injuries which, through their instrumentality, might be inflicted upon the rising republic. This feeling towards the whites, and especially to the people of the United States, had a deeper foundation than mere prejudice or self-interest. Tecumseh was a patriot, and his love of country made him a statesman and a warrior. He saw his race driv-en from their native land, and scattered like withered leaves in an autumnal blast; he beheld their morals debased, their independence destroyed, their means of subsistence cut off, new and strange customs introdu-ced, diseases multiplied, ruin and desolation around and among them; he looked for the cause of these evils and believed he had found it in the flood of white immigra-tion which, having surmounted the towering Alleghe-nies, was spreading itself over the hunting grounds of Kentucky, and along the banks of the Scioto, the Miami and the Wabash, whose waters, from time im-memorial, had reflected the smoke of the rude but populous villages of his ancestors. As a statesman, he studied the subject, and, having satisfied himself that justice was on the side of his countrymen, he tasked the powers of his expansive mind, to find a re-medy for the mighty evil which threatened their total extermination.

The original, natural right of the Indians to the oc-cupancy and possession of their lands, has been recog-nized by the laws of congress, and solemnly sanctioned by the highest judicial tribunal of the United States. On this principle, there is no disagreement between our government and the Indian nations by whom this country was originally inhabited.*

In the acquisition of these lands, however, our government has held that its title was perfect when it had purchased of the tribe in actual possession. It seems, indeed, to have gone further and admitted, that a tribe might acquire lands by conquest which it did not occupy, as in the case of the Iroquois, and sell the same to us; and, that the title thus acquired, would be valid. Thus we have recognized the principles of international law as operative between the Indians and us on this particular point, while on some others, as in not *allowing* them to sell to individuals, and giving them tracts used as hunting grounds by other tribes beyond the Mississippi, we have treated them as savage hordes, not sufficiently advanced in civilization to be admitted into the family of nations. Our claim to forbid their selling to individuals, and our guarantying to tribes who would not sell to us in our corporate capacity, portions of country occupied as hunting grounds, by more distant tribes, can only be based on the right of discovery, taken in connection with a right conferred by our superior civilization; and seems never in fact to have been fully acknowledged by them. It was not, at least, admitted by Tecumseh. His doctrine seems to have been that we acquired no rights over the Indians or their country either by discovery or superior civilization; and that the possession and jurisdiction can only be obtained by conquest or negociation. In regard to the latter, he held that purchase from a single tribe, although at the time sojourners on the lands sold, was not valid as it respected other tribes. That no particular portion of the country belonged to the tribe then within its limits—though in reference to other tribes, its title was perfect; that is, possession excluded other tribes, and would exclude them forever; but did not confer on the tribe having it, the right to sell the soil to us; for that was the common property of all the tribes who were near enough to occupy or hunt upon it, in the event of its being at any time vacated,

---

* 6 Wheaton's Reports, 515.

and could only be vacated by *the consent of the whole.* As a conclusion from these premises, he insisted that certain sales made in the west were invalid, and protested against new ones on any other than his own principles.

It must be acknowledged that these views have much plausibility, not to grant to them any higher merit. If the Indians had been in a nomadic instead of a hunter state, and in summer had driven their flocks to the Allegheny mountains—in winter to the banks of the Wabash and Tennessee rivers, it could scarcely be denied that each tribe would have had an interest in the whole region between, and as much right as any other tribe to be heard on a question of sale. The Indians were not shepherds, wandering *with* their flocks of sheep and cattle in quest of new pastures, but hunters, roaming after deer and bison, and changing their location, as the pursuit from year to year, or from age to age, might require. We do not perceive a difference in principle in the two cases; and while we admit the difficulty of acquiring their territory on the plan of Tecumseh, we feel bound also to admit, that as far as its preservation to themselves was concerned, his was the only effective method.

In its support he displayed in council the sound and logical eloquence for which he was distinguished—in war the prowess which raised him into the highest rank of Indian heroes.

At what period of his life he first resolved upon making an effort to stop the progress of the whites west of the mountains, is not certainly known. It was probably several years anterior to the open avowal of his plan of union, which occurred in 1805 or '6. The work before him was herculean in character, and beset with difficulties on every side; but these only quickened into more tireless activity his genius and his patriotic resolution. To unite the tribes as he proposed, prejudices must be overcome, their original manners and customs re-established, the use of ardent spirits utterly abandoned, and finally, all intercourse with the whites cut off. Here was a field for the display of the highest moral and intellectual powers. He had already gained the reputation of a brave and sagacious warrior, a cool headed, upright and wise counsellor. He was neither a war nor a peace chief, and yet he wielded the power and influence of both. The time had now arrived for action. To win savage attention, some bold and striking movement was necessary. He imparted his plan to his brother, a smart, cunning and pliable fellow, who adroitly and quickly prepared himself for the part he was appointed to play, in this great drama of savage life. Tecumseh well understood, that excessive superstition is every where a prominent trait in the Indian character, and readily availed himself of it. Suddenly, his brother begins to dream dreams, and see visions, he is an inspired Prophet, favored with a divine commission from the Great Spirit; the power of life and death is placed in his hands; he is the appointed agent for preserving the property and lands of the Indians, and for restoring them to their original, happy condition. He commences his sacred work; the public mind is aroused; unbelief gradually gives way; credulity and wild fanaticism begin to spread in circles, widening and deepening until the fame of the Prophet, and the divine character of his mission, have reached the frozen shores of the lakes, and overrun the broad plains which stretch far beyond the Mississippi. Pilgrims from remote tribes, seek, with fear and trembling, the head-quarters of the mighty Prophet. Proselytes are multiplied, and his followers increase in number. Even Tecumseh becomes a believer, and, seizing upon the golden opportunity, he mingles with the pilgrims, wins them by his address, and, on their return, sends a knowledge of his plan of concert and union to the most distant tribes. And now commenced those bodily and mental labors of Tecumseh, which were never intermitted for the space of five years. During the whole of this period, we have seen that his life was one of ceaseless activity. He traveled, he argued, he commanded: to-day, his persuasive voice was listened to by the Wyandots, on the plains of Sandusky—to-morrow, his commands were issued on the banks of the Wabash—anon, he was paddling his bark canoe across the Mississippi; now, boldly confronting the governor of Indiana territory in the council-house

U 2

at Vincennes, and now carrying his banner of union among the Creeks and Cherokees of the south. He was neither intoxicated by success, nor discouraged by failure; and, but for the desperate conflict at Tippecanoe, would have established the most formidable and extended combination of Indians, that has ever been witnessed on this continent. That he could have been successful in arresting the progress of the whites, or in making the Ohio river the boundary between them and the Indians of the north-west, even if that battle had not been fought, is not to be supposed. The ultimate failure of his plan was inevitable from the circumstances of the case. The wonder is not that he did not succeed, but that he was enabled to accomplish so much. His genius should neither be tested by the magnitude of his scheme, nor the failure in its execution, but by the extraordinary success that crowned his patriotic labors. These labors were suddenly terminated in the hour when the prospect of perfecting the grand confederacy was brightest. By the battle of Tippecanoe—fought in violation of his positive commands and during his absence to the south, —the great object of his ambition was frustrated, the golden bowl was broken at the fountain; that ardent enthusiasm which for years had sustained him, in the hour of peril and privation, was extinguished. His efforts were paralyzed, but not his hostility to the United States. He joined the standard of their enemy, and fought beneath it with his wonted skill and heroism. At length the contest on the Thames was at hand. Indignant at the want of courage or military skill, which prompted the commander of the British forces to shrink from meeting the American army on the shore of lake Erie, he sternly refused to retreat beyond the Moravian towns. There, at the head of his warriors, he took his stand, resolved, as he solemnly declared, to be victorious, or leave his body upon the field of battle, a prey to the wolf and the vulture. The result has been told. The Thames is consecrated forever, by the bones of the illustrious Shawanoe statesman, warrior and patriot, which repose upon its bank.

In whatever aspect the genius and character of Tecumseh may be viewed, they present the evidence of his having been a remarkable man; and, to repeat the language of a distinguished statesman and general, who knew him long and intimately, who has often met him in the council and on the field of battle, we may venture to pronounce him, one of those uncommon geniuses which spring up occasionally to produce revolutions, and overturn the established order of things; and, who, but for the power of the United States, would, perhaps, have been the founder of an empire which would have rivalled that of Mexico or Peru.

Printed in the United States
113594LV00006B/33/A

9 780766 163447